Regional Parallelism and Corruption Scandals in Nigeria

Muhammad Jameel Yusha'u

Regional Parallelism and Corruption Scandals in Nigeria

Intranational Approaches to African Media Systems

palgrave
macmillan

Muhammad Jameel Yusha'u
Uni Focus Academy
Kano, Nigeria

ISBN 978-3-030-07159-2 ISBN 978-3-319-96220-7 (eBook)
https://doi.org/10.1007/978-3-319-96220-7

Softcover re-print of the Hardcover 1st edition 2018

Cover credit: vkovalcik/iStock/Getty Images Plus
Cover design by Ran Shauli

This Palgrave Macmillan imprint is published by the registered company Springer Nature Switzerland AG
The registered company address is: Gewerbestrasse 11, 6330 Cham, Switzerland

To Bayero University, Kano
Where my intellectual journey began

Preface

This is the first major study that applies a comparative approach to media systems research in Africa from an intranational rather than cross-national perspective by studying the media systems of three countries. Nigeria, Kenya and South Africa. This is quite important because previous studies in comparative media research such as Hallin and Mancini's *Comparing Media Systems* (2004), Blumler and Gurevitchs's *Crisis in Public Communication* (1995) and Hallin and Mancini's *Comparing Media Systems: Beyond the Western World* (2012) and the famous *Four Theories of the Press* by Siebert et al. (1956) focused on cross national comparative research.

Africa has a different historical journey, with most of the countries created by colonial borders, combining nations within nations, yet under the same national flag. Nigeria is a typical example of this where the amalgamation of the country in 1914 brought together different nations into a single nation state. However, the character of the media still reflects the context of the pre-colonial borders.

This book was written in three different phases. The first phase was between 2005 and 2009 when I was at the University of Sheffield in the United Kingdom, which coincided with the release of the seminal work of Daniel C Hallin and Paolo Mancini, *Comparing Media Systems: Three Models of Media and Politics* (2004). What I found quite fascinating about *Comparing Media Systems* was the authors' admission that the conventional theories of the press, particularly the famous *Four Theories of the Press* by Siebert et al. (1956), were inadequate to explain media systems around the world.

This was a revelation because it started the process for exploring one of the questions I had since I was an undergraduate student in mass communications. One of my favourite courses was the theories of mass communications, yet I always felt that the attempt to situate the Nigerian media system within the four theories of the press was too inadequate to address the kind of media environment that operates in the country. When I took a teaching appointment at Bayero University, Kano, my students asked me the same question. Do we have an authoritarian media system, a Soviet model, social responsibility or libertarian model?

These are theories that originate in Europe and were written under a political climate, historical context and economic environment that is radically different from the one obtained in Africa. Therefore, there is need for more research to understand how the media operates in other systems. I was enticed by Hallin and Mancini's humility to admit that the book does not provide all the answers and cannot be applied without modification.

"We do believe that much of the analysis will be of interest to those studying other regions…we will also stress that we don't intend any of this analysis simply to be applied to other systems without modification" (p. xiv), explained Hallin and Mancini.

I am certainly one of those who took a strong interest in studying the media systems of other regions. As much as I want to use a model that originates from Africa, I also believe that scholarship has no borders. Knowledge is a trust and it has been passed from generation to generation, and even some empires where built based on the intellectual foundation provided by people from other cultures, regions and nationalities.

Therefore, the work of Hallin and Mancini serves as a foundation that can be applied with modification to test the media systems of other cultures. That is exactly what I did in this book. As readers will find out, I made several references to the foundation laid by Hallin and Mancini, but I have departed, modified their paradigm and tried as much as possible to explore the Nigerian media system, and by extension South Africa and Kenya, in order to find the right answer to the question on the type of media system that obtains in Africa.

During this phase, I attended major conferences such as the International Communication Association (San Francisco 2007), International Summer School in Political Communication and Electoral Behaviour (University of Milan 2007) International Association of Media and Communication Research (Stockholm 2008), Media, Communication and Cultural Communication Association PGN Conference (University of Sussex

2008) and American Political Science Association's 6th Annual Pre-Conference in Political Communication (Harvard University 2008).

These conferences proved extremely useful as I had the opportunity to meet leading scholars in political communication as well as researchers working on media systems. I benefited immensely from their contributions, which have been integrated into this book.

The second phase of writing this book took place between 2010 and 2016 when I published several articles in academic journals and wrote book chapters about the subject of this book. I thank the anonymous reviewers and the editors of *African Journalism Studies*, *Journal of African Media Studies*, *Journal of Global Mass Communication* as well Palgrave Macmillan and Routledge with whom I published some book chapters. The constructive suggestions I received I am sure have contributed in making this book what it is.

The third phase of writing this book was what I call the miracle of Cartagena. I have physically been out of the academia since 2012, but my heart has not moved an inch from it. I had planned to attend the International Association of Media and Communication Research Conference in Cartagena, Colombia, in 2017 but there was some difficulty in obtaining a visa.

While I live and work in the Middle East, I had to obtain the visa from the Colombian Embassy in Ghana 72 hours before the start of the conference. I must thank the organisers of the Cartagena conference for ensuring that I received the visa. When the visa was issued, I was in neighbouring Côte d'Ivoire and I had to purchase the travel ticket from Abidjan. Although most of the airlines were fully booked I managed to get a flight; however, the price would shake the credit card of any researcher let alone a self-funded one like myself. It was my longest flight ever as I flew from Abidjan to Addis Abbas–Jeddah–Dubai–New York and Cartagena within those 72 hours. Finally, I made it to Cartagena.

One of the first people I met at the conference was Shaun Vigil of Palgrave Macmillan. I immediately engaged him in conversation and told him about my interest in publishing this book. After a short but fruitful discussion, I wrote the proposal that finally resulted in the publication of this book in Cartagena. I must therefore start by thanking Shaun for the interest, advice and friendship throughout the process of publishing this book. No flight was too long if it would lead to a modest scholarly contribution like this.

Glenn Ramirez was my line editor at Palgrave. I enjoyed working with him, his speed and ability to turn things quickly is one of my takeaways in the journey to writing this book. I also thank the anonymous reviewers for the book as well as the team at Springer who were constantly in touch throughout the proofing process. I received a lot of support from different individuals and from research bodies to undertake part of this research. I would like to thank the University of Sheffield Excellence Exchange Scheme, the Kano State Scholarships Board, Bayero University Kano and the Aminu Kano Centre for Democratic Research and Training, which hosted me during part of this research. Mubarak Elegbede, Habeeb Amuni and Olatunji Yusuf helped with the names of some local language newspapers, I am grateful for their effort.

I must also thank the contribution of University of Sheffield professors and lecturers: Dr. John Steel provided constructive comments on this book and continued to provide support throughout the process of writing this book. I am equally grateful to Professor Ralph Negrine; Professor Karen Sanders; Professor Jackie Harrison; and Professor Martin Conboy, who was instrumental in introducing me to critical discourse analysis, which I have embraced and applied in many of my research publications. I would also like to thank South Africa's Professor Herman Wasserman and University of Westminster's Dr. Winston Mano for their contribution to this book and providing support in many ways.

Habeeb Pindiga was extremely supportive; he helped with contacts for interviews, sent me several reading materials and provided useful suggestions. Joseph Burite, Bashir Saad, Houssam Bizri, Nur Abdullah, Muttaqa Yusha'u, Abbas Yusha'u and Mujahid Yusha'u have provided tremendous support including research and transcription of the interviews. I received tremendous support while carrying out this research in one form or another from my teachers especially Professor Abdalla Uba Adamu, Malam Ibrahim Ado-Kurawa, Dr. Abubakar Danlami Alhassan, Professor Haruna Wakili, Dr. Gausu Ahmad, and my friend Malam Ghazali Abdullahi.

In the first quarter of 2018, I spent several weeks writing and researching parts of this book at King Fahad Public Library. My sincere appreciation to the staff for their support.

Writing this book took away the precious time of my family. It certainly reduced the phone calls to my parents who have endured my absence from Nigeria for well over a decade. They have seen me through and gave me the training and upbringing that every child would hope for. I am sure they will be pleased at the sight of this book, and also all my brothers and sisters. Thank you all.

No one suffered from the writing of this book like my wife, Hauwa Sarkina, a great friend and an unquestionable believer in my success. She provides motivation and always believes that I can do better. My daughter Asma equally deserves commendation; she sometimes had to bear with my endless lectures on this book at such a young age, listening to me patiently discussing such terms like regional parallelism or polarized pluralism that perhaps make little sense to her now. So, also, my little Aishah who normally pops into my study area to have more time to play with her dad, only to be disappointed with his commitment to meet the deadline for writing this book.

There are too many friends, colleagues, neighbours and well-wishers who have supported or provided words of encouragement. I apologise in advance if you did not see your name, but certainly you are not forgotten.

All views expressed in this book are strictly personal and do not represent the position of my present or previous employers. I bear responsibility for any shortcomings in the book, and I hope any observation will be communicated to me so that I can take measures to rectify it in future research.

Thank you.

Kano, Nigeria Muhammad Jameel Yusha'u

Reference

Siebert, F. S., Peterson, T., & Schramm, W. (1956). Four Theories of the Press. The Authoritarian, Libertarian, Social Responsibility and Soviet Communist Concepts of What the Press Should ne and Should Do. Urbana and Chicago, University of Illinois Press.

Contents

List of Tables

CHAPTER 1

Introduction: Corruption Scandals and Intranational Framework for Media Systems Research in Africa

Background

In the 1990s, many African countries started a transition from military rule or from one-party dictatorship, to multiparty elections that brought new governments into power. Some countries—such as Ghana, Senegal, Malawi, Niger, Benin and many others—conducted a series of elections that brought in a new era for them, even if there were little change in the living conditions of the people. From 1989 to 1997, at least 75% of African countries conducted multiparty elections (Burchard 2014).

Nigeria, the most populous country in the continent, and the largest economy in the continent after rebasing its economy in 2014 (BBC News 2014), launched a transition to civilian rule in 1998 after the death of its military leader, General Sani Abacha. On May 29, 1999, the newly elected president Olusegun Obasanjo, a former military head of state, was sworn in. Obasanjo was the first civilian president since Shehu Usman Aliyu Shagari, who was overthrown in December 1983 by the incumbent Nigerian President, Muhammadu Buhari, then a Major General in the Nigerian army.

One of the promises made by President Olusegun Obasanjo was to tackle corruption, and he established two bodies, the Economic and Financial Crimes Commission (EFCC) and the Independent Corrupt Practices Commission (ICPC).

The EFCC, established through an Act of Parliament in 2002, became operational in 2003. It was headed by a senior police officer, Nuhu Ribadu.

M. J. Yusha'u, *Regional Parallelism and Corruption Scandals in Nigeria*, https://doi.org/10.1007/978-3-319-96220-7_1

In one of major revelations made about the level of corruption in Nigeria, Nuhu Ribadu made the following statement to the US Congress: "Between 1960 and 1999, Nigerian officials had stolen or wasted more than $440 billion.[1] That is six times the Marshall Plan, the total sum needed to rebuild a devastated Europe in the aftermath of the Second World War."[2]

From 1999 to 2018 there have been several allegations of corruption against top Nigerian government officials, including some of the recent allegations against former petroleum minister under the administration of Goodluck Jonathan, Mrs. Diezani Alison-Madukwe. The former Central Bank governor of Nigeria, Sanusi Lamido Sanusi, had in 2013 written a letter to former president Goodluck Jonathan alleging that US $20 billion in revenues owed to the state had not been remitted by the Nigerian state oil company. An allegation the minister denied, but admitted that the amount not remitted was US $10.8 billion, which was to be paid for subsidies (Reuters 2013). Another major allegation was that against former national security advisor to former president Goodluck Jonathan, Sambo Dasuki, who was accused of embezzling US $2 billion meant for the purchase of arms against the violent Nigerian militant group, Boko Haram (BBC News 2015). Both cases are now under investigation by the Muhammadu Buhari administration.

What is noteworthy about these allegations of corruption is that there is no gender, regional or religious difference among Nigerian elites when it comes to these accusations of corruption. Alison-Mduekwe is a female Christian from Southern Nigeria, while Sambo Dasuki is a male Muslim from Northern Nigeria. This point is important because Nigeria is a country that is diverse, and regionalism and ethnicity (Ogingwo 1980; Yusha'u 2010) are major components in the psyche of the country. The

[1] This figure excludes the country's 1999–2009 income; many Nigerians, including Major General Muhammadu Buhari (retd), believe that the country's income generated during this period was the highest since the 1914 amalgamation because of the surge in global oil prices before they fell due to the global economic crisis. He stated this in an interview with the BBC Hausa Service on 25 May, 2009.

[2] Nuhu Ribadu was the former chairman of the EFCC in Nigeria. He was removed from office by former president Umaru Musa Yar'Aduwa through the former Inspector General of Police, Mike Okiro. He was sent on a course at the National Institute of Policy and Strategic Studies (NIPSS), and later removed and demoted from Assistant Inspector General of Police to Deputy Commissioner of Police. He made the quoted statement to the US House Committee on Financial Services on May 19th, 2009. The full report is available at: http://www.saharareporters.com/index.php?option=com_content&view=article&id=2780:capital-loss-and-corruption-the-example-of-nigeria-&catid=42:exclusive&Itemid=160 downloaded 21/05/09.

news media though is supposed to be different. It is supposed to serve as a watchdog, focusing on truth and nothing but the truth for the benefit of society. But is the Nigerian media living up to this expectation, or is it blinded by primordial sentiments clouded in ethnicity and regionalism? What is the situation in other major African economies like South Africa and Kenya? We shall soon find out in this study that aims to explore the nature of media systems in Africa.

Why This Book?

There is a scholarly thirst for a media system study from an African perspective. This book is about the coverage of corruption scandals in the Nigerian press with an eye in other countries like South Africa and Kenya. It seeks to compare the reporting of corruption scandals by the northern and the Southern Nigerian newspapers in order to gain a deeper understanding of the country's media system.

Before the amalgamation of Nigeria in 1914 by British Colonial Governor Frederick Lugard, the protectorates of Northern and Southern Nigeria were independent of each other (Smith 1964), yet the establishment of institutions and the political character of the country, including the news media is still influenced by this colonial mindset. Nigeria is a complex, multi-ethnic and multi-religious country in West Africa. The issue of corruption is one of the problems bedevilling the country. The media, the press in particular, reflects and reports the happenings of a society; in addition, it also serves as a watchdog. Yet despite the purported function of the media as a watchdog, there are little or no major studies about the way the press reports allegations of corruption scandals in Nigeria. Therefore, there is the need for research that will explore the nature of such corruption scandals and develop a framework that will contribute towards guiding further research in scandal reporting.

The changing nature of society at the end of the twentieth century and the beginning of the twenty-first century has necessitated the need for different countries to evaluate their progress and position themselves in the struggle for development. The revolution in information and communication technology, the challenges of globalisation, the emergence of free market economies and the merger between international corporate organisations have all combined and made it easier for many countries to look inward and find out some of the reasons hindering their progress (see de Sardan 1999 for more on corruption in Africa).[3]

One of the key problems that hinders economic development is the phenomenon of corruption, particularly in African countries (Commission for Africa Report 2005). The phenomenon of corruption manifests itself in different forms ranging from accepting bribes, violation of procedure to enhance private benefit, intervention by political leaders in the judicial process, false claims or lack of execution of contracts and so on (Doig and Theobald 2000).

However, to understand the phenomenon of corruption, we need to consider other factors in our contemporary setting that might affect the way the act of governance is conducted, such as the transformations society is undergoing in politics, media, culture and technology (Tumber and Waisbord 2004a, b).

The report of the Commission for Africa[4] has discussed some of the reasons why corruption retards the progress of a country. The report identified a lack of good governance, transparency and accountability as a result of the massive corruption, which is becoming associated with the identity of many African countries. Section 4.5 of the report states:

> Corruption is a by-product of weak governance. It manifests itself in many ways…Much of it takes place at the grassroots level and affects people's daily lives, for example through bribes paid to bureaucrats, or non-delivery of services to poor people. The corrosive effect of corruption undermines all effort to improve governance and foster development. (Commission for Africa Report 2005: 142)

Nigeria, being one of the most influential African countries, is also in the forefront among the countries that suffer from endemic corruption, of which, according to the 2017 corruption perception index of Transparency International, Nigeria is at the bottom, ranking number 148 (Transparency International 2017).[5]

[3] In his research entitled *A Moral Economy of Corruption in Africa*, de Sardan also suggested six things which he thinks will explain corruption in Africa. They are (1) corruption complex, (2) a common routine, (3) stigmatisation of corruption, (4) cumulative and expansionist, (5) absence of correlation on the extent of corruption, and (6) considered legitimate by perpetrators.

[4] The Commission for Africa was established by the British Government to study the problems bedevilling African countries and how to find solution to them.

[5] In the 2017 Corruption Perceptions Index published by Transparency International, Nigeria ranked number 148 out of 180 countries. See https://www.transparency.org/news/feature/corruption_perceptions_index_2017 retrieved 14/05/2018.

This research, therefore, intends to study the coverage of corruption in Nigeria as covered by both southern and northern newspapers. Following the introductory section in this chapter there are five further sections. The first section is a brief history of Nigeria from pre-colonial and colonial to post-colonial times. The second section covers political culture, which is essential in comparative research because scholars of comparative study see it as an integral part of cultural studies. The third section reviews the literature and the way other academic fields like sociology, political science, law and organisational communication view the definition of corruption. The fourth section looks at the meaning of scandal, which is the communication perspective of corruption, the fourth estate role of the media and investigative journalism. The final section reviews the different approaches used by media scholars from the era of the *Four Theories of the Press* to Hallin and Mancini's *Media Systems Theory*, who used comparative research to understand various media systems; these approaches are discussed and modified, and a comparative methodology based on the specificity of the Nigerian media landscape is proposed for the purpose of an intra-national comparative research.

A Brief History of Nigeria

Nigeria is a diverse country whose contemporary name can be traced back to the colonial era. Prior to colonialism the regions that constitute present-day Nigeria already existed, with their different cultures and civilisation. About a thousand years ago, the northern part of the country came into contact with Islam, which later spread to the south-western part of the country (Library of Congress Country Studies 2006).[6] Around 1800 there was an Islamic reform led by Uthman Dan Fodio which saw the establishment of an Islamic caliphate that lasted until the British forces conquered the region in 1903. The slave trade which occurred from the 1650s to the 1860s was also an integral part of Nigerian history. There was a political structure, with each city having an emir or king in the north and south-west, and the sultan as the head of the entire caliphate also in the north, while in the south-eastern part of the country leadership style was by gerontocracy.

[6] The Library of Congress Country Study is available online at: http://rs6.loc.gov/frd/cs/ngtoc.html

The creation of modern-day Nigeria can be linked to the 1884–1885 Berlin Conference when Nigeria fell under British Control. In 1914, Governor General Frederick Lugard amalgamated the southern and northern protectorates to form what is now called Nigeria. In the southern part of Nigeria Lugard did not meet much resistance, while in the north there was a lot of resistance, as Lugard confirmed in an interview recording stored in the BBC archives (BBC Witness 2014). Lugard introduced indirect rule in the Northern Region which left the emirs to maintain their position as long as they followed the instructions of the colonial government.

Nigeria gained independence from Britain on October 1, 1960, with Dr. Nnamdi Azikwe as the ceremonial governor general and Sir Abubakar Tafawa Balewa as the prime minister. The major political parties at independence were the Northern People's Congress, which established government in the Northern Region under the leadership of Sir Ahmadu Bello; Action Group, which was predominant in the Western Region and led by Chief Obafemi Awolowo (now called south-west); and the National Consensus for Nigerian Citizens was predominant in the eastern part of the country (now called south-east and south-south) under the leadership of Dr. Nnamdi Azikwe.

It is important to note that during the period of the struggle for independence, and the years after, the relationship between these regions was characterised by strong rivalry and competition. Each of the regions tried to assert its relevance and hegemony over the other, which contributed to shaping the country's political culture, as we shall discuss later. The Northern Region was predominantly Muslim, and the premier of the region Ahmadu Bello was a descendent of Uthman Dan Fodio, who established the Sokoto Caliphate. Even though there are Christians, especially among the minority ethnic groups, many of whom held ministerial appointments, the influence of Islam cannot be divorced from the way the region was run. The Western Region on the other hand, has a significant population of both Muslims and Christians, and so the premier of the region, Chief Obafemi Awolowo chose to emphasise the politics of ethnicity and regionalism rather than religion. On the other hand, Dr. Nnamdi Azikwe, who came from the east, started his movement as a nationalist struggle, and his party had been accepted in many parts of the country. This changed with the emergence of three major political parties, particularly the Action Group (Western Region), NCNC (Eastern Region) and NPC (Northern Region).

The first republic was aborted in a military coup by some young officers of the Nigerian army on January 15, 1966, majority of whom were Igbo.[7] During the coup, major politicians from the north, including the prime minister, Sir Abubakar Tafawa Balewa, and the premier of the Northern Region, Sir Ahmadu Bello were assassinated. Other politicians assassinated included Chief Ladoke Akintola, the premier of the Western Region. Later, the senior members of the Nigerian army led by Lt General Aguiyi Ironsi took over the mantle of leadership, but his style of leadership was seen to be favouring his ethnic group, the Igbo, and in July 1966 there was a counter-coup by young officers of northern extraction, which saw the assassination of General Ironsi. Lt Colonel Yakubu Gowon became the Head of State and since then the story has been that of coups and counter-coups.

After Gowon took over in 1966, the military governor of the Eastern Region, Colonel Odemegwu Ojukwu, announced his intention to break away from Nigeria and establish the Republic of Biafra, and that resulted in a 30-month civil war that ended in 1970. General Gowon was overthrown by General Murtala Muhammad in July 1975. On February 13, 1976, General Murtala was assassinated and his deputy Lt General Olusegun Obasanjo took over and continued with the transition programme started by Murtala. On October 1, 1979, General Obasanjo handed over power to Alhaji Shehu Shagari, who was later overthrown by Major General Muhammadu Buhari on December 31st, 1983, a few months after winning a second term in a controversial election. Buhari was overthrown in a palace coup on August 27, 1985, by General Ibrahim Babangida.

General Babangida continued ruling until August 26, 1993, after he annulled the June 12 presidential election and established an Interim National Government headed by Chief Earnest Shonekan. After three months General Sani Abacha, in a broadcast to the nation, announced the resignation of Chief Shonekan, and his own appointment as the new head of state. General Abacha died on June 8, 1998, and the Chief of Defence Staff General Abdusalami Abubakar was sworn in as the new head of state. General Abubakar started a transition to civilian administration, and on May 29, 1999, Chief Olusegun Obasanjo, who was head of state between

[7] Igbo is one of the three major ethnic groups in Nigeria. The remaining two are Hausa and Yoruba. It is estimated that there more than 250 different ethnic groups across Nigeria, some of which include Kanuri, Efik, Fulani, Ijaw, Tiv, etc.

1976 and 1979, and newly released from prison for his alleged involvement in a coup to overthrow General Abacha, was sworn in as the new president. After two terms in office Obasanjo was succeeded by Umaru Musa Yar'Adua on May 29, 2007.[8]

President Yar'Adua died on May 10, 2010, after being sick for many months. He was succeeded by his vice president, Goodluck Jonathan who completed the presidential term started by Yar'Adua. Goodluck Jonathan ran for the presidential election in 2011 and was declared winner by the Independent National Electoral Commission, in an election that was marred by allegations of fraud which resulted in violence and protests in the northern part of the country. In 2015, Goodluck Jonathan was defeated by Muhammadu Buhari in a historic election that saw the transfer of power from an incumbent political party, the People's Democratic Party (PDP), to the opposition All Progressive Congress (APC). Goodluck Jonathan received a lot commendation for conceding defeat and congratulating his opponent, a gesture which is rare in African politics.

Prior to independence, agriculture was the main source of revenue, but with the discovery of oil in commercial quantities, oil is now the main source of revenue. The World Fact Book estimates the Nigerian population to be around 190 million as of July 2017 (World Fact Book 2018). The predominant religions are Islam and Christianity with some indigenous religious practices present.

Political Culture

The concept of political culture was introduced in the 1950s (Laitin 1978) and received further attention in the 1960s, particularly in the political science literature with the works of Almond, Verba, Coleman and other political scientists who wanted to explore the patterns of behaviour that determine political action (see Mamadouh 1997; Mudambi and Navarra 2003; Canel and Sanders 2006).

Importance of meaning is crucial in the discourse on political culture and is mostly applied nationally because the state plays an important role in driving the political process. Understanding cultural differences is important in fashioning out ways of ensuring a healthy political atmosphere because those differences contribute in comprehending the national political culture (Mamadouh 1999).

[8] The election that brought Yar'Adua to power was marred by controversy because of the allegation of rigging and fraud.

According to Mamadouh (1997), "The main advantage of the concept 'political culture' is to point out that political behaviour has to be seen in cultural context. Political behavior is directed by *interpretations* and *preferences*, not by bare facts and interests." Mamadouh further states that "the concept political culture is generally used to refer to specific cultural patterns in a specific state. Doing politics – participating in the political decision-making process – is not the same everywhere", "the concept of 'political culture' reminds us that in each state there is a specific way of doing politics and that it is related to its cultural background.". (1997: 17–18 emphasis original).

Other works on political culture, like Wegener (2000), Sharkansky (1969) and Werlin and Eckstein (1990), have discussed the phenomenon of political culture from individual attitudes to its reflection on the state, how relations between leaders and followers affect culture and the patterns of people's orientation when it comes to political action. It includes the understanding of values and the perception of history in political life.

It is the variation of cultures in different constituencies of a given country that is fused to produce the national political culture, which is defined "as the pattern of successive alliances embedded in a specific cultural context, it can be seen as a dialogue or conversation between rationalities (and alliances): some cultural biases are loudly voiced, others are muted. Differences are rooted partly in the cultural context" (Mamadouh 1999: 479).

The political culture in Nigeria is an integral part of the evolution of the Nigerian state. Nigerians are very proud of their country and are quite passionate about its development. Political discourse is a common practice among peers, though people also tend to judge things from ethnic and regional perspectives as influenced by their religious beliefs. It can be argued that the Nigerian political culture is a juxtaposition of scepticism, ethnic, regional and religious loyalty. The scepticism comes from the loss of faith in political office holders. The citizens have lost faith in the political leaders doing the right thing, especially from the mid-1980s. Political leaders, military or civilians are seen as opportunists who use the state as a means of enriching themselves. This behaviour is also reflected in the media coverage of issues in Nigeria as editorials and comments from columnists tend to doubt the sincerity of government actions. One of the reasons for the issues stated above is identified by Aluko (2002) as corruption. Therefore, according to him "the institutionalization of corruption in Nigeria is not without its telling effects on the emerging political culture and behavior" (p. 396).

"Power shift", which is the phrase used by politicians and journalists to describe the transfer of power from one region to the other, has become a common language in Nigeria. The political parties have an informal arrangement of alternating the office of the president between the northern and the southern part of the country. Although this is not part of the constitution, it shows the influence of regionalism and ethnicity in Nigeria. Even the ruling party, the APC, which claims not to recognise the power-sharing arrangement is indirectly practising it because the party has faced several challenges related to zoning of political offices. In the 2019 elections, there are more candidates from Northern Nigeria expressing interest in the presidency because of this informal arrangement among Nigerian elites. It is likely that there will be more candidates from Southern Nigeria expressing interest for the presidency in the 2023 elections. This is one of the strategies used by politicians to maintain a stronghold on political power and mobilise voter support.

It is important to note that despite some of the differences between people, there are areas of cultural interaction, and even where cultures overlap. The political behaviour of the politicians interrelates with each other. A politician from the north seeking for votes in the south is prepared to dress to look like someone from the south. A politician from the south seeking for votes in the north will be happy to receive a traditional title in the north. Politicians from different parts of the country try to portray themselves as godly people; Christians seeking the blessing of the church and Muslims from the mosque. When accused of wrong doing, such as corruption, people will seek prayers from religious leaders and their local community.

Defining Corruption

Corruption is increasingly becoming a subject of academic discourse partly because of the impact it is having on the economy by reducing the incentive for investment, the cost of transactions (Seligson 2002), and providing an environment dictated by a questionable approach to issues of economic and political magnitude. The complex nature of corruption has also made it difficult for scholars to agree on a single definition of corruption because of the differences in culture, attitude and environment. What is seen as a corrupt act in one society may be normal in another society. The attitude in culture and behaviour could include the shift in attitude or ideology from good to bad (Nye 1967). Researchers also tend to look at corruption as an indication of the failure of the system in a given society (Hans 1998).

Bayley (1966) looks at some of these differences in his discussion of the effect of corruption in a developing nation. Bayley differentiates between western and non-western conception of what may be a corrupt act. Using the definition by Webster's dictionary which defines corruption as "inducement [as of public official] by means of improper consideration [as bribery] to commit a violation of duty" as a reference point, Bayley states that these improper considerations could include nepotism and misappropriation, but according to him, these could pose a dilemma to somebody from a non-western background from India or an African country to whom using one's position to get jobs for friends, kinsmen or region may signify an act of loyalty to the community which should be appreciated rather than condemned (pp. 720–721).[9] Bayley therefore sees corruption as culturally conditioned.

The study by Sandholtz and Koetzle (2000) also agree with Bayley on the cultural context of corruption. Their study questions the criteria to be used by a researcher in determining which action is corrupt. They suggested the three approaches used by political scientists in studying corruption. These approaches are the public interest, public opinion and legal norm. The public interest approach to defining corruption looks at the behaviour of the public official in discharging his responsibility and the extent to which he violates public interest. The public opinion approach defines corruption by weighing it against public opinion and so corruption is what the public consider as corrupt. The legal approach explains corruption in terms of the violation of rules on how to observe public duties. The difficulty with the three approaches to understanding corruption would be in defining public interest, and who should define the public interest—is it the elite, the media or the ordinary members of the public? Also, how can the public opinion be sufficiently weighted to represent the view of the majority?

Discussing corruption in a democratic society, Jain (2001) also states that the first problem with the issue of corruption is defining it. He

[9] The position of Bayley may still be relevant in many developing countries, but the explanation may go beyond behaviour and culture, perhaps due to the fragile nature of the economies of these countries where equal opportunity may not be provided to citizens. Thus, people use their positions to secure employment for those that are closer to them tribally or geographically.

identifies three types of corruption which can help in understanding the phenomenon of corruption. They are grand corruption, bureaucratic corruption and legislative corruption (pp. 73–75). Grand corruption refers to the use of political power by the elites in creating economic policies that favour their interest. They do this by channelling resources to those sectors where it is easier to make personal gain. Jain further explained that it is difficult to identify this kind of corruption unless a bribe is exchanged, because the resources are channelled in the name of a public service.

Bureaucratic corruption is corruption by civil servants who interact both with political elites and members of the public; for example, a member of the public could be coerced into giving a bribe in order to speed the process of administering an official task, or it could take the form of paying bribes to members of the judiciary so as to lessen a legal penalty. Legislative corruption according to Jain involves influencing the voting pattern of legislators to serve the interest of some groups, or the members of the executive who are desperate to get particular legislation through.

A different approach to the understanding of corruption was provided by Luo (2004) by looking at corruption from an organisational perspective. According to Luo "the disciplines that deal with corruption each have fundamental paradigms, which they bring into the analysis of the phenomenon. Sociologists hold that the roots of corruption are social and cultural, and that corruption hinders public welfare and social development. Political scientists maintain that nontransparent institutions, low paid public servants and a shortage of independent and well-functioning market mechanisms are antecedent of corruption. Legal scholars focus on the type of legal system and its enforcement. Macroeconomists focus on weak economic institutions and lack of transparent institutions as root causes" (pp. 119–120).

Luo believes that to understand corruption we need to look at organisations and the corrupt practices they are indulged in, especially profit-driven organisations who are willing to give bribes either to public servants, legislators or other government officials. Luo further argued that unless the issue of organisational corruption is addressed, it would be difficult to eradicate corruption, because unlike individuals, organisations cannot be arrested, they can only face legal sanction. Luo therefore defines corruption as "an illegitimate exchange of resources involving the use or abuse of public responsibility for private ends" (p. 121).

But Luo's definition does not differ much from other definitions of corruption apart from the emphasis given on organisations as indicated earlier. It seems there is consensus among scholars that corruption is simply the use of public office for private gain (see Jain 2001; Anderson and Tverdova 2003; Bohara et al. 2004; Golden and Picci 2005; Wu 2005; Chang 2005; Luo 2004). Most of the differences are in the arrangement and rearrangement of words, but the meaning remains the same.

Broadly speaking, the classifications discussed above fall within the theory of political corruption (Philip 1997, 2002). Although the political corruption theory indicates the difficulty in defining political corruption, it does, however, suggest that such forms of corruption, like public interest, public office and market definitions of corruption, fall within the category of political corruption. This is important because, as will be discussed later, the cases of corruption scandals that will be studied revolve round the typologies discussed above.

While political corruption "involves substituting rule in the interests of an individual or group for those publicly endorsed practices which affect an ordered resolution to conflicting individual or group interests" (Philip 1997: 458), other schools of thought may see this as a simplistic approach to understanding corruption. Critics, like those who belong to the Marxist school of thought, will see it differently. They will rather look at the whole phenomenon of corruption as a struggle between classes: the ruling class, who are the elites, and the working class or the masses. In his discussion on Marx and Engels on the State, Sanderson (1963) states, "the state was for Marx essentially coercive. It was, he held in the first volume of *Capital*, 'the concentrated and organised force of society.'" (p. 947, emphasis original). Therefore, from Marxist perspective, corruption can be seen as a means by which the managers of the state exploit resources in the process of accumulation in order to maintain their hold on the working class. In his view this trend will continue until the working class destroy the state and replace it "with their own dictatorship" (Sanderson 1963: 953).

However, there are scholars who express concern over the Marxist approach to understanding corruption. According to Hollander (1982):

> It was the great historic promise of Marxism to inspire societies that would not only eliminate economic exploitation and inequality but also create such social harmony that the necessity of maintaining social order by force will disappear, allowing the state to "wither away." Not only Marx and Engels, but even Lenin believed (up to appoint, at any rate) that this was a realistic

> prospect…it is one of the great ironies of history that the attempt to translate Marxism-Leninism into reality provoked far more resistance and consequently far more political violence and coercion than had been foreseen. (p. 327)

Other scholars like Jowitt (1983) in his article "Soviet Neotraditionalism: The Political Corruption of a Leninist Regime; and White (1996) in his article "Corruption and the Transition from Socialism in China", have expressed similar reservation about the ability of states run on Marxist philosophy, dealing effectively with the exploitation of resources, or to say it more explicitly, corruption in their societies.

An important point to note is that scholars influenced by Marxist approach in analysing media discourses have used different approaches in studying media contents. Key among these approaches is the application of the political economy theory. According to Golding and Murdock (2000), "critical political economists follow Marx in shifting attention from the realm of exchange to the organisation of property and production, both within the cultural industries and more generally. They do not deny that cultural producers and consumers are continually making choices, but point out that they do so within wider structures" (p. 73).

The political economy approach is built on a premise that uses a critical approach in studying the dynamic nature of the economic structure, the ideological content of the media, and the nature of the operation of the media industry. It is interested in the ownership and control of the media, and pays attention to the linkage of the media industry with the economic and political system (McQuail 2005).

Golding and Murdock have made an important distinction between "mainstream economics" and political economy. According to them these differences can be categorised into four. "First, it is holistic; second, it is historical; third, it is centrally concerned with the balance between capitalist enterprise and public intervention; and finally—and perhaps most importantly of all—it goes beyond technical issues of efficiency to engage with basic moral questions of justice, equity and the public good" (pp. 72–73).

In essence, the political economy approach studies communication content, not by simply concentrating on the nature of ownership of the media, or the interest of the elites who own these media organisations, but also by looking at the interplay between journalism as a practice, and the forces within the society, whether political or economic, that shape the way media content is produced. Different studies have used this approach in studying media content. One such study is the work of Edward Herman and Noam Chomsky, in which they put forward a propaganda model (2002). The study recognised what it called news filters, such as (a) the size and nature of ownership of the media; (b) advertising as a means of income generation for the media; (c) the reliance of the media on sources, such as government and business owners, as a credible means of generating stories; (d) flak; and (e) anticommunism, through which information must pass (Herman and Chomsky 2002).

What the political economy approach in studying media and communication does is to empirically study how media content reflect such journalistic values like honesty, impartiality, objectivity and so on, in comparison to such other determinants like ownership of the media, elite interest, corporate interests and other socio-economic factors that directly or indirectly influence the work of the journalist.

This is important for this book in the sense that this study is interested in such factors that shape journalism practice in Nigeria, like regionalism, clientelism and so forth. While the political economy approach claims to be holistic, as stated by Golding and Murdock (2000), there is need for a fresh approach to the study of journalism by looking at the media in terms of the internal complexities within the society, especially in non-Western societies, where the nature of the economy and the challenges faced by the news media may vary. It is also important to identify new approaches to the study of journalism beyond the conventional theories like the political economy or the normative theories of the press that have been used in the study of journalism for decades. This is one of the reasons why this book takes a different theoretical approach in studying the coverage of corruption scandals in the Nigerian press, even though some elements of the political economy approach might be relevant in the analysis.

Corruption should be seen, therefore, as a social, political, economic and governance problem, to which any society can be vulnerable, irrespective of ideology, political or economic system. The extent of corruption may differ depending on the system, but theoretical assumptions may not fully provide effective solutions.

While corruption normally takes place between individuals or social groups, once it catches the attention of the media, and the allegation of corruption generates public awareness (as explained in the next section), then it has become a scandal, which is the subject of this research within a Nigerian context.

Corruption Scandals, the Fourth Estate and Investigative Journalism

With the definition of corruption provided by scholars, coupled with the interest of the media in revealing to the public the acts of corruption, it is now necessary to focus on why the media consider it a duty to explore and inform the people about what is considered to be corrupt and scandalous.

Scandal is a word which refers to acts of corruption that have become public knowledge through the news media. Scandal is "the publication of information about corruption" (Tumber and Waisbord 2004a: 1032). It is also used when reporting acts of transgression and violation of moral codes. These transgressions could be corrupt practices that public officials are trying to hide, excessive use of power to maintain political relevance or in some cases involving extra-marital relationships.

The word *scandal* has a religious connotation as "the word was first used in a religious context in the Septuagint, the Greek version of the Old Testament" (Thompson 2000: 12). According to Thompson, the word *scandal*, which appeared in English language in the sixteenth century, is used to describe a religious person who discredited the religion, or the action of the followers of the religion who begin to doubt their belief in the Creator, to any defamatory action or an abominable behaviour that is frowned upon by the people (Thompson 2000). Thus scandal "involved a transgression of moral codes which could be, but did not have to be, religious in character, and with reference to which the action or the event was denounced" (Thompson 1997: 39). It is a behaviour that is "in conflict with society's moral standards" (Funk 1996: 2).

Thompson offered a working definition of scandal, which he defined as "*actions or events involving certain kinds of transgressions which become known to others and are sufficiently serious to elicit public response*" (Thompson 2000: 13, emphasis original). As such, scandal is not hidden. Many corrupt practices and actions that violate the norms of the society are conducted in secret, but they may not qualify as scandals until they have been exposed to the public.

Once the cover of secrecy is removed, that's when scandal sets in, and in the words of Lull and Hinerman (1997) that is when "the secrets of desire are unlocked, the curtains of privacy are pulled back. The unspoken is articulated, observed and pondered" (p. 3). Jimenez (2004) states that "the word *scandal* in colloquial language is used in two different senses.

On one hand it is used to qualify certain behaviour that deviates from norm. In this sense, we call certain behavior scandalous before it brings about social reprobation at all. *Scandalous* is, in this usage, synonymous with *deviate*. On the other hand, by the word scandal we also refer to the social reaction brought about by the public knowledge of behaviour qualified as deviate" (p. 1100, emphasis original).

Scandal is also about calling to order the representatives of the people when they deviate from the trust given to them by the people. If the response received from them as a result of the scandal is convincing to the public, they may regain public confidence; otherwise, they will elicit public disapproval which will make them lose both the trust of the people and the position they are holding (Jimenez 2004). In the words of Tiffen (2004) "the accused must often either suffer no tangible punishment or else suffer the political equivalent of capital punishment, having their public career terminated by resignation" (p. 1172).

Lull and Hinerman (1997) identified ten criteria that constitute a scandal. The criteria include violation of social norms, some people have to be identified as the perpetrators of the scandal, their actions should clearly aim at satisfying their personal desires, there should be individuals who committed the acts, the actions should be done deliberately, they must take responsibility for their action, the events should have an effect on the persons involved, such actions have to be widely reported in the mass media, they should be structured and narrativised as stories, and finally the stories must elicit public responses by attracting public attention and wide discussion.

In this age of communication and information revolution, where citizens have access to information through the news media, the activities of public officials are easily placed under public scrutiny. According to Canel and Sanders (2006) "in this atmosphere the reputation of the leaders becomes vulnerable. Here lies the scope for scandal" (p. 50).

The news media, therefore, take on this vulnerability of the political leaders and turn the scandals into issues of national discussion. According to Thompson (2000: 78–83), the media does that for a number of reasons including their commercial interest, the desire of some individuals to use scandal stories in order to satisfy some political objectives, the professional ethics of journalism which seek to promote factuality and entertainment, and finally the competitive rivalry that exists between the media organisations.

Looking at each of these factors within the Nigerian context, it can be stated that the majority of the newspapers are privately owned, and any scandalous story that might promote the paper and attract a wider audience is likely to make the front page.

Esser and Hartung (2004) look at the phenomenon of scandal from a communication perspective. They see "*scandal* as the intense public communication about real or imagined defect that is by consensus condemned, and that meets universal indignation and outrage" (p. 1041, emphasis original). Esser and Hartung's view is that for scandal to be worth its name, it has to be made public by someone who views the action as scandalous. Esser and Hartung call those who reveal the story to the public as "denouncers", that is, those "who contradict defenders" (p. 1044), and according to them, these denouncers can be categorised into four groups:

> The first group is composed of the opposition to the political system who may hope to undermine the legitimacy of the system by continuously stressing its shortcomings...A second group of denouncers is composed of politicians from other parties or companies in competition ...A third group at first glance less obvious, is composed of rivals in one's own party, company, or organisation...The fourth group of denouncers is composed of journalists in the mass media. Aside from political motives, this group also has a professional inclination to suggest scandal, for the control of government and the exposure of deficiencies are among the most important functions of the mass media. (pp. 1044–1045)

Therefore, these four groups aid the news media in its search for scandal stories either through interviews or leaks or both so that the transgression can be brought to the attention of the public. This is because no matter how grave an offence or the violation of moral code is, once it is ignored by the mass media, such violation cannot be termed a scandal "especially in times when publicity is synonymous with mediated publicity, the media wield unmatched power in converting secret acts of wrongdoing into scandalous actions. If it is hard to imagine a scandal without media attention, it is because of the capacity of the media to produce and distribute information that reaches mass audiences" (Waisbord 2004: 1077); hence, the ability of the media to put before the electorates "the scandal of politics" (Schudson 2004: 1236–1237), which might perhaps explain why "news about official wrongdoing enjoys substantial advantage over other news about wrongdoing because it fits standard journalistic principles about the newsworthiness of official actions" (Waisbord 2004: 1087).

Even though publicity is what counts in media scandals, and lack of attention by the media might symbolise the death of the scandal, beyond that Waisbord suggests, "Scandals might also illustrate views that we live in a postmodern world in which mediated signs have replaced (political) reality and that politics has moved from traditional to mediated agoras" (p. 1078).

But some scholars are critical of the news media, which they see as dependent on news sources rather than the initiator of stories. For example, Liebes and Blum-Kulka (2004) suggest that scandals are revealed through "whistle-blowing", "entrapment", and "spotlighting or mainstreaming"—"whistle-blowing is when an insider for idealistic or political or personal motives, volunteers information about a carefully hidden dark secret, damaging to the perpetrator"; "entrapment is when a reporter, for professional or political or personal motives, break a tacit or explicit agreement with a source"; and "spotlighting or mainstreaming" occurs "when a source or a reporter spotlights information that may even be widely known) to prove the violation of a norm, the abuse of which is ignored". Liebes and Blum-Kulka also sees live broadcasting as another form of whistle-blowing which "disintermediates the reporter by addressing the public directly" (p. 1154).

The argument by Liebes and Blum-Kulka is that the power of the media in reporting scandals might be exaggerated since the sources of news play an active role in revealing the acts of transgression, and in some cases, it is the journalist who violates an agreement in order to satisfy either personal motives or the commercial interest of his medium.

Whatever the case, you cannot discuss the issue of scandal in the twenty-first century without referring to the media. The media has established itself as the trumpet of an information society, and for the world to know the existence of a scandal or any related news, it must pass through this inevitable medium. This is not to downplay the relevance of other sources or avenues that play a vital role in scandalising stories, but because news about scandals satisfies the criteria news editors would like to see on their desks, and beyond that the media sees itself as the fourth estate of the realm.

As a result of that, the fourth estate is now a common term used by journalists, politicians and public affairs commentators to refer to the watchdog role of the media in society. The media in this case is assumed to be the unelected representative of the people that combined the dual role of profit-making and service to the people. This role played by the media varies from one society to another depending on the independence of institutions, culture and style of governance.

A number of journalists who understand the debate about the watchdog role of the media see their role as that of strengthening the fourth estate conception of journalism which is attributed to Edmund Burke, who stated in the eighteenth century during a session of the English Parliament that "*there are three estates in parliament, but in the reporters' gallery yonder sits a fourth estate more important than they all. It is not a figure of speech or witty saying; it is a literal fact, very momentous to use in these times*". (Carlyle 1841 cited in Donohue et al. 1995: 118, emphasis original).

The other three branches referred to by Edmund Burke are the executive, the legislature and the judiciary. These three arms, according to the postulations of the fourth estate, cannot function properly without the fourth, which is the media. According to de Albuquerque (2005), "this division of power system needs communication between the branches, and between the government and the public, and the news media are the main way to accomplish that role" (p. 497).

However, what is indisputable is that for the media to achieve this position, it must be critical of the powers that be, investigating and discovering wrongdoings that people's representatives would wish remain hidden and, as stated by Shultz (1998), the press lives by disclosures and is up-to-date by having the correct information on the happenings in a country, and turns such happenings into the property of the people.

Investigative Journalism

Investigative journalism is required if the media is to deserve the fourth estate description. Even though there are different conceptions on the meaning of investigative journalism, it is worth noting that for news to be investigative it requires a distinctive effort beyond reliance on leaks and the use of other secondary sources of information. But as journalist Bob Green states, investigative journalism requires exploring information as a result of the effort of the journalist and such information must be relevant to the public (Waisbord 2000).

It involves aggressive follow-up, as stated by Calvert (1999), that "some stories you make five calls, on some twenty. When you are making a hundred, that's investigative journalism. The story may land in your lap—it's the substantiation that makes it an investigative story, because when you realise people are lying to you, blocking you, then you have to find different ways of getting hold of the information and it can take a lot longer.

Also, you have to be careful when you are making serious allegations against people, then the evidence really matters" (cited in de Burgh 2000: 18).

Investigative journalism that satisfies such criteria succeeds in changing the mood of the public, the news horizon and serves as a reference point that will help in deterring erring officials from violating public trust to satisfy personal desires. This kind of journalism turns news stories into scandalous issues that will attract the wrath of the public. Therefore, it can be argued that investigative journalism, as stated by Waisbord (2000), "is one form of journalistic discourse that deals with moral questions".

Investigative journalism is distinct from routine journalism that relies on press conferences, press releases, interviews and other conventional ways of news-making, whose main aim is to convey the messages received through official proceedings. (For more on routine journalism see Harcup and O'Neill 2001.[10]) Investigative "journalists occupy a vital role as educators and keepers of the public conscience, serving as watchdogs forever on the lookout for corruption, incompetence, and abuses of power" (Brennen 2000: 109–110). "To be termed 'investigative', journalism usually involves extensive research by one or more journalists to uncover matters which affect the citizenry of the society in which the journalist lives and of which the society generally does not approve but is unaware". (de Burgh 2003: 806).

Investigative journalists are seen as the mirrors of the society who use their conscience in uncovering wrongdoings that would likely remain hidden to the public. Investigative journalists are fearless and courageous, they are disliked by the mighty and the powerful as well as those in positions of authority. Journalists involved in investigative journalism are seen as the custodians responsible for depending the values of the society that might be violated by those in authority; one of their aims is to see that wrongdoers are duly punished (de Burgh 2003) because of the argument that investigative journalism is done to promote the interest of the public (Goddard 2006). Investigative journalism seeks to discuss and interpret the value of justice and affirm the importance or otherwise of right and wrong, innocence and guilt by analysing, criticising and interpreting the case under journalistic investigation (Ettema and Glasser 1988).

[10]Tony Harcup and Deirdre O'Neill did a study on the factors that determine what is news in Britain? They did the study by revisiting earlier news values proposed by Galtung and Ruge in the 1960s. The study was interesting, but as explained by scholars on investigative journalism, investigative journalism is different from everyday reporting, and that is the position of this research.

Citing the criteria provided by Ettema and Glasser (1987), Ekstrom (2002) discussed the steps followed by investigative journalists which serve as evaluative criteria in determining the worthiness of the investigative story. "*First*, they assess various tips and ideas. Are they credible? Can they be turned into a good story? But also: Will the reportage achieve something? In the *second* step, information is collected and evaluated with respect to its value as evidence. There is a hierarchy of evidentiary weight… in the *third* step, pieces of the story are fitted together into a narration… *Fourth*, the journalists make a final evaluation of the story as a whole. Alternative narratives, alternative explanations are tested, and the staff test the story for possible faults. The result is then a sufficiently justified story" (pp. 271–272 emphasis original).

The political climate in Nigeria from independence to date has not been scandal-free especially when we consider the definition that explains scandal as "corruption revealed" (see Tumber and Waisbord 2004a, b). Various governments, both military and civilian, faced a number of accusations about corruption. The media on its part has not been silent on these issues, especially the newspapers, most of which are privately owned. But unlike many developed countries, such as the United States and Britain, where the media has to some extent been successful in bringing down public officials, the extent to which that is achieved in Nigeria as a developing country is a subject of debate.

To borrow from the South American continent whose countries may possibly go hand in hand with Nigeria in grappling with leadership challenges where in the words of Waisbord, "there is widespread skepticism about the honesty of public officials and where denunciations of wrongdoing have become regular in recent years, exposes may have less impact than in situation where government officials are expected to obey the law and or are seen as decent and trustworthy persons" (2000: xvii).

The characterisation by Waisbord may serve as an explanatory reason that may hinder the effort of the newspapers, even if they expose the wrongdoing of government officials, because of the scepticism from the public to whom doing the right thing by public office holders seems unusual, and doing the wrong thing is the order of the day.

That notwithstanding, the media, though itself not free from problems as we shall discuss in Chaps. 6, 7 and 8 in the case of Nigeria, or South Africa and Kenya in Chaps. 4 and 5, continued to be vigilant of government at different levels whether during the military or civilian administrations.

Intranational Comparative Research in Africa: The Case of Nigeria

Most of the media studies conducted using comparative approaches are cross-national in nature to bring out the similarities and differences in the way the media operates in different countries (Blumler and Gurevitch 1995; Hallin and Mancini 2004; Canel and Sanders 2006).

One of the problems identified by mass media researchers is the likelihood of employing the theories developed in a different political and socio-cultural settings and then applying them in another setting, thinking they can be applied without any difficulty (Hallin and Mancini 2004). To depart from this tradition in order to understand vividly the media environment of other countries and the relationship between the media and other institutions, Blumler and Gurevitch proposed certain criteria for cross national comparative analysis. "Degree of state control over mass media organisations", "degree of mass media partisanship", "degree of media-political elite integration" and "the nature of the legitimizing creed of media institutions"(p. 62), are the four frameworks proposed by Blumler and Gurevitch which can be used to comparatively study the operation of the media in different countries.

Prior to the research by Blumler and Gurevitch, the work of Siebert, Peterson and Schramm (1956), popularly known as the *Four Theories of the Press* was the dominant study that was used in comparative political communications research. The four theories proposed by them, authoritarian, libertarian, social responsibility and the Soviet Union theories were adopted to explain media systems even in societies that have a political system completely different from those in Europe and North America.

Hallin and Mancini strengthened the approach in comparative research by refining the work of Blumler and Gurevitch in their study of media systems in Western Europe and North America. They identified the ethnocentric nature of previous media researches and their assumption of universality, and they suggested four criteria for comparative research which they thought could be applied in other settings with modification. The proposed framework by Hallin & Mancini include (1) the development of media markets, with particular emphasis on the strong or weak development of mass circulation press; (2) political parallelism; that is, the degree and nature of links between the media and political parties or, more broadly, the extent to which the media systems reflect the major political divisions in the society; (3) the development of journalistic professionalism; and (4) the degree and nature of state intervention in the media system (p. 21).

While the examples cited above have been conducted cross-nationally in parts of Europe and North America, the point of departure with this book is that it is within an intranational setting, hence the need for further modification of the framework to be used. Looking at the historical peculiarities of Africa and Nigeria in particular, it can be stated that many African countries are nations within nations, comprising different tribes, religious affiliations and other ethno-regional differences. For example, countries like Sudan (especially before the seperation of South Sudan), Cameroon, Côte d'Ivoire, Nigeria and many other countries in Africa comprise regional dichotomies, each region with a different political and cultural precolonial history, but united under one umbrella during colonialism.

The internal divisions within these countries suggest that they have not gone beyond the political convenience created at independence in order to hand over political power to indigenous citizens, but the struggle for self-assertion continued (see Chaps. 4, 5, and 8 for more on the regional, tribal and racial challenges inherited by some of African countries, which continue to shape their media landscape). The media that according to Hallin and Mancini, "no analyst would argue that journalism anywhere in the world is literally neutral" (p. 26), is likely to reflect on these divisions. Hence, the likelihood for the emergence of distinct journalism cultures that may need to be explored using a comparative approach.

In Nigeria this struggle is reflected among the various regions of the country, even though some of the regions are ahead of others in establishing media organisations, but the rivalry among the regions results in each region establishing any institution established by the other competing region. Although the military has abolished the old regional structure and created states, the operational mindset of the media is still influenced by that rivalry and struggle for self-assertion.

Because of the stated reasons, a framework for comparative study is proposed, modified on the works of Hallin and Mancini (2004), but created on the historical and political peculiarities of Nigeria. The proposed framework includes:

(a) The emergence of nationalist press and the search for political independence; this is about the emergence of nationalist newspapers which contributed in the struggle for independence and the mobilisation of the public on various issues affecting their well-being.

(b) The development of regional/ethnic media to enhance post-independence competition among the regions; this explains the establishment of regional media organisations before and immediately after independence to protect the interests of various regions.
(c) Regional parallelism and clientelism; this explains how the media develops a regional identity, and also establishes a clientelist relationship with politicians or people with a particular socio-political interest. This is a modification of Hallin and Mancini's political parallelism framework.

This modified framework will guide this research from the onset. The first and second categories, that is the development of nationalist press, and the emergence of regional media will be discussed from a review of the literature by drawing from the works of scholars who worked on the Nigerian media, its history, politics and so on. It would also be explored in other African countries such as Kenya and South Africa. The third category, regional parallelism, will be explored by using primary data. This will be done by conducting in-depth interviews with journalists, as well as an analysis of some of the newspapers by means of critical discourse analysis.[11]

This book therefore is divided into nine chapters. In Chap. 2 the discussion focuses on providing an overview of the state of the media in Africa and the historical origin of communications in Africa right from the development of traditional communications up to the emergence of the mass media. The history of the media in other African countries like Ghana, Kenya and South Africa is explored. The notion of development communication, which is a common feature in developing countries, is discussed and examples of studies that focus on corruption scandals in Africa are provided.

Chapter 3 discusses the historical landscape of Nigerian newspapers, the evolution of newspapers and the role played by Nigerian newspapers in the search for independence from Britain. It explains the nature of ownership of the media between the private and public sectors, the role of military and the challenges of press freedom in Nigeria. The chapter explores the role of the Nigerian media in returning the country to civilian administration, issues of national survival, and standing for the country by

[11] See Chap. 4 for detailed discussion of the methodology.

challenging those military and civilian leaders that attempted to change the constitution in order to stay beyond their welcome.

The media system in South Africa is the subject of Chap. 4. Discussions here focus on the development of the media during apartheid, the classification of the media between white and black press as well as the role of media in South Africa in the liberation struggle. One of the things that emerged after the end of apartheid was the development of tabloid journalism. What was the reason for that and who are the readers? Where are the media owners that supported the apartheid regime, and do they continue to publish, and who are their new audiences? These are questions the chapter will answer. The South African Media System will be located within one of the three models of media and politics suggested by Hallin and Mancini (2004).

Kenya is the subject of Chap. 5. This is a country that has several similarities with Nigeria and other Sub-Saharan African countries. What is the history of the country, and how does that history shape its media landscape? Who are the owners of the media, and what role does the media play during the election violence that followed multiparty elections in the 1990s and 2000s? The chapter will also compare the Kenyan media system within the media systems paradigm suggested by Hallin and Mancini (2004).

The subject of Chap. 6 is a critical discourse analysis of the stories on the coverage of corruption scandals in Nigeria. Attention is paid to the Petroleum Technology Development Fund (PTDF) scandal involving former president Olusegun Obasanjo and his former deputy Atiku Abubakar. It also discusses the former governors' scandal. Was the media neutral in the coverage or was it influenced by regionalism and ethnicity. Is the media itself free from the corruption it claims to expose? These are questions that are addressed.

This study has conducted interviews with 24 journalists from Nigeria, Kenya and South Africa. In Chap. 7 issues that emerged from the qualitative interviews are discussed. The chapter particularly focuses on journalistic practices, such as investigative journalism to find out whether media applies these practices, or whether it simply promotes armchair journalism. What are the challenges faced by the media and how can they be addressed?

Following the outcome of the interviews with journalists, Chap. 8 examines the concept of regional parallelism in the Nigerian press. It defines regional parallelism and explains its characteristics, such as location, elite influence, unevenness in newspaper ownership and so on.

Challenges, such as corruption within the media itself, bad working conditions, poor pay and weak capital base are explored.

In the concluding chapter, Chap. 9, a comparative analysis between Nigerian, Kenyan and South African media systems is conducted within the Hallin and Mancini models. This will help us to understand whether European and North American theories can work in Africa or not, and what would be the alternative.

References

Aluko, M. A. O. (2002). The Institutionalising of Corruption and Its Impact on Political Culture and Behaviour in Nigeria. *Nordic Journal of African Studies, 11*(3), 393–402.

Anderson, C. J., & Tverdova, Y. V. (2003). Corruption, Political Allegiances, and Attitudes Toward Government in Contemporary Democracies. *American Journal of Political Science, 47*(1), 91–109.

Bayley, D. H. (1966). The Effects of Corruption in a Developing Nation. *The Western Political Quarterly, 19*(4), 719–732.

BBC News. (2014). Nigeria Becomes Africa's Biggest Economy. Retrieved May 14, 2018. Available at http://www.bbc.com/news/business-26913497

BBC News. (2015). Nigeria's Dasuki 'Arrested Over $2bn Arms Fraud'. Retrieved May 14, 2018. Available at http://www.bbc.com/news/world-africa-34973872

BBC Witness. (2014). The Creation of Modern Nigeria in 1914. Retrieved May 14, 2018. Available at https://www.bbc.co.uk/programmes/p01q3c13

Blumler, J. G., & Gurevitch, M. (1995). *The Crisis of Public Communication*. London/New York: Routledge.

Bohara, A. K., Mitchell, N. J., & Mittendorf, C. F. (2004). Compound Democracy and the Control of Corruption: A Cross-Country Investigation. *The Policy Studies Journal, 32*(4), 481–499.

Brennen, B. S. (2000). What the Hacks Say: The Ideological Prism of US Journalism Texts. *Journalism, 1*(1), 106–113.

Burchard, S. M. (2014). *Democracy Trends in Sub-Saharan Africa, 1990–2014*. Institute for Defense Analysis. Alexandria. Retrieved May 14 2018.

Canel, M. J., & Sanders, K. (2006). *Morality Tales: Political Scandals in Britain and Spain in the 1990s*. Cresskill: Hampton Press.

Chang, E. C. C. (2005). Electoral Incentives for Political Corruption Under Open-List Proportional Representation. *The Journal of Politics, 67*(3), 716–730.

Commission for Africa. (2005). Our Common Interest: Report of the Commission for Africa. Available at http://www.commissionforafrica.org/english/report/introduction.html. Downloaded 24 Jan 2007.

de Albuquerque, A. (2005). Another 'Fourth Branch': Press and Political Culture in Brazil. *Journalism, 6*(4), 486–504.

de Burgh, H. (Ed.). (2000). *Investigative Journalism: Context and Practice*. London: Routledge.
de Burgh, H. (2003). Kings Without Crowns? The Re-emergence of Investigative Journalism in China. *Media, Culture and Society, 25*, 801–820.
de Sardan, J. P. O. (1999). A Moral Economy of Corruption in Africa? *The Journal of Modern African Studies, 37*(1), 25–52.
Doig, A., & Theobald, R. (2000). *Corruption and Democratisation*. London: Frank Cass.
Donohue, G. A., Tichenor, P. J., & Olien, C. N. (1995). A Guard Dog Perspective on the Role of Media. *Journal of Communication, 45*(2), 115–132.
Ekstrom, M. (2002). Epistemologies of TV Journalism: A Theoretical Framework. *Journalism, 3*(3), 259–282.
Esser, F., & Hartung, U. (2004). Nazis, Pollution, and No Sex: Political Scandals as a Reflection of Political Culture in Germany. *American Behavioural Scientist, 47*(8), 1040–1071.
Ettema, J. S., & Glasser, T. L. (1988). Narrative Form and Moral Force: The Realisation of Innocence and Guilt Through Investigative Journalism. *Journal of Communication, 38*(3), 8–26.
Funk, C. L. (1996). The Impact of Scandal on Candidate Evaluations: An Experimental Test of the Role of Candidate Traits. *Political Behaviour, 18*(1), 1–24.
Goddard, P. (2006). 'Improper Liberties': Regulating Undercover Journalism on ITV, 1967–1980. *Journalism, 7*(1), 45–63.
Golden, M. A., & Picci, L. (2005). Proposal for a New Measure of Corruption, Illustrated with Italian Data. *Economics & Politics, 17*(1), 37–75.
Golding, P., & Murdock, G. (2000). Culture, Communications and Political Economy. In J. Curran & M. Gurevitch (Eds.), *Mass Media and Society* (pp. 70–92). London: Arnold.
Hallin, D. C., & Mancini, P. (2004). *Comparing Media Systems: Three Models of Media and Politics*. Cambridge: Cambridge University Press.
Hans, K. H. (1998). Governmental Mismanagement and Symbolic Violence: Discourses on Corruption in the Yucatan of the 1990s. *Bulletin of Latin American Research, 17*(3), 367–386.
Harcup, T., & O'Neil, D. (2001). What Is News? Galtung and Ruge Revisited. *Journalism Studies, 2*(2), 261–280.
Herman, E. S., & Chomsky, N. (2002). *Manufacturing Consent. The Political Economy of the Mass Media*. New York: Pantheon.
Hollander, P. (1982). Research on Marxist Societies: The Relationship Between Theory and Practice. *Annual Review of Sociology, 8*, 319–351.
Jain, A. K. (2001). Corruption: A Review. *Journal of Economic Surveys, 15*(1), 71–121.
Jimenez, F. (2004). The Politics of Scandal in Spain: Morality Plays, Social Trust, and the Battle for Public Opinion. *American Behavioural Scientist, 47*(8), 1099–1121.

Jowitt, K. (1983). Soviet Neotraditionalism: The Political Corruption of Lenninist Regime. *Soviet Studies, 35*(3), 275–297.
Laitin, D. D. (1978). Religion, Political Culture, and the Weberian Tradition. *World Politics, 30*(4), 563–592.
Liebes, T., & Blum-Kulka, S. (2004). It Takes Two to Blow the Whistle; Do Journalists Control the Outbreak of Scandal? *American Behavioural Scientist, 47*(9), 1153–1170.
Lull, J., & Hinerman, S. (1997). The Search for Scandal. In J. Lull & S. Hinerman (Eds.), *Media Scandals: Morality and Desire in the Popular Culture Marketplace* (pp. 1–33). Cambridge: Polity Press.
Luo, Y. (2004). An Organisational Perspective of Corruption. *Management and Organisation Review, 1*(1), 119–154.
Mamadouh, V. (1997). Political Culture: A Typology Grounded on Cultural Theory. *GeoJournal, 43*, 17–25.
Mamadouh, V. (1999). A Political-Cultural Map of Europe. Family Structures and the Origins of Differences Between National Political Cultures in the European Union. *GeoJournal, 47*, 477–486.
McQuail, D. (2005). *McQuail's Mass Communication Theory*. London: Sage.
Mudambi, R., & Navarra, P. (2003). Political Culture and Foreign Direct Investment: The Case of Italy. *Economics of Governance, 4*(1), 37–56.
Nye, J. S. (1967). Corruption and Political Development: A Cost-Benefit Analysis. *The American Political Science Review, 61*(2), 417–427.
Ogingwo, W. (1980). 'We' and 'They': A Study of Ethnic Stereotypes in Nigeria. *Sociologus, 30*(2), 97–123.
Philip, M. (1997). Defining Political Corruption. *Political Studies, XLV*, 436–462.
Philip, M. (2002). Conceptualising Political Corruption. In A. J. Heidenheimer & M. Johnston (Eds.), *Political Corruption: Concepts and Contexts* (pp. 41–57). New Brunswick: Transaction Publishers.
Reuters. (2013). Special Report: Anatomy of Nigeria's $20 Billion Leak. Retrieved May 14 2018. Available at https://www.reuters.com/article/us-nigeria-election-banker-specialreport/special-report-anatomy-of-nigerias-20-billion-leak-idUSKBN0LA0X820150206
Sanderson, J. (1963). Marx and Engels on the State. *The Western Political Quaterly, 16*(4), 946–955.
Sandholtz, W., & Koetzle, W. (2000). Accounting for Corruption: Economic Structure, Democracy, and Trade. *International Studies Quarterly, 44*, 31–50.
Schudson, M. (2004). Notes on Scandal and the Watergate Legacy. *American Behavioural Scientist, 47*(9), 1231–1238.
Seligson, M. A. (2002). The Impact of Corruption on Regime Legitimacy: A Comparative Study of Four Latin American Countries. *The Journal of Politics, 64*(2), 408–433.
Sharkansky, I. (1969). The Utility of Elazar's Political Culture: A Research Note. *Polity, 2*(1), 66–83.

Shultz, J. (1998). *Reviving the Fourth Estate: Democracy, Accountability & the Media*. Cambridge: Cambridge University Press.
Siebert, F. S., Peterson, T., & Schramm, W. (1956). *Four Theories of the Press. The Authoritarian, Libertarian, Social Responsibility and Soviet Communist Concepts of What the Press Should ne and Should Do*. Urbana/Chicago: University of Illinois Press.
Smith, M. G. (1964). Historical and Cultural Conditions of Political Corruption Among the Hausa. *Comparative Studies in Society and History, 6*(2), 164–194.
The Library of Congress Country Study. (2006). Available at http://rs6.loc.gov/frd/cs/ngtoc.html. Downloaded 9 Aug 2006.
The World Fact Book. (2018). Africa-Nigeria. Retrieved May 14 2018. Available at https://www.cia.gov/Library/publications/the-world-factbook/geos/ni.html
Thompson, J. B. (1997). Scandal and Social Theory. In J. Lull & S. Hinerman (Eds.), *Media Scandals: Morality and Desire in the Popular Culture Market Place* (pp. 34–64). New York: Columbia University Press.
Thompson, J. B. (2000). *Political Scandal: Power and Visibility in the Media Age*. Cambridge: Polity Press.
Tiffen, R. (2004). Tip of the Iceberg or Moral Panic? Police Corruption Issues in Contemporary New South Wales. *American Behavioural Scientist, 47*(9), 1171–1193.
Transparency International. (2017). Corruption Perception Index 2017. Retrieved 14 May 2018 available at https://www.transparency.org/news/feature/corruption_perceptions_index_2017
Tumber, H., & Waisbord, S. (2004a). Political Scandals and Media Across Democracies, Volume I. *American Behavioral Scientist, 47*(8), 1032.
Tumber, H., & Waisbord, S. (2004b). Political Scandals and Media Across Democracies, Volume II. *American Behavioral Scientist, 47*(9), 1143.
Waisbord, S. (2000). *Watchdog Journalism in South America: News, Accountability, and Democracy*. New York: Columbia University Press.
Waisbord, S. (2004). Scandals, Media, and Citizenship in Contemporary Argentina. *American Behavioral Scientist, 47*(8), 1072.
Wegener, B. (2000). Political Culture and Post-communist Transition—A Social Justice Approach: Introduction. *Social Justice Research, 13*(2), 75–82.
Werlin, H. H., & Eckstein, H. (1990). Political Culture and Political Change. *The American Political Science Review, 84*(1), 249–259.
White, G. (1996). Corruption and the Transition from Socialism in China. *Journal of Law and Society, 23*(1), 149–169.
Wu, X. (2005). Corporate Governance and Corruption: A Cross-Country Analysis. *Governance: An International Journal of Policy, Administration and Institutions, 18*(2), 151–170.
Yusha'u, M. J. (2010). Regional Parallelism and the Reporting of Corruption in the Nigerian Press. *Journal of African Media Studies, 2*(3), 353–369.

CHAPTER 2

An Overview of the State of Media in Africa

Introduction

Unlike the erroneous assumption that treats Africa as one country (Nothias 2016), the media in Africa is quite diverse and has evolved differently from region to region and culture to culture. The diversity of the media in Africa can be seen from the diversity of the continent itself. You have the English-speaking Africa, whose media organisations have the tendency to follow the British style of adversarial journalism as can be seen in Nigeria, Kenya, Ghana and so on. You have the francophone countries in Africa where countries like Senegal, Guinea and Cote d'Ivoire can be grouped, and by extension Arab countries in North Africa that were colonised by France, like Algeria, Morocco and Tunisia. Yet the latter have a distinct cultural, religious and linguistic peculiarities.

The media has developed in phases from colonial to postcolonial times. It has gone through a period of serious dictatorship during the military era and even under civilian dictatorship, yet the liberalisation of media environments in the 1990s brought a new scenario that saw the beginning of deregulation. Private media organisations were established, and an improvement was noticed in press freedom. The revolution in information and communications technology saw the establishment of more media organisations on the Internet (Mabweazara et al. 2014; Yusha'u 2014) all over the continent.

Despite these developments, several challenges remain and more needs to be done to ensure a more sustainable media environment. In this

M. J. Yusha'u, *Regional Parallelism and Corruption Scandals in Nigeria*, https://doi.org/10.1007/978-3-319-96220-7_2

chapter we shall discuss the evolution of the media landscape in Africa not just from a contemporary perspective, but from traditional times before the advent of colonialism that contributed to the establishment of modern media organisations. A historical overview of some countries will be provided in order to have a better understanding of the historical trends in the establishment of media organisations. Since this book is studying media systems in Africa using the coverage of corruption scandals in order to understand the character of the media in Africa, a brief account of corruption scandals in the continent will be discussed. The notion of communication and national development has always been part of the discussion on the evolution of media in developing countries, not just the African continent; this chapter will highlight that aspect in light of the development of media systems in the continent.

Traditional Communication in Africa

Prior to the emergence of newspapers, radio, television and now the Internet, there has always been a method of traditional communication in Africa. According to Wilson (1987), these methods of traditional communication in Africa were neglected with the intervention of colonial rule, while researchers interested in the nature of communication in Africa seldom pay attention to this significant area of study.

One of the ways of transmitting messages in African societies is through the town crier who performs various roles that can today be likened to what contemporary media professionals, such as correspondents, spokesmen, newsagents, postmen and press secretaries do. Wilson categorised the forms of communication used by the town crier in the Calabar province of Southern Nigeria into idiophones, membranophones, aerophones, symbolography, signals, signs, objectifics, colour music, extra-mundane communication, symbolography and symbolic displays (Wilson 1987).

In Northern Nigeria, the use of the town crier is common, but he doesn't have to use instruments in many instances; rather, he utilises his voice to send across messages, usually at night in various corners of the town. The responsibility is usually given to those with high pitch in their voice. Other methods employed in some African settings include the use of smoke, or the beating of drums to signify the commencement or expiration of an event.

However, there are variations among African societies on how the traditional means of communication are utilised due to differences in culture, religion, ethnicity and environment. Wilson argued that one of the problems faced by the traditional method of communication includes "lack of standard technical vocabulary in the description, analysis and conceptualisation of the media/channels and processes of the traditional communication system" (Wilson 1987: 98).

Other factors identified by Wilson which militate against the advancement of the traditional system of communication in Africa comprises the difficulty in using a single code to identify the communication channels due to linguistic problems, coupled with the mixture of foreign languages with indigenous ones. He suggested, however, some solutions open to scholars interested in exploring the traditional system of communication. These options according to him are "(i) retaining and using indigenous names along with descriptive labels in one of the international languages especially the one spoken in the researcher's country; (ii) using only descriptive labels in the former colonial language spoken in the country of the researcher; and (iii) inventing or coining alternative words, perhaps based on known models of related media/channels and then validating these coinages at international conferences through promulgation" (Wilson 1987: 98).

In his study on communication and national development in Africa, Blake (1979) is of the opinion that the problem with communication studies in Africa is due to the colonial legacy inherited in African countries which concentrates more on the electronic medium of communication, in particular radio and television. This, according to Blake, has made African countries to neglect the study of African traditional communication which has been in existence precolonially, and he thinks that with research new methods of communication can be created.

Blake suggested that among the strategies that need to be employed in order to develop the traditional system of communication is to have a pedagogical structure that focuses on the development of this important area, an initiative which he thinks countries like Ghana, Nigeria and some other African countries have embarked upon by establishing communication departments in their universities.

It can be said that Blake is to a large extent right in suggesting a pedagogical approach, but at the moment there are various communication departments, not only in the countries he has mentioned but in many other African countries, yet there is little improvement in the development of these traditional means of communication. This may partly be due to other social problems affecting the continent like economic retrogression, corruption and bad leadership. These problems may contribute to undermining the efforts of the institutions of learning who are supposed to invent new ideas for the refinement and reconstruction of these communication tools.

African Media and National Development

Many scholars believe that the media plays an important role in national development, and that this can be seen from the attention African countries pay to the use of the media in various national development initiatives despite the little resources available to them (Boadu 1981).

This has, therefore, created a debate about the role of the media in the development of Africa. This debate attracts attention partly because the excuse given by many African leaders is that the media should be a tool for development, and therefore excessive criticism might render this noble goal impotent. But some scholars argued that this is not possible because "the continent has relied on a notion of development and development agendas that are foreign to the bulk of its people both in origin and objectives, and that have not always addressed the right issues or done so in the right manner. The second reason is that development communication researchers have adopted research techniques designed to answer to the needs of Western societies and which do not always suit African cultures or societies that are in the main rural and non literate"(Nyamnjoh 2010: 2).

Nyamnjoh's research studied the nature of African media using a critique of the modernisation theory; a thesis which he asserts does not fit into the African system. He therefore calls for a participatory method of communication that will look at the nature of communication in Africa before the emergence of contemporary mass media. Such method of participatory communication, according to Nyamnjoh, will involve the less privileged Africans in whose name development communication proposals are suggested, and they can therefore communicate and present their problems in the language they understand.

This position was taken by Nyamnjoh because of a research conducted by UNESCO in some developing countries which include Columbia, Brazil, India, Senegal, Peru, India, Iran, Tanzania Canada, Tobago and the Philippines. The outcome of the research suggested that in none of the ten countries mentioned did the idea of rural communication originate from the local population. The idea is usually decided by the government or development agencies after which the method of communication is settled upon using the media of their choice.

Tettey (2006) looked at the role of the media in Africa from a different perspective. His study focuses on the role the media play in the democratisation process, in particular the role of the private press. According to Tettey, he chose to use the term private press rather than independent press in Africa because a number of the press serve the interests of their proprietors or ethnic groups rather than the larger public interest. This problem is compounded by the state ownership of radio, television and newspapers which claim to practice development journalism, an idea which gives various governments in Africa the freedom to interfere in the activities of the media despite constitutional provisions guaranteeing the freedom of the press.

The proponents of this school of thought use the modernisation paradigm to advance their argument. To them—since African countries are seeking to find a solution to their political and economic problems—so that they can be in the position to compete with the more economically advantaged countries, many of whom were previously their colonial masters, one of the tasks before them is to modernise. However, the criticism against the scholars who champion this idea is that they overlook the extent of the role the government should play in national development, and this uncritical position gave many African countries the opportunity to control the media in Africa without room for criticism and policy assessment. This does not mean that the situation is the same everywhere in Africa. Rather, there are some variations among countries; especially countries like Nigeria and Kenya where the media were a bit more critical of African leaders during the early days of independence. But the general picture of reporting, especially in the print media, was more of propaganda than a genuine desire to inform and educate the people (Hyden and Leslie 2002).

While the government-owned media serve as the mouthpiece of the authorities, the private media, despite its allegiance to its proprietors and ethnic loyalty, contributes toward checking the excesses of those in authority. This has in turn resulted in a conflicting relationship between the private press and the various governments in Africa. In terms of the contribution made by the press, studies have shown that it was newspapers that spearheaded the debate on the one-party state in countries like Tanzania and uncovered various cases of corruption in Cameroon. As pointed out by Tettey, "the media have been very active in exposing activities within the state that would otherwise have been unknown to the citizenry. Through these kinds of information, the people were able to measure the pronouncement of politicians against their deeds, and hence make informed judgements about the political future of those individuals. The likelihood of exposure is also instrumental in at least, making government officials more circumspect in their activities. What we see therefore, is a certain measure of imposed accountability on the part of these officials which they did not have to worry about in the past" (Tettey 2006: 10).

In their study on the media and two waves of democracy in Africa, Hyden and Okigbo (2002) reviewed the role of the media in Africa and in particular the media contribution towards democratisation. They divided the wave[1] into a first and second wave. The characteristics of the first wave was determined by internal power struggle in search of independence yet determined by the colonial rule; in the first wave the print media was effective, but radio was less effective because it was not common. Hyden and Okigbo discussed the first web from two fronts, first as "as mouthpieces of nationalist cause" and two "as creators of discursive realm" (p. 32).

The media, especially the print, served as a mouthpiece for nationalism because a number of the principal actors involved in the nationalist struggle have some connection with the print media either as proprietors themselves, or they share some form of ideological semblance, and according to Hyden and Okigbo, there are about three models that can explain this. The first model looks at the emergence of newspapers in the indigenous languages of African people because of the absence of coverage on issues that matter most to the African population in the newspapers controlled by colonial governments. Examples of this include the relationship between former nationalist Jomo Kenyata with *Muigwithania* (the reconciler) journal, which became the mouthpiece for the nationalist movement in Kenya with its monthly publication. In Uganda there were such indigenous newspapers like *Munno*, *Taifa Empya* and *Kizito*. In Tanzania, the newspaper *Mfanyakazi* (the worker) also played a prominent role in the nationalist struggle. These indigenous newspapers became popular, especially where the press in the colonial language ignores the needs of the indigenous population. However, these kinds of newspapers were more available in east and southern Africa than in West Africa.

[1] Quoting Huntington (1991: 15), Hyden and Okigbo defined *wave* as a group of transitions from one type of regime to another that occur within a specified period of time and that significantly outnumber transitions in the opposite direction during that period of time (Hyden and Okigbo 2002: 31).

The second model discussed by Hyden and Okigbo under the media as mouthpiece of nationalism looks at the use of the colonial language by Africans to satisfy their needs. This was made possible because in other parts of Africa like Nigeria and Ghana, there were no European settlers as the case was in southern Africa. Therefore, the newspapers became sympathetic to nationalist struggle, especially in English-speaking Africa. The French policy of assimilation in francophone Africa also helped the indigenous populations to exploit the French language for indigenous purposes, but not as much as the newspapers were able to achieve in English-speaking Africa.

The third model according to Hyden and Okigbo was the contribution of the metropolitan press in the struggle for independence. But this was more effective in the French-speaking countries, due to elected representatives from Africa serving in France having access to the editors of these metropolitan newspapers, and because of the divided public opinion within France itself. Those on the right wanted the colonies to remain under colonial control, while the socialists wanted independence for African countries.

This was the climate under which many African countries gained their independence, a climate in which the effort of the rising African elite to ensure self-rule was supported by the emergence of newspapers. Citing Hachten (1993), Bourgault (1995) looked at the development of the press from the mid 1950s to late 1980s, in which from "1956 just a few years before most nations became independent, Helen Kitchen reported the presence of 100 daily African newspapers. The number of dailies increased during the 1960s, the decade of African independence. The USIA reported 150 dailies in 1966, and Hachten reported 160 in 1969. The 1970s with its high number of military coups, was a poor decade for African newspaper survival. According to Burton, there were 116 dailies in 1975–76. But by the 1980s, newspapers were again on the upswing. The *World Press Encyclopaedia* counted 124 dailies in 1980. And by the end of the 1980s, the press appeared to be bouncing back from its low point in the 1970s. The UNESCO *Statistical Handbook* reported 200 dailies on the African continent in 1988" (p. 153).

The beginning of the 1990s saw a transformation in the nature of journalism in many African countries due to the deregulation of media ownership in many African countries. Independent media organisations began to emerge. This created a competitive media environment in both the print and electronic media and a platform for political pluralism flourished gradually. This was happening at a time when there was serious economic decline in many African countries. But many of the media organisations managed to survive, and those that couldn't succeed were replaced by new ones. These privately-owned newspapers played a significant role in the political development of many African countries by questioning government policies believed to be detrimental to the stability of these countries, and the process of reversing the old trend, where many African governments thought their decision was beyond any form of scrutiny, was set (Hyden and Leslie 2002). The role of the private media became like an indirect reconsideration of the notion of national development, which may be useful in its essence, but misused by many African elites for egoistic reasons.

As discussed by Hyden and Leslie, another factor that contributed to the emergence of private and to some extent independent press in Africa was the availability of new technologies, more sophisticated printing machines and computers, and the spread of satellite communication making access to information much easier. This access to information showcases the happenings around the world, a factor that might have contributed in accelerating the growth of more private media institutions in many African countries.

The Press in Some African Countries

The development of the press in Africa differs across countries, in some parts of Africa, the government, both colonial and postcolonial has total monopoly over the press. In some countries, the nature of media ownership was shared, with the government having total control over the broadcast media, and the press privately owned. Still, the media is more active in some countries than others, and Ghana, South Africa and Kenya can serve as a representative example of media ownership that combines government monopoly, private ownership, and various challenges that face the media in Africa, in particular during colonial struggle, military rule, and the liberalisation of media ownership (see Hyden and Leslie 2002; Hyden and Okigbo 2002; Ochilo 1993). These three countries are relevant because they share certain features with Nigeria. Apart from being English-speaking countries, they both share a colonial past, with South Africa breaking away from apartheid in 1994. All the countries are multi-ethnic, multi-regional or even multiracial.

As in Nigeria, newspapers in Ghana were a colonial creation. In a study on the media of mass communication and the third republic constitution in Ghana, Twumasi (1981) traced the history of newspapers in Ghana to 1822; this was when the British colonial governor, Charles McCarthy established an official paper called *The Royal Gold Coast*[2] *Gazette*. But the paper lasted for only two years. And the next newspaper to emerge was in 1857, the paper also ceased to exist between 1873 and 1874. But in the same year James Huton Brew founded *The Gold Coast Times* which appears every two weeks but went out of circulation in 1885, though it was replaced by another paper called *Western Echo*. Dr. J.B. Danqua established the first daily newspaper, *The Times of West Africa*, and from that period onward newspapers continue to flourish throughout the nineteenth and twentieth centuries. There was an increase in ownership by indigenous Africans, though the colonial government continued to monitor the nature of news coverage in the newspapers.

However, this trend in private ownership of the press could not last, government control and ownership was about to set in, principally for three reasons that occurred during colonial rule and just after independence, as identified by Twumasi (1981). These three developments gave birth to the idea of state ownership and political control of the media. The first was the introduction of radio broadcasting by the then colonial governor, Arnold Hodson, who wants the retransmission of BBC programmes in Accra. Hodson's plan was to have a radio transmission that would counter the emerging influence of the nationalist press which was becoming more radical in its reporting. But this effort ended up serving as groundwork for government monopoly on broadcasting by successive governments.

The second reason was the establishment of newspapers by British newspaper proprietors in Ghana in the 1950s, in particular by Cecil King, of the London Mirror group. At that time there were two leading nationalist parties, The United Gold Coast Convention (UGCC), and the Convention People's Party (CPP). The papers established by the London Mirror Group were *Daily Graphic* and *Sunday Mirror*; the two papers tried to ensure an even reporting between the two parties, but on the eve of independence, the CPP perceived the two papers as being critical of their party and also undermining the independence movement.

The third development was the emergence of new elites who had various professional backgrounds, some as teachers, market women and the

[2] Gold Coast was the former name of Ghana.

larger members of the society. These emerging elite were socialists in orientation, and were part of the CPP, and led by Kwame Nkrumah who himself was a journalist and founder of the *Accra Evening News*. These new elite and their newspapers like *Morning Telegraph* and *Daily Mail* were opposed by the Mirror Group and members of the UGCC who already publish newspapers like *National Times*, *Talking Drums* and the *Ashanti Pioneer*. And after independence, some of the papers were purchased by the Nkrumah-led government, and others were banned (see Twumasi 1981); hence, laying the foundation for total control of the media by indigenous Africans in Ghana.

Like many African countries, Ghana was affected by successive military regimes, who by their nature ensured the retention of government control of the media. Various military administrations in Ghana tried to come up with community-oriented newspapers so that the information gap between rural and urban areas could be bridged. As confirmed by Boafo (1987) "content analytical studies have indicated that news and information about events from urban centres, especially news concerning the political leadership and other socio-economic elite, occupy disproportionately more space in the press and more air time in the broadcast media in Ghana than news and information about events in the rural communities" (p. 29). And this situation may not be peculiar to Ghana because, in many African countries, the literacy rate is higher in urban areas, and because economic opportunities are concentrated in the urban areas, rural urban migration could also affect the success of community newspapers because of the possibility of rural dwellers who have some skills, or a higher literacy level, migrating to the metropolitan areas of the country.

These community newspapers as discussed by Boafo (1987), like *The Densu New Times* and *The Akora New Era* were published by the University of Ghana School of Communication. One of the aims of these newspapers was to promote adult literacy and community integration. However, the community newspapers could not last due to inadequate funding and other problems associated with newspaper publishing in Africa.

This trend continued until the late 1980s and early 1990s when the deregulation and liberalisation, especially of the broadcasting industry, started gaining ground. As discussed by Heath (1999), the issue of broadcasting policy in Ghana was not on the public agenda before 1993. For more than sixty years, broadcasting was owned and controlled by the government using the Ghana Broadcasting Corporation (GBC). Broadcasting was seen as a means of ensuring national cohesion, promoting development and ascertaining national stability. An approach that is common in many African countries.

With the promulgation of a new constitution in 1993, which clearly states that "there shall be no impediments to the establishment of private press or media; and in particular there shall be no law requiring any person to obtain license as a prerequisite for the establishment or operation of a newspaper; journal or other media for mass communication or information; article 162 (3)", room was created for public debate, which resulted in series of negotiations between the National Democratic Congress's government (NDC), whose motive was informed by the desire to deregulate the electronic communication sector, and another section of the elite who believe in the efficacy of public service broadcasting (Heath 1999: 312).

As discussed by Heath, various committees were set up, and conferences were held in order to arrive at an acceptable position on the establishment of private media organisations. The conclusion was to allow for the proliferation of more private media houses. As a result of this, by 1998 more than 45 FM stations have been approved with 29 already on air. Despite challenges such as technology and manpower facing the new media organisations, today, the new approach to media ownership is becoming part of the political life of Ghana.

The emergence of the media in Kenya and its landscape is not different from Ghana, Nigeria or South Africa. The media was similarly created by the missionaries and upheld by the colonialists. Reverend Robert Stegal was among the first missionaries to establish a newspaper called *Taveta Chronicle* in 1895. Other newspapers that followed were the *Leader* in 1899, owned by the British East Africa Company, followed by *Uganda Mail*, which was published in Mombasa. The basic objective of these newspapers was to provide information for the purposes of the missionaries and colonial administrators. Added to this was the emergence of newspapers by the Asian communities that settled in Kenya, but their attempt to establish newspapers was seen by the indigenous Kenyans as an effort to consolidate their grip on the country as done by the colonialists (Ochilo 1993).

According to Ochilo (1993), three patterns of media ownership emerged in Kenya after receiving political independence. The first pattern of ownership represents the swapping of roles between colonial administrators and their African successors. In this case, ownership and control of the media was maintained by the Africans who took control of political power. Such institutions as the *Kenya Broadcasting Corporation* and newspapers like *Kenya Times* remained under government control. The essence of communication was based on the promotion of national unity, stability and development.

The second type of ownership according to Ochilo was the privately owned newspapers. These newspapers like the *Nation Group* and the *Standard* were financially autonomous, and so they can exercise a degree of control and editorial independence. But they were not totally immune from government interference since the government provide political representation to the owners, and where that fails, they were threatened with libel laws.

The third pattern of ownership involves "the indigenous magazines and weeklies such as the *Weekly Review, Finance, the Nairobi Law Monthly, Parents* and *Step*. This category depends on the goodwill of the government of the day as their capital base is weak. They have less circulation confined mainly to most urban centres and consequently do not draw a great deal of commercial advertising from the seemingly saturated small readership in the urban centres of Kenya" (Ochilo 1993, pp. 24–25).

Although Kenya is normally cited as an example when it comes to private ownership of the media because to some extent Jomo Kenyatta, who became president at independence, "tolerated, if not valued, a free press" (Hyden and Leslie 2002: 9), which paved the way for the newspapers to ascertain their political independence, the government exercises more control over the broadcast industry, especially in the 1990s when the Kenyan African National Union (KANU), was in power. It controls the privately owned television station, while still exercising undue influence over the Kenya Broadcasting Corporation (KBC) such that the KBC was once accused of siding with the government by the Election Monitoring Unit of the country, both in 1992 and 1997 (Van der Veur 2002).

As for South Africa, which is seen today as a leading player not just in Africa but globally, after breaking away from apartheid in 1994, one of the defining moments particularly for media ownership, press freedom and the setting of a platform for a vibrant media organisation was the section in the then interim constitution of South Africa, which states the following:

> Every person shall have the right to freedom of speech and expression, which shall include freedom of the press and other media, and the freedom of artistic creativity and scientific work, and all media financed by or under the control of the state shall be regulated in a manner which insures impartiality and the expression of a diversity of opinion.[3]

[3] Cited in Giffard et al. (1997).

As discussed by Giffard et al. (1997) South Africa has the history of one of the oldest newspapers in Africa with the first newspapers established in Cape, the *Cape Town Gazette* and *Commercial Advertiser* in 1800. Since then many newspapers have been established, including the *Eastern Province Herald* (1845), *Natal Witness* (1846), *Natal Mercury* (1852) and so on. These are the newspapers published in the English language. There were also many newspapers established in the 1800s that were published in the Afrikaans language. These newspapers, which were established by "anti-slavery white liberals" as a reaction to the English press include, among others, *Die Zuid African* (1828), and *Di Patriot* (1876) (Giffard et al. 1997, pp. 80–83). Today South Africa has one of the most vibrant media industries in Africa published in different regions and languages.

One distinct feature of the South African press is its political affiliation and "ethnic" loyalty. As discussed by Steenveld (2007), the newspapers have a professional approach but they still maintain their ethnic or regional identity. According to her, "although the press was commercialized, and a common professional ideology of independence was adopted, each press maintained its ethnicised political identity, which was shaped by its relation to the apartheid state" (p. 109).[4] Steenveld's work is very relevant to this book in that she made reference to Hallin and Mancini's work about the way the media established a kind of "parallelism" with a particular societal identity. This corresponds with the situation in Nigeria, where the newspapers also develop regional identity despite their national outlook (see Chaps. 6, 7 and 8 for a discussion on regional parallelism and ethnic bias of Nigerian newspapers).

What the issues raised in different countries discussed in this chapter is the complex nature of the media in Africa. While it has a shared history of colonialism and struggle for independence, different countries have internal peculiarities which may have some semblance with other countries but may also remain a distinct feature of the country. This is relevant because sometimes there is the tendency, especially for those who have little understanding of Africa, to view it as a single country. This is a point that Nyamnjoh (2005) drew attention to; according to him, "we must not fuel

[4] For a discussion on the changes in South African media, especially due to democratisation and the changing nature of the economy which makes newspapers to pay attention to profit-making, see Tomaselli (2002).

the tendency to mistake Africa for a country, or to assume that states and the media on the continent are so alike that a few casual generalisations suffice to capture their characteristics and interactions" (p. 32).

Certainly, there are lots of similarities among African media, such as the establishment by colonial administrators, and the challenges of censorship under colonial, postcolonial, military and civilian administrations. But there are differences politically, regionally, economically, and in religious beliefs. A country like Senegal that has never experienced military coup since independence cannot be compared with a country like Mauritania that suffers continued military intervention. Tunisia, though an Arab country, cannot be generalised with Egypt or Sudan despite being predominantly Arab and Muslim. An interesting work that depicts these complexities is the edited collection on *Press Freedom and Communication in Africa* (1997) by Festus Eribo and Willian Jong-Ebot. The work studied press freedom in Africa according to anglophone, francophone, Arab-speaking and lusophone countries, which clearly exposes the similarities and differences in the nature and character of the media in Africa.

In many African countries, the media faces a lot of challenges. Key among those challenges is the issue of corruption which pervaded different countries, and the media—whether press or broadcast—is part of that society, yet there are few studies paying attention to how the media covers cases of corruption, and whether the media itself is corruption-free. A study by Ronning (2009) looks at the politics of corruption and the media in Africa. The research discussed the issue of corruption and the role of the media to possibly serve as a deterrent. The research also focused on one of the central issues discussed in this research; that is, investigative journalism, which is needed in order to uncover the wrongdoings in order to educate the public. However, one shortcoming of the work by Ronning is that it looks more generally at corruption and the media in Africa, rather than focusing on a specific case study. But that is understandable in that he is trying to promote a debate so that more researchers will pay attention to the issue, and this is where this research will make additional contribution to the literature on corruption and the media in Africa by specifically focusing on Nigeria, and looking at how journalists see their role as the conscience of the society, and the way the media frames the stories about corruption.

Studies on Corruption Scandals

Some scholars are of the view that *Watergate*, the scandal that forced the former US president, Richard Nixon, to resign was a turning point in the study of scandals because of the role played by the press. Since then, within the US there have been series of scandals, and as argued by Schudson, scandals are not peculiar to democracies only, they can be found in other countries that may not be seen as advanced democracies (Schudson 2004).

As such, scholars paid attention to the coverage of scandals and the nature of corruption in different parts of the world. For instance, Righter and Burke (2007) conducted their work on combating corruption by promoting ethics in the United States. Canel and Sanders (2006) studied political scandals in Britain and Spain by paying attention to the nature of coverage in the press of the two countries. Spector's (2005) edited work, *Fighting Corruption in Developing Countries,* did a sector-by-sector analysis on corruption, from the justice system, to education, health, political parties, environment, and so on. Johnson (2004) did a comparative analysis of corruption in four countries: India, Russia, United States and Israel. So it can be seen that corruption can be found in different sectors of society; some of the differences between countries are in what Klitgaard (1988) calls "cultures clash".

Scholars have shown that many African countries suffer from different forms of corruption. Blundo et al. (2006) conducted a study on corruption in West Africa. The research they conducted in Senegal, Niger and Benin revealed some similarities and differences because the countries share historical linkages, for being former French colonies, and they also have cultural ties. Petty corruption, in which people receive gratification for a job they are paid to do is found in different sectors of the countries studied. This is relevant to this book in that as we shall see corruption within the media is one of the challenges the Nigerian press is facing. Journalists receive bribes for a job they are paid to do.

Doig and Theobald (2000) focus their research on corruption and democratisation. Their study also paid attention to African countries, and although they mentioned Nigeria as among the corrupt countries in the world going by Transparency International's rankings, they suggest that lack of data from other West African countries makes generalisation difficult.

Some studies on corruption have focused specifically on Nigeria. Olaleye-Oruene (2007) studied corruption as a cultural phenomenon in Nigeria. He sees present-day corruption in Nigeria as a colonial legacy.

According to him, it was the style of European countries that partitioned Africa at the Berlin conference in 1884–85 that promoted corruption because of the competition among European multinational companies working in Africa. His study also cited different scandals in Britain involving members of parliament, as evidence that corruption is a legacy of colonialism, because Britain was Nigeria's colonial master.[5]

Chiluwa (2007) conducted a study of how the press in Nigeria frame the discourses of political scandals in their headlines. His study focused specifically on weekly magazines like *Tell, The News* and *Newswatch*. Apart from the rhetoric and strategies used in the headlines of these magazines, the study concluded that "news headlines are however influenced by personal bias of the individual journalists as well as the overriding professional and social ethics of the news magazine itself" (p. 70).

The study by Chiluwa is particularly useful because this book will be studying the headlines of some Nigerian newspapers in order to find out how they frame the headlines about the scandals under study (see Chap. 6). Chiluwas's study would have been more useful if he had compared the north and the south, but that is understandable since his study focused on weekly magazines, and there are so few of them in the north, and they are on and off the market.

Conclusion

In conclusion the following can be discerned about the media in Africa.

1. African newspapers share a relatively common history, because they emerge as a result of missionary activities or colonisation or both.
2. The immediate leaders of Africa after independence simply carried on where the colonial governments stopped and ensured government monopoly of the media. This can be seen in terms of the laws inherited from colonial governments, which continued to be applied by indigenous postcolonial governments. This is further illustrated by Nyamnjoh (2005):

[5] In 2009, just before the local elections, there were series of reports in the British press led by the *Daily Telegraph* about the expenses of MPs, known as the expenses scandal. On July 23, George Galloway, and former British Defence Secretary Geoff Hoon exchanged words during BBC's *Question Time* programme, on the allegations of British involvement in the BAE arms scandal between Britain and Saudi Arabia.

> Postcolonial states in Africa have had much more in common with their colonial counterparts than is often acknowledged by those eager to present Africa as a reluctant student of western achievements in democracy—a few examples will illustrate the point. At the time of independence in francophone Africa, nationalist leaders had a rich repertoire of colonial censorship laws from which to draw inspiration, in the interest of continuity. For example, a highly repressive version of a October 1923 decree regulating the press in France survived independence in much of French Africa—And although the English colonial administrators were usually seen to be relatively less interventionist, they bequeathed to their colonies a legacy of an 'official secrets act', which has over the years made it extremely difficult for the media in anglophone Africa to obtain official information through declarations by or interviews with civil servants (p. 35)

3. There is a division in the nature of ownership, in that the newspapers are mostly privately owned, while the government controlled the broadcast industry prior to liberalisation in the 1990s.
4. Most African countries share the notion of using the media for national development, and that was what defined the nature of media operation after independence.
5. The 1990s brought a shift in the nature of ownership because of the deregulation and liberalisation of the broadcast industry (see Ogundimu 2002).

References

Blake, C. (1979). Communication Research and African National Development. *Journal of Black Studies, 10*(2), 218–230.

Blundo, G., et al. (2006). *Everyday Corruption and the State: Citizens & Public officials in Africa*. London/New York: Zed books.

Boadu, S. O. (1981). Mass Media and Modernisation: An Assessment of Theoretical problems. *Journal of Black Studies, 12*(2), 193–200.

Boafo, S. T. K. (1987). Democratising Media Systems in African Societies. The Case of Ghana. *Africa Media Review, 2*(1), 24–37.

Bourgault, L. M. (1995). *Mass Media in Sub-Saharan Africa*. Bloomington/ Indianapolis: Indian University Press.

Canel, M. J., & Sanders, K. (2006). *Morality Tales: Political Scandals in Britain and Spain in the 1990s*. Cresskill: Hampton Press.

Chiluwa, I. (2007). News Headlines as Pragmatic Strategy in Nigerian Press Discourse. *The International Journal of Language Society and Culture*, 63–71.

Doig, A., & Theobald, R. (2000). *Corruption and Democratisation*. London: Frank Cass.

Giffard, A., Beer, D., Arnold, S., & Steyn, E. (1997). New Media for the New South Africa. In F. Eribo & W. Jong-Ebot (Eds.), *Press Freedom and Communication in Africa*. Trenton: Africa World Press Inc.

Heath, C. W. (1999). Negotiating Broadcasting Policy: Civil Society and Civic Discourse in Ghana. *International Communication Gazette, 61*(6), 511–521.

Hyden, G., & Leslie, M. (2002). Communications and Democratisation in Africa. In G. Hyde, M. Leslie, & F. F. Ogundimu (Eds.), *Media and Democracy in Africa* (pp. 1–27). New Brunswick: Transaction Publishers.

Hyden, G., & Okigbo, C. (2002). The Media and the Two Waves of Democracy. In G. Hyden, M. Leslie, & F. F. Ogundimu (Eds.), *Media and Democracy in Africa* (pp. 29–53). New Brunswick: Transaction Publishers.

Johnson, R. A. (2004). *The Struggle Against Corruption: A Comparative Study*. New York: Palgrave Macmillan.

Klitgaard, R. (1988). *Controlling Corruption*. Berkeley: University of California Press.

Mabweazara, H., Mudhai, O. F., & Whittaker, J. (2014). *Online Journalism in Africa. Trends, Practices and Emerging Cultures*. London: Routledge.

Nothias, T. (2016). How Western Journalists Actually Write About Africa: Reassessing the Myths of Representation About Africa. *Journalism Studies, 19*(8), 1138–1159.

Nyamnjoh, F. (2005). Media and the State in Africa: Continuities and Discontinuities. In P. Kareithi & N. Kariithi (Eds.), *Untold Stories: Economics and Business Journalism in African Media* (pp. 32–48). Johannesburg: Wits University Press.

Nyamnjoh, F. B. (2010). Re-thinking Communication Research and Development in Africa. Available at https://s3.amazonaws.com/academia.edu.documents/30970433/nyamnjoh-2.pdf?AWSAccessKeyId=AKIAIWOWYYGZ2Y53UL3A&Expires=1537011291&Signature=4dKayn%2BEtpcZpK7wcgYO0dhbZaU%3D&response-content-disposition=inline%3B%20filename%3DRethinking_Communication_Research_and_De.pdf. Retrieved 15 Sept 2018.

Ochilo, P. J. O. (1993). Press Freedom and the Role of the Media in Kenya. *Africa Media Review, 7*(3), 19–33.

Ogundimu, F. F. (2002). Media and Democracy in 21st Century Africa. In G. Hyden, M. Leslie, & F. F. Ogundimu (Eds.), *Media and Democracy in Africa* (pp. 207–236). New Brunswick: Transaction Publishes.

Olaleye-Oruene, T. (2007). Corruption in Nigeria: A Cultural Phenomenon. *Journal of Financial Crime, 5*(3), 232–240.

Righter, W. L., & Burke, F. (2007). *Combating Corruption, Encouraging Ethics: A Practical Guide to Management Ethics*. Lanham: Rowman & Littlefield.

Ronning, H. (2009). The Politics of Corruption and the Media in Africa. *Journal of African Media studies, 1*(1), 155–171.

Schudson, M. (2004). Notes on Scandal and the Watergate Legacy. *The American Behavioral Scientist, 47*(9), 1231–1238.

Spector, B. I. (2005). *Fighting Corruption in Developing Countries*. Bloomfield: Kumarian Press.

Steenveld, L. (2007). The SAHRC' Enquiry into Racism in the Media: Problematising State-Media Relationships. *Ecquid Novi: African Journalism Studies, 28*(1&2), 106–126.

Tettey, W. J. (2006). The Politics of Media Accountability in Africa: An Examination of Mechanism and Institutions. *The International Communications Gazette, 68*(3), 229–248.

Tomaselli, K. G. (2002). Media Ownership and Democratisation. In G. Hyden, M. Leslie, & F. F. Ogundimu (Eds.), *Media and Democracy in Africa* (pp. 129–155). New Brunswick: Transaction Publishes.

Twumasi, Y. (1981). Media of Mass Communication and the Third Republic Constitution in Ghana. *African Affairs, 80*(318), 13–27.

Van der Veur, P. R. (2002). Broadcasting and Political reform. In G. Hyden, M. Leslie, & F. F. Ogundimu (Eds.), *Media and Democracy in Africa* (pp. 81–105). Uppsala: Transaction Publishers.

Wilson, D. (1987). Traditional Systems of Communication in Modern African development: An Analytical Viewpoint. *Africa Media Review, 1*(2), 87–104.

Yusha'u, M. J. (2014). The Internet, Diasporic Media, and Online Journalism in West Africa. In H. Mabweazara, O. F. Mudhai, & J. Whittaker (Eds.), *Online Journalism in Africa. Trends, Practices and Emerging Cultures* (pp. 207–221). London: Routledge.

CHAPTER 3

Historical Landscape of Nigerian Newspapers

Introduction

Writers, journalists and commentators on African history have studied the emergence of contemporary Africa. These writers, like Nnamdi Azikwe for example, see contemporary Africa as a child of both colonial rule and the desire of man to dominate others. This desire culminated in making stronger societies to rule over weaker ones for a number of reasons. These reasons include the availability of resources needed by the strong societies, which are available in the weaker societies, or to extend the control of an empire in the struggle for the control of territories; this and other reasons have "aided in giving impetus to imperialism which culminated in the acquisition of colonial empires" (Azikwe 1931: 288), and majority of African States became part of the colonial empires.

Yet the acquisition of these African States by the colonial powers resulted in a clash of interest between the colonialists and the natives. The colonialists wanted to ensure control of the territories they occupy, while the natives see the effort of the colonialists as an infringement on their freedom, and therefore agitated for the right to self-rule. Many Africans experienced forced labour without compensation, especially in South Africa. In Congo, people were asked to work and give a fifth of their time and land free for the benefit of the Dutch government. In Algeria people were enslaved and their labour made for the benefit of the French Government. In countries like Kenya, up to 300,000 to 600,000 acres of land were taken and leased to the British citizens only. In Nigeria, the

M. J. Yusha'u, *Regional Parallelism and Corruption Scandals in Nigeria*, https://doi.org/10.1007/978-3-319-96220-7_3

natives of Lagos were not allowed to live or come near the areas where the British settled (Azikwe 1931).

Many of the colonies were conquered through violence, and any attempt at resistance by the people was met with serious consequences, such as the incident in Satiru village, where the people attempted to resist the British forces and many lives were lost, including the head of the Caliphate. In some areas, taxes that took away almost 50% of the farmers' output were imposed. "In French Africa until 1946, all Africans but a few citizens were under a regime of administrative law whereby they were subject to summary justice with no right of appeal. In 1914 Lugard specifically outlawed the representation of defendants by lawyers in the magistrates' courts of the South where a British model judiciary had been installed, albeit with massive problems and defects. In the Congo and the Portuguese territories, too, the Africans have no access to metropolitan style legal institutions. These existed only for European inhabitants or in the case of the Portuguese territories the handful of *assimilados*. They were made available to Africans only on the eve of independence or immediately afterwards" (Crowder 1987: 16, emphasis original).

The relationship between colonial governments and the native inhabitants therefore became antithetical. People were simply looking for the ways to assert their independence and govern themselves in their own way. It was in these tough times that some educated Africans saw the need to invest in the press and use it as an avenue to fight for their rights and struggle for independence. It was in these difficult moments that nationalists, like Herbert Macaulay and Nnamdi Azikwe, emerged in Nigeria and complemented the effort of newspapers that originally began as missionary platforms but later also became part of the struggle for self-assertion.

Another important point to note also is that some of the nationalists who fought for independence took over the mantle of leadership in Africa, but instead of changing the system, they continued with the legacy of their colonial predecessors; so, instead of experiencing relief, the struggle by the press started afresh, this time between two groups that were hitherto together struggling for independence. As stated by Crowder (1987) "the colonial state was not only conceived in violence, but it was maintained by the free use of it". Some of the African governments continued with this legacy. The kind of violence used by African leaders may not necessarily be bloody; it may take the form of imprisonment and other means of prosecution which resulted in silencing many journalists and in some cases even death. The emergence of military rule in many African countries a few years after political independence also did not help matters. It is by reflecting on these historical realities that we can understand the challenges the press is facing, not only in Nigeria but in Africa as a whole and many developing nations. (See Ado-Kurawa 2005 for a discussion on the historical evolution of Nigeria.)

The Emergence of Newspapers in Nigeria

Most discussions of media practice and ownership in Nigeria starts from colonial times which as stated by Olayiwola (1991) "was dominated by missionaries, colonial administrators, nationalists, political parties, politicians and private foreign organisations. During the colonial period, the press served as a medium of sustained public debate and political protest, an uncompromising advocate of administrative and political reforms, and a seething critic of the excesses of the colonial order. By its political activities, the press not only stimulated the emergence of nationalist movements but also played a prominent role in the constitutional development of modern Nigeria" (p. 35).

Developing a culture of literacy is extremely important in developing the readership that will sustain the newspaper industry. In the case of Nigeria, the story is mixed. As discussed by Abubakar (2011), in Northern Nigeria, there was a system of education in Arabic language centuries before the arrival of the British. Scholars have been spreading education using the Arabic language in Hausa, Fulfulde and Kanuri. But they were very suspicious of the English language after the arrival of the British because of its connection with missionary activities. This literally disenfranchised people from Northern Nigeria from partaking in the development of the newspaper industry. The colonial administrators also never encouraged the development of a strong education culture of Western education in the region.

This is where the southern part of Nigeria had major advantage by accepting and utilising the opportunity offered in the English language, or the use of Latin letters to communicate in local languages. As discussed by Omu (1978), the first printing press in Nigeria was established in 1846 by the Presbyterian mission in Calabar. It was eight years after the establishment of the printing press in Calabar that Reverend Henry Townsend established another printing press at a mission compound in Abeokuta and started the publishing of *Iwe Irohin* in 1859.

So, we can argue that the establishment of *Iwe Iroyin fun Awon Ara Egba ati Yoruba* (The Newspaper for the Egbas and Yorubas) by Reverend Henry Townsend in Abeokuta[1] (Babalola 2002: 405) initiated the process of establishing newspapers in Nigeria. *Iwe Iroyin*, as the paper was normally called, publishes in both Yoruba and English languages.

In 1863, another newspaper called *The Anglo-African* edited by Robert Campbell was established. *Iwe Irohin* focused its attention on fighting slavery while *The Anglo-African* was more interested in news about the problems of that time (Babalola 2002). In the words of Omu (1968) *The Anglo-African* is the real first indigenous press that marks the beginning of newspaper journalism in Nigeria.

According to Babalola, "The blossoming of the Nigeria Press started seventeen years later in the exigencies of socio-political and economic activities. The first newspaper of this period was by Andrew Thomas, who came out with the '*The Lagos Times*' on 10th November 1880. This bi-monthly newspaper was used to aggregate public opinion on topical issues. Fifteen months later after Blackall Benjamin began the publication of *The Lagos Observer*. This was followed closely by *The Eagle*, which made its debut on March 31, 1887 when Adolphus Mark started *The Mirror*" (Babalola 2002: 405 emphasis original). In 1908, another newspaper called *The Nigerian Chronicle* was established followed by *The Nigerian Pioneer*, then *Nigerian Daily Times* in 1926 established by Nigerian Printing and Publishing Company edited by Earnest Ekoli. The government took over *The African Messenger*, and Dr. Nnamdi Azikwe who later became the first ceremonial President of Nigeria established The *West African Pilot* in 1936.

The colonial government established *Gaskiya Tafi Kwabo* in 1939, and it became the first known newspaper from Northern Nigeria. Although prior to that, there were other newspapers such as 'Yar Gaskiya (The Truth), published in ajami (Hausa in Arabic script), and another newspaper called *Suda*, both of which were established in the 1940s (Yahaya 1988 in Abubakar 2011).

Chief Obafemi Awolowo pioneered the Publishing of *The Nigerian Tribune* in 1946 (Babalola 2002; Ado-Kurawa 2006).

Several newspapers have emerged between the 1950s and 1970s, though many of them did not survive. They include *Nigerian Outlook*, *Nigerian Citizen*, *The Herald*, *Afriscope*, the *Times International* (Ado-Kurawa 2006).

[1] Abeokuta is the Capital of Ogun State in Nigeria.

The late 1970s and early 1980s saw the establishment of commercially inclined newspapers, such as the *Guardian, Vanguard*, the *Punch, Triumph*[2] and the *Concord.* Most of these newspapers exist to date except the *Concord.* From the late 1980s to late 1990s more newspapers joined the market, such as *Democrat, Reporter, Thisday,* and *Weekly Trust.*[3] Neither *Democrat* nor *Reporter* survived.[4] With the return of Nigeria to civilian rule in 1999, many newspapers were established (Tables 3.1 and 3.2).

One characteristic of those who established the early newspapers in Nigeria was that they were people who having studied in Europe and America, returned home to help fight for the independence of the country, and some of them, like Dr. Nnamdi Azikwe, received journalism training. According to Jones (1979):

> Here we have a small body of men…who became successful and professional business men, others with a flair for journalism (but in most cases with no head in business) were able to establish their own newspapers and presses. Their financial resources were minimal, their circulation figures were reckoned in hundreds rather than thousands and few of their papers survived more than a few years until after the First World War. But their influence was out of all proportion to their size. (pp. 562–563)

This process that saw Nigerians who individually established their own newspapers to struggle for independence, might have set the precedence for individual ownership of newspapers and later commercial ownership which is more prevalent in Nigeria today, as most of the newspapers are privately owned. Oso (1991) traced the historical roots of the commercial interest in the newspaper industry in Nigeria and according to him, "The capitalisation of the Nigerian press and its subsequent commercialisation

[2] *Triumph* was owned by Kano State Government; it was very popular in the 1980s, but collapsed during the leadership of Governor Rabiu of Kwanakwaso of Kano State between 2011 and 2015. It is now being published periodically, but certainly not at the standard it was known for.

[3] The *Weekly Trust* is the first private newspaper from Northern Nigeria that survived from the 1980s to date. It has since developed into a daily newspaper, *Daily Trust.* See Chap. 7 for the reasons why some journalist think the newspaper was able to survive despite the fact that it is based in the north.

[4] See Chap. 8 for discussion on the reasons for the death of newspapers in Nigeria. *Democrat* and *Reporter* were established in the north. Some of the respondents interviewed suggested why they think newspapers do not survive in the north.

Table 3.1 List of active Nigerian newspapers in 2018

Name	*Location*	*Region*	*Publisher*	*Platform*
Daily Trust https://www.dailytrust.com.ng/	Abuja	North	Media Trust	Print and Online
Peoples Daily http://www.peoplesdailyng.com/	Abuja	North	Peoples Media	Print and Online
New Telegraph https://newtelegraphonline.com/	Lagos	South	Orji Uzor Kalu	Print and Online
Vanguard https://www.vanguardngr.com/	Lagos	South	Sam Amuka	Print and Online
The Nation http://thenationonlineng.net/	Lagos	South	Bola Tinubu	Print and Online
The Guardian http://guardian.ng/	Lagos	South	Alex Ibru	Print and Online
Leadership https://leadership.ng/	Abuja	North	Sam Nda-Isaiah	Print and Online
Tribune http://www.tribuneonlineng.com/	Ibadan	South	African Newspapers of Nigeria	Print and Online
Blueprint https://www.blueprint.ng/	Abuja	North	Muhammad Idris	Print and Online
Thisday https://www.thisdaylive.com/	Lagos	South	Nduka Ogbabaina	Print and Online
National Mirror https://www.nationalmirroronline.net/	Lagos	South	Emeka Obasi	Print and Online
Independent https://independent.ng/	Lagos	South	James Ibori	Print and Online
Punch http://www.punchng.com/	Lagos	South	Sam Amuka and James Aboderin	Print and Online
Champion http://www.championnews.com.ng/	Lagos	South	Emmanuel Iwuanyanwu	Print and Online
Daily Sun http://sunnewsonline.com/	Lagos	South	Orji Uzo Kalu	Print and Online
National Daily https://nationaldailyng.com/	Lagos	South	Mr Chris	Print and Online
Triumph	Kano	North	Kano State Government	Print and Online
Business Day	Lagos	South	Frank Aigbogun	Print and Online

Table 3.2 Online Nigerian newspapers by 2018

No	*Online newspaper*	*Website*
1	Sahara Reporters	http://saharareporters.com/
2	Premium Times	https://www.premiumtimesng.com/
3	Daily Nigerian	https://dailynigerian.com/
4	Daily Focus	https://www.dailyfocus.ng/
5	Elendu Reports	http://247ureports.com/
6	News Diary	https://newsdiaryonline.com/
7	News Digest	www.newsdigest.ng
8	Nigeria News Digest	www.nigerianewsdigest.com
9	Greenbarge Reporters	http://www.greenbreporters.com/
10	The Cable	https://www.thecable.ng/
11	Daily Post	http://dailypost.ng/
12	Solacebase	https://www.solacebase.com/
13	The Will	https://thewillnigeria.com/news/

started with the arrival of *Daily Times* in 1926. The paper was established by European financial interests represented in the Lagos Chamber of Commerce in alliance with some wealthy Nigerians. A wealthy and influential Nigerian Lawyer, Sir Adeyemo Alakija, who was opposed to the radical wing of the nationalist movement as embodied in Herbert Macaulay and his outspoken paper the *Daily Service,* was made the chairman. Before the arrival of the *Daily Times,* most of the earlier newspapers were owned and managed as one-man businesses, the owner being the editor, reporter and, in most cases, the printer" (p. 43). Another factor identified by Oso which helped in tilting the newspaper ownership towards private management is the issue of professionalism, which makes journalists follow certain principles and values in producing news.

Even though the ownership of the press in Nigeria was largely in private hands, there were some changes, especially after the involvement of the military in politics. In 1975, the Federal Military Government took over two major national dailies, *New Nigerian* and the *Daily Times.* These takeovers gave other state governments the resolve to establish their own newspapers, and coupled with military decrees and other government sanctions, the press suffered from attaining journalistic independence (Ette 2000).

Two things can be identified with Nigerian Newspapers, one positive and the other negative. Perhaps due to the influence of Nigerian newspapers in fighting for independence, the industry one can argue is to a large extent united on issues of national importance. This can be seen in the stand of the newspapers on many issues of national debate, such as the International Monetary Fund (IMF) debate in the 1980s when the federal government wanted to take a loan from the IMF, government sensitisation programmes like Operation Feed the Nation, Green Revolution and War Against Indiscipline (Olayiwola 1991). Other issues include their role in returning to civilian rule, ensuring the defeat of political leaders who want to elongate their tenure in office, and so on. This can be seen as a positive development (see also Shettima 1993).

On the other hand, as identified by Oso (1991), the newspapers are divided by ethnic, political and regional influences. This has in some situations contributed in dividing the people along ethnic and regional affiliations which in many instances does not help the stability of the country especially in times of ethnic or religious crises (see Chap. 5 on the Kenyan media system, which shows a similar trend). The way the newspapers report some crisis results in retaliatory attacks on innocent individuals, as exemplified by Isioma Daniel's article in *Thisday* newspaper, the ethnic crises involving various ethnic groups in, for example, Lagos, Kano, Kaduna, Ogun, Onitha and Maiduguri. Whatever the case, the Nigerian newspaper industry is an influential force in the discourse and deliberation on the Nigerian nation state.

Just as Nigeria is a diverse country, so are the newspapers. Beyond the north/south dichotomy in newspaper ownership in Nigeria (see Chap. 8 on regional parallelism for a more detailed discussion on the regional divide of Nigerian newspapers), there are differences in ownership and political orientation which can help us to understand the Nigerian media system. The following classification will therefore be useful in understanding Nigerian newspapers. The newspapers can be classified into at least four categories. These categories are not exhaustive, but they cover the active newspapers: clientelist-political, commercial newspapers, diaspora and online newspapers and the local or indigenous language newspapers. I have excluded the government owned newspapers because most of them have vanished; the few that exist are not as active as they were in the 1980s.

The clientelist-political newspapers are those established by politicians, former or existing government executives while holding public office or immediately after leaving office. Their owners have business, family and political interests even if there is an unlikely visibility of their interest in the coverage provided by these newspapers. In this category falls newspapers like *The Nation* owned by former Lagos State governor, Bola Ahmad Tinubu; the *Independent* owned by former Delta State governor, James

Ibori—one of the few governors to serve a prison term in London as a result of an investigation into money laundering, The Compass (now defunct) established by former Ogun State governor Gbenga Daniel; *New Telegraph* and *Daily Sun* owned by former Abia State governor Orji Uzo Kalu; the *Champion* newspaper owned by Chief Emmanuel Iwuanyanwu, a powerful politician from South Eastern Nigeria; and the *Tribune*, owned by the family of former premier of the defunct Western Region of Nigeria, Chief Obamfemi Awolowo. Defunct newspapers, such as the *Concord* owned by Chief MKO Abiola, and the *Reporter* owned by former presidential aspirant, Shehu Musa Yar'Adua belong to this category.

Some of these newspapers, particularly those established after the return of the country to civilian rule in 1999, have a feature: allegation of corruption. As some of the interviewees for this book stated, the Economic and Financial Crimes (EFCC) Commission has traced funds directly taken from the state treasury to establish some of these newspapers (see Chaps. 7 and 8 for details). Although these newspapers are owned by politicians, they are run and managed by professional journalists.

The commercial newspapers are privately owned newspapers managed by professional journalists. Their motive just as in the Liberal Model in the media system theory discussed by Hallin and Mancini (2004) is profit making. They are most of the English-speaking newspapers in Nigeria and have survived the longest. In this category are newspapers like *Daily Trust*, *Punch*, *Vanguard*, *Guardian*, *Thisday*, *Leadership*, *Peoples Daily* and *Blueprint*. Even among these groups there are variations. *Leadership* and *Thisday* can be subclassified as clientelist-commercial due to the strong relationship between the owners of the two newspapers with political establishment. The owner of the *Leadership* newspaper, Sam Nda Isiaiah, was a presidential candidate in the 2015 presidential election under the banner of the ruling All Progressive Congress (APC). Also see Chaps. 7 and 8 for further discussion on *Thisday* newspaper and its clientelist tendencies.

The online and diasporic newspapers are advocacy-type newspapers established online by the diaspora community or journalists within Nigeria. They incorporate professional journalism into their work. The background of the owners and managers differ with some coming from a more advocacy background, such as Sahara Reporters, and others from a more professional journalism background like *Premium Times, the Cable* and *Daily Nigerian*. Yet activism, whether in a more adversarial or soft form, is an important aspect of their journalism. Kperogi (2011) did a detailed study on the nature of advocacy journalism and he believes their practice is closer to the fearless journalism that some newspapers in Nigeria were known for during the independence struggle as well as in the military era. According to him the philosophy of Sahara Reporters itself suggest that:

> Sahara Reporters is an online community of international reporters and social advocates dedicated to bringing you commentaries, features, news reports from a Nigerian-African perspective. A unique organization, founded in the spirit of Article 19 of the Universal Declaration of Human Rights, comprising of ordinary people with an overriding commitment to seeking the truth and publishing it without fear or favor. Because its core members are unapologetic practitioners of advocacy journalism, Sahara Reporters also serves as an umbrella outlet for objective reporting of verifiable and accurate news and untainted social commentaries for anyone wishing to exercise their freedom of speech in the public interest and common good. (Sahara Reporters 2018)

Although these online newspapers are yet to be accepted as the mainstream media like the traditional newspapers in Nigeria and Africa, they should not in any way be underestimated, looking at the global trends. Because the model of newspaper business is changing drastically. Rupert Murdock has opted for online subscription for his newspapers, while *The Guardian* is working on goodwill. The *London Evening Standard* has joined the free newspaper market (Sambrook 2017). The *Independent* has become online and stopped the print edition. Although Nigerian newspapers are still vibrant, the online newspapers might hold the future.

The diasporic and online newspapers also are diverse. Some like the *Daily Nigerian* are somewhat close to the clientelist newspapers due to the open relationship between their owners with politicians. The founder of Sahara Reporters, Omoyele Sowore, has joined politics ahead of the 2019 elections, will Sahara Reporters maintain its advocacy journalism? Even the most professional among the online newspapers, *Premium Times*, has strong connections with politicians like the former EFCC chairman, Nuhu Ribadu. These are tendencies that are clientelist in nature and close to the Polarised Pluralist Model suggested by Hallin and Mancini (2004).

The last category are the local language newspapers published in Hausa, Yoruba, Igbo or any other Nigerian language. It is not out of place to state that unlike Kenya (as discussed in Chap. 5) where the local language media are quite influential especially during elections, in Nigeria, the English language newspapers carry the day. The local language newspapers cover different interests from culture, religion and news and current affairs. Some of the English language newspapers publish the local language newspapers as part of the strategy to expand their markets.

Among the active local language newspapers are *Aminiya, Alfijir, Leadership Hausa, Daily Nigerian Hausa, Solacebase Hausa, Rariya, Premium Times Hausa, Hausa Online, Almizan, Madubi, Mikiya, Jakadiya, Jakadan Fasaha* and *Jaridar Dimukuradiyya* published in the Hausa language. In the Yoruba language there are newspapers like *Irohin Yoruba, Alaroye, Akede Odua, Akede Agbaye* and *Iroyin Owuro*, while existing Igbo Language newspapers include *Iroko* and *National Light* (partly English).

Nigerian Newspapers and the Struggle for Independence

One of the important landmarks of the Nigerian newspapers is their role in the struggle for independence. Any serious study on the attainment of Nigeria's independence must acknowledge this fact, because of the role the papers played in serving as the mouthpiece of Nigerian nationalists. When the struggle for independence became stronger and the Nigerian elite became part and parcel of the struggle, it was the newspapers that took a frontline position and gave themselves the role of an anti-colonial mouthpiece, which later resulted in the detention and maltreatment of a number of journalists. The earlier role of the newspapers which took the form of religious proselytisation changed and became a nationalist struggle that criticises the legitimacy of colonial rule (Oyovbaire 2001).

As stated earlier, the Nigerian press was created under colonial circumstances, and the nature of newspapers and their content reflected that circumstance. According to Malaolu (2004), colonial rule started with the arrival of missionaries; later European traders came into the African continent and found it to be a potential area for commerce because of the abundant natural resources the African continent is endowed with. By the middle of the nineteenth century direct rule by colonialists has already taken shape; the use of law enforcement agencies to ensure compliance to colonial rule and particularly the payment of taxes has become commonplace. In Nigeria, the inhabitants of the colonised areas were angered by these policies, because they were created and enforced without consulting them. Any attempt by the people to organise themselves into pressure groups was curtailed, and the Nigerian press emerged in this circumstance.

Therefore, from inception Nigerian press "was a militant press: bellicose in temperament, belligerent in posturing and adversarial in language and perception. Where the police force was supportive of the authority, the press pitched its tent with people. It was resolute in its determination for political emancipation for the people. It was passionate in its demand for self-government. It was unrelenting in its battle against all vestiges of oppression, both local and foreign, it was, and still largely is, fearless, vibrant and nationalistic press" (Malaolu 2004: 5).

Even the first newspaper, *Iwe Irohin*, established by Reverend Henry Townsend in 1859 in Abeokuta for evangelical purposes, faced some challenges that forced the paper to take a radical stand on some issues such as the slave trade, where the move to abolish slavery was popular at that time. *Iwe Irohin* did so through powerful editorial and opinion writings, a fact that was acknowledged by Dr. Nnamdi Azikwe, editor of the *West African Pilot*. The paper later became the centre of attention (for various interest groups looking for Nigerian independence) and the medium for airing the viewpoint of the Nigerian intelligentsia (Malaolu 2004).

Idemili (1978) studied the role of Nigerian newspapers in the struggle for independence with an emphasis on the *West African Pilot*. Idemeli states that when the *West African Pilot* made its debut in 1937, there were newspapers already on the ground, like *Nigerian Daily Times* and the *Daily Service*, but the most critical of them was the *West African Pilot*, partly because Azikwe founded the paper in order to serve two purposes: first to concentrate on the struggle for independence, and second to serve as a business outfit.

The contribution made by the *West African Pilot* went beyond the struggle for independence; the paper also changed the face of Nigerian journalism by introducing a new approach in its production, such as the use of large photographs and sourcing news from wire services like Reuters. It also introduced other initiatives that transformed the use of language and caused Nigerian journalism to follow in the footsteps of American journalism. The *West African Pilot* carried several editorials that questioned some of the policies of the colonial government after World War II on issues that have to do with the liberty and general well-being of the citizens of the British Empire because of their contribution to the war, also because members of the colonies have lost their lives to bring peace to various localities. For instance, the *West African Pilot*, according to Idemili, carried an editorial in the 1940s entitled "Even Mr. Churchill" in which it states:

> When in the House of Commons, Mr. Winston Churchill explained application of the Atlantic Charter, in words like these: "At the Atlantic meeting, we had in mind primarily restoration of sovereignty, self government and national life of the States and nations of Europe...That is quite a separate problem from the evolution of self-government institutions in regions and people's which owe allegiance to the British Crown". Our Prime Minister made us wonder whether the Atlantic Charter is, after all to use the phrase of the "London Chronicle" a symbol of hypocrisy.
>
> That a British Prime Minister could utter such a statement during an unparalleled destructive war which has cost colonial peoples their material resources and manpower is, indeed, a revelation. What, now, must we expect to be our fate after the war? Must we believe in platitudes? Indeed the four freedoms must be said to be good enough for "the States and nations of Europe" but when the interpretation and application of this principle are applied to us, "that is a quite separate problem".

One of the most significant contributions made by the press that earned it respect and a special position in the history of newspaper journalism was how it successfully pioneered the birth of the National Council of Nigeria and Cameroons (NCNC), with Herbert Macaulay as the leader and Nnamdi Azikwe the editor of the *West African Pilot* as Secretary General, an effort that was seen as the beginning of the struggle for independence from Britain (Idemili 1978).

Beyond struggling for independence, the emergence of a political party whose original base was a newspaper could also mean the beginning of what Hallin and Mancini (2004) would call "political parallelism", a situation where the ideological inclination of a media organisation corresponds with the stand of a political party, as obtained in many European countries.

However, as pointed out by Idemili, when the *West African Pilot* achieved some success in the struggle for independence, new powerful politicians emerged in other regions, namely Chief Obafemi Awolowo[5] in the Western Region and Sir Ahmadu Bello[6] in the Northern Region. The emergence of these two powerful politicians changed the focus of the *West African Pilot* from attacking the colonial government into attacking opposition politicians and their party platforms. An attempt that can be

[5] Chief Obafemi Awolowo was the Premier of the defunct Western Region.

[6] Alhaji Sir Ahmadu Bello was the Premier of the defunct Northern Region.

interpreted as the beginning of tribal politics on the pages of newspapers in Nigeria based on regional divide. Nigerian newspapers in the struggle for independence also engaged themselves not only with self-governance from Britain, but on issues relating to internal politics whether initiated by the colonial government, or in the struggle to ensure the supremacy of one region or the other in precolonial Nigeria.

Adebanwi (2004) discussed one of such issues that drew the attention of the newspapers, and according to him the status of Lagos which was made to be the capital of Nigeria after the amalgamation of Nigeria in 1914 became the centre of attention. Two leading newspapers, the *West African Pilot* led by Nnamdi Azikwe and the mouthpiece of National Council for Nigeria and Cameroon (NCNC), and the *Daily Service* supporting Earnest Ikoli and Obafemi Awolowo, and equally the mouthpiece of Action Group (AG) engaged each other. The *West African Pilot* used its influence to write editorials and news stories demanding that every part of Nigeria should have a share of the capital, while the *Daily Service* wanted Lagos to be part of the Western Region. According to the *Daily Service*, "to submit to the severance of Lagos from the West would amount to economic and fiscal suicide on the part of the people and Government of the Western Region"; it therefore criticised the Colonial Secretary Mr. Lyttleton for favouring the idea of making Lagos an independent entity. *Daily Service* argued that "Lagos, an indisputable Yoruba City owned by the West, is to remain a lone star…And in arriving at his decision, Mr Lyttleton disregards all historical facts and constitutional precedent" (Adebanwi: 87–88).

The *West African Pilot* disagreed with the position of *Daily Service*, *Pilot* states in its September 10, 1953 editorial that Lagos has a special position in the mind of every Nigerian, because the *Binis*[7] consider it part of their ancient empire, and people from the Northern Region consider Lagos as a place developed using their resources, particularly groundnut and cotton that were booming then in the international market. For the members of the Eastern Region, according to the *Pilot*, Lagos was not only built with their revenue, but with their blood as well; while the attachment of the people of the Western Region to Lagos stems from historical and geographical ties, and therefore Lagos is considered a home for entire sections of the country (Adebanwi 2004).

[7] An ethnic group in Nigeria.

Though Adebanwi criticised the stance of the *West African Pilot* on the position of Lagos, particularly the assertion of the paper that the Northern Region contributed to the development of Lagos through the resources of the region like cotton and groundnut. According to Adebanwi the Northern Region was amalgamated with other regions because of lack of resources in the region. The position of Adebanwi is flawed on two fronts. First, it may be a denial of history to think that the north had no resources when, indeed, it was the groundnut, cotton and other agricultural outputs of the region together with those of other regions that were used to build Lagos. At a point when the colonial government was starved of funds, it borrows money from the northern businessmen who, prior to independence, were engaged in trade across various parts of Africa. Secondly Adebanwi's argument failed to understand the reason why Britain amalgamated the regions that later became present-day Nigeria. According to Arnold (2005), "in 1914 there was no historical basis for Nigerian unity except British imperial convenience" (p. 189).

The debate about the position of Lagos,[8] then the seat of political power, reflects the nature of media location as well, which later comes to make an impact on the world view of Nigerian media. According Oyovbaire (2001), the Nigerian press inherited a legacy after independence which is adversarial and in constant opposition to the political class, and the opposition continued after independence when Nigerians took over from the colonialists. For this reason, a section of the Nigerian political elite began to dislike the nature of reportage of the Nigerian media and it was later given the name "Lagos press". Oyovbaire concludes that "there was also the fact that the origins and dominant location of the media created for it an instrument for the propagation of a role, which was nationalistic yet geo-politically partisan. This is the inheritance at independence in the relationship between the media and the political process" (p. 2).

The concentration of the media in a particular geopolitical location has created a complex image that combined so many features that are an integral part of the historical formation of Nigeria, yet might be seen to be alienating other interests that are also part of the historical formation and

[8] The capital of Nigeria has been shifted from Lagos to Abuja after the recommendation of a committee established by General Murtala Muhammad to advise for a new capital acceptable to all Nigerians, and Abuja was selected, being at centre of the country. In 1991 Abuja took over as the nation's new capital, and Lagos still maintains its position as the commercial centre of the Nigeria.

the realities of today's Nigeria. This complex nature was captured by Oyovbaire (2001), where he categorically states that "the south-west of the country is the materialist location of the Nigerian media which coincides with the Yoruba nationality, early evangelisation of Christianity, propagation of western education and establishment of seat of colonial and post-colonial government together with the large and flourishing market forces and patronage which aided the locational stimuli of the media". Oyovbaire saw this situation as shaping the material strength and readership of the Nigerian media and according to him therefore, "the readership audience for marketing its role, mandate and products was the southwest initially, and even when in contemporary times other audiences could be located outside the southwest, this historical location continued to provide the arrowhead for opinion formation, legitimisation of media contents, agitation and agenda-setting. From this perspective…the media is highly rooted in south-western Nigeria or in the famous Lagos-Ibadan axis…provides the materialist base for the worldview of the media" (p. 7). See Chaps. 7 and 8 for a detailed discussion on the influence of location in the Nigerian newspaper landscape.

This, however, does not mean that every newspaper or other media organisations are owned by people from the southwest geopolitical zone; rather, a number of the influential newspapers like the *Guardian* and *Thisday* are owned by Alex Ibru from the South-South and Nduka Obaigbena also from the South-South region (see Chap. 8 for discussion on the complexity of Nigerian newspapers). None of them is Yoruba by ethnicity, but the location of the newspapers is Lagos and as such they become influenced by the factors identified by Oyovbaire. However, gradual changes are occurring in the newspaper industry since the capital of Nigeria relocated to Abuja. Some newspapers owned by those from the Northern Region like *Leadership* and *Daily Trust* are currently gaining ground. In the past a lot of privately owned newspapers emerged in the north, but they couldn't survive.

The Media and Press Freedom in Nigeria

The concept of press freedom has been discussed by many scholars and media practitioners. It is a concept that is still relevant in media discourse because of the role information dissemination is playing in the political life of many countries. The media has become the vehicle responsible for informing and educating the citizenry. It is the mediator between citizens and those holding political authority, and the ability of the media to discharge this responsibility without hindrance depends on how free it is to operate in any given society.

The media therefore upholds freedom of expression which "is the right of the individual and the entire community to engage in active, challenging and robust debate about all issues pertaining to the 'normal and harmonious functioning of society'. The sort of political debate encouraged by the right to free expression will inevitably generate a speech that is critical of, and even offensive to those who hold public office or are intimately involved in the formation of public policy. A law that is targeting speech that is considered critical of the public administration by virtue of the individual who is the subject of the expression, strikes at the very essence and content of freedom of expression. Such limitations on speech may affect not only those directly silenced, but society as a whole" (Inter-American Commission 1994 cited in Perkins 2002: 11).

Gunaratne (2002) reviewed various scholarly works on the meaning of press freedom. Such scholarly works traced the discussion on press freedom to the libertarian theory of the press by Siebert et al.; others look at press freedom as the freedom to express opinion without interference and challenging the various branches of government by making them accountable to their actions, those who have those views essentially see the role of the press as that of the fourth estate of the realm.

Gunaratne (2002) further looks at press freedom beyond the ability of the media or the individual to express themselves, but as a role that bears some responsibilities. It carries some responsibilities because societies are different, and these differences must be taken into consideration in producing media outputs. Others do not even accept the notion of press freedom, but the freedom of the individual to freely express himself, hence the need to differentiate between press freedom and individual freedom.

This position might be apt because the process of development between one society to another might not be the same. Equally important is the fact that societies that lived under authoritarian regimes, military dictatorship or have minimal level of civic education, therefore their understanding of press freedom may not be the same. For instance, the kind of freedom enjoyed by the press in the economically developed countries may perhaps be detrimental in some developing countries that are looking for direction, and what they need is a press that complements their development effort.

According to Nossek and Rinnawi (2003), applying the Western model of the relationship between media and society may not be applicable in non-Western societies because of the gradual phase of development. It will therefore take time before the media catches up, and if the crises in Africa, Asia and South America are anything to go by, it makes it more difficult for the press in developing countries to tread in the footsteps of their Western counterparts. The only problem with this position is that sometimes political authorities take advantage of this situation to interfere in the activities of the media in order to cover some corrupt practices.

Once the political authorities succeed in completely silencing the media, there is the likelihood of higher level of corruption, as supported by a study conducted in around 130 countries by Ahrend (2002). The study shows the likelihood of having high levels of corruption where there is low level of press freedom. The study further stated that "there is strong evidence that more press freedom leads to less corruption, and no evidence that more corruption leads to less press freedom. Increasing press freedom is thus an important indirect mechanism for fighting corruption" (p. 17).

Some scholars see as a sign of press freedom a press that is critical of the politicians, state agencies and corporate bodies. To them the press should question when they see evidence of corruption, incompetence or non-delivery of service to the people they claim to represent. Criticising questionable behaviour is not a sign of disrespect because there is difference between personalities and the office they hold; if they behave well, the media should cooperate and where they go wrong, their misdeeds must be voiced out (Tomaselli 2003).

There are several ways in which the extent of the freedom enjoyed by the media can be evaluated. Wu (2003) discussed the criteria provided by Freedom House in his study of systematic determinants of international news flow between developed and developing countries. The criteria include "(1) whether laws or administrative decisions influence the content of news media; (2) the degree of political influence or control over content; (3) economic influences on the media by government or private entrepreneurs; and (4) the degree of oppression, ranging from the murder of journalists to censorship" (p. 15).

Tettey (2006) balanced the argument by looking at the role of the media from a public interest perspective. His position is that there are certain values in the society which must be protected, and the role of the media here is to act with a high degree of responsibility, being critical where the society foresees a problem, and tactical in discussing issues that might cause hostilities. From this perspective therefore, freedom of the press is a duty that firstly, makes the media accountable to the people, and second it should hold itself responsible where it is wrong.

It is therefore the responsibility of the media to ensure that "those who occupy positions of responsibility in the state are made to respect those provisions and freedoms" (Tettey 2006: 232), but on the other hand media should be made accountable for its mistakes.

The struggle for press freedom and independence of the media in Nigeria is a historical process which dates to colonial administrations. Nationalism and the struggle for independence was what gave Nigerian newspapers the ability to seek for freedom of the press. This effort transformed into a confrontation between the colonial government on one hand, and on the other, the Nigerian elite who felt alienated by the colonial government. Nationalism became the backbone of the struggle for the autonomy of the press, the search for independence and the base for political communications processes that became the vehicle to independence. It was at this period that people like Nnamdi Azikwe joined the journalism profession and began to emerge as national leaders whose writings attract attention and commands the respect of the people. It can therefore be stated that the nationalist struggle in Nigeria was a symbol of the strength of the Nigerian media (Nnaemeka 1990).

This, however, does not mean that the press had its affairs conducted smoothly without any interference from the colonial administration. According to Omu (1968), "the relations between the newspaper press and the government in British West Africa up to the end of the First World War exemplify the press freedom dilemma. In Sierra Leone, the Gold Coast,[9] and Nigeria, where popular newspapers were started in the 1850s and 1860s, Africans, the Colonial Governments and the Colonial Office were participants in what was probably the most momentous drama in early pre-independence history of the territories" (p. 281).

A number of journalists in British West Africa faced press prosecution, such as Charles Bannerman, founder of the *West African Herald* in the Gold Coast in 1862. He was held in contempt of court after criticising a judicial ruling. Colonial officers at various times seek permission to establish taxes when they hear about the establishment of newspapers in Lagos, which some of them described as "dangerous instruments in hands of semi-civilised Negroes" (Omu 1968: 288).

[9] Gold Coast was the former name of Ghana.

According to Omu, other editors like J.B. Benjamin of the *Lagos Observer* were jailed even before their cases had been ascertained before the judiciary. The emergence of more newspapers in Lagos, and the way they opposed the colonial government, led to the establishment of press laws. In 1908, after an article by Herbert Macaulay which was critical of the government, a new law of sedition was established which called for reasonable discussion of government policies by the press yet allows for the punishment of those who write articles that may likely steer public discontent. "The new bill covered familiar clauses about exciting hatred towards the Queen of Britain [England] and the government of Southern Nigeria; but it also provided by implication that no black man should show hostility to a white man: 'Whoever…promotes or attempts to promote feelings of enmity or hatred between different classes of …Nigeria, shall be punished'" (p. 293).

Other bills introduced then include the one that prohibits criticism against government officials. The penalty for anyone who contravenes the provisions of the two bills is two years' imprisonment. This angered a lot of people, including some traditional holders who ordered for the translation of the document in Yoruba language. At a meeting of the Legislative Council, about three members who were known hitherto for their pro-government stand had to work out of the chamber in protest for the introduction of the bill. The bill, however, was passed on November 9, 1909. But the rejection of the bill by a cross section of the population reduced its impact; as such there was only one prosecution from the time the bill was passed into law to the departure of the colonial governor. Therefore, when Lord Lugard became the Governor-General he faced a lot of criticism from the Nigerian pres; at the time he even complained about the kind of freedom Nigerian newspapers enjoy. Lugard said he could not tolerate the kind of liberty the press enjoyed; he stated this in a letter he wrote to his wife on October 16, 1913 (Omu 1968).[10]

During the post-independence era, Nigerian newspapers continued with the struggle. What changed, however, was that several of the former political actors prior to independence were the ones occupying the spaces left by the colonialists. This created some tension and even affected the credibility of the press, because those who remained in opposition trans-

[10] The critical stand against the media by the colonial government was also reflected by various military governments who were jittery of the press in Nigeria. See Ogbondah (2003) for a detailed discussion on the relationship between the military and the Nigerian press.

ferred their hostility from the previous colonial governments to the new government run by Nigerians. They depicted the government as evil and one in which the principal actors promote their personal interest (Nnaemeka 1990).

In order to challenge the critical nature of the Nigerian press, the government decided to invest heavily in the media by establishing newspapers and radio stations to compete with the privately owned press. But "despite the government'[s] substantial investment in capital and human resources to promote and sustain pro establishment newspapers and radio and television programming, the nationalists' tradition of a virile, independent and privately owned press continued as distinguishing characteristics of the post independent, political communication structure in Nigeria" (Nnaemeka 1990: 317).

Another challenge faced by the press in Nigeria relates to the constitutional provisions of the various constitutions in Nigeria, which have been the subject of debate for a long time. Though many scholars and writers claim that the Nigerian press is one of the freest in Africa, many journalists are still not satisfied with the level of protection provided to the press by the Nigerian constitution. One of the heated debates took place in 1976 during the process of drafting a new constitution for the country when the military decided to hand over to civilians. The constitution drafting committee decided that journalists should not be superior to other Nigerians; therefore the provision for freedom of expression suffices the requirement to uphold and maintain the independence of the press. Therefore, the post-independent constitutions of Nigeria, 1963 and 1979 constitutions did not go beyond the normal provisions for freedom of expression (Agbaje 1990).

Ogbondah (2004) conducted a comparative study on the constitutional provisions of press freedom between Nigeria and Ghana. His study showed that in the case of Ghana there has always been a provision for press freedom in the constitution which stated clearly that people should be free to express their opinion and establish media organisations. The constitution went further to provide provisions that discouraged censorship, or the need to have a licence when establishing private media organisations. The constitution of Ghana also provides clauses that prohibit interference against the decisions of editors, nor should they be questioned or harassed for the opinion they have expressed or be subjugated for the content of their publication (Ogbondah 2004).

The 1999 constitution in Nigeria also made provisions for press freedom in section 39 (1), which stated that Nigerians have the right to freedom of expression and the freedom to have an opinion and even impart their ideas on others without any interference. Subsection 2 of the section also provides Nigerians with the freedom to establish media organisations and disseminate their messages without influence from others. What, however, differs between the constitutions of Nigeria and that of Ghana is that subsection 3 of the Nigerian constitution made provisions for the non-disclosure of information which is "reasonably justifiable in a democratic society". Ogbondah therefore concludes that:

> Comparatively, I conclude that Ghana's effort at ensuring press freedom and protection of fundamental human rights in their constitution is more substantive than Nigeria's. For example, while the constitution of Ghana, like that of Nigeria, guarantees press freedom, the Ghanaian constitution goes further to outlaw press censorship. Beyond that, it emphatically states that government-owned media are obligated to provide fair opportunities to all political parties to present their views. In addition, the constitution of Ghana, unlike that of Nigeria, makes specific provisions guaranteeing editorial independence in the press. And unlike the Nigerian constitution, Ghana's states that it is an offence for the state to control or interfere with editorial content as it is also an offence for journalists to be harassed. (p. 25)

Ogbondah's study has clearly depicted some of the weaknesses of the Nigerian constitution concerning press freedom. Of interest here is the provision by the Ghanaian constitution for fair coverage by government-owned media. This is one area where the Nigerian media is yet to come on board, because the government-owned media, whether print or broadcast, end up being the mouthpiece of the government in power. Where editors take a position that differs from that of the government, they may be sacked, and in the case of private media, the media organisation might be raided by security agents or the journalists who carried the reports might face detention or prosecution.

In 2006, during the controversial debate for the extension of the tenure of the executives from two terms of four years each as provided in the 1999 constitution to three terms of four years, the editor of the government-owned *New Nigerian*, Mahmoud Jega was sacked immediately because of a headline by the *New Nigerian* celebrating the defeat of the constitution amendment bill in the national assembly.[11] Africa Independent Television (AIT) was also raided on May 14, 2006, by security agents for giving live coverage of the debate on the constitutional amendment, which many analysts believed was responsible for defeating the amendment bill. Reporters Without Borders, a non-profit advocacy organisation based in Paris even issued a press release condemning the security raid and urging Nigerian officials to restrain themselves from making "attacks on journalists critical of a proposed constitutional amendment to allow former president Olusegun Obasanjo to run for a third term".[12] The situation is the same in many states in Nigeria where members of the opposition have no say in the government-owned media.

However, there is more to it when it comes to discussion on press freedom in African countries. While government interference is one of the major impediments against independent journalism, there are also internal problems within the media that need to be tackled. Such problems as discussed by Alhaji Babatunde Jose, one of the former leading Nigerian journalists, include self-control and lack of professional training (see Chaps. 7 and 8 for analysis and discussion on the lack of professional training among Nigerian journalists).

According to Jose, "self-control by the press, whether in London, New York, Cairo, Rome, Bonn or Lagos is an important factor in the maintenance of press freedom. It is especially important where society is still largely traditional and where the democratic process as you know it… is still foreign" (Jose 1975: 260). The second problem faced by journalists in Africa according to Jose is that they don't have enough professional training and equipment to carry their duties, yet you see African journalists carrying on in their front pages serious allegations of sleaze and corrupt practices against senior government officials, while they don't have the required training to carry out investigations in order to prove such allegations (Jose 1975). That's why, according to Jose his paper took the slogan of "Militancy without hostility" (p. 260).

So, the challenges faced by the press in Nigeria should be seen from two perspectives, internal and external. The internal challenges faced by the Nigerian media are essential requirements of what it means to be in

[11] See a story by the BBC on the third term debate which was defeated the attempt by former president Obasanjo to succeed himself, by the national assembly on May 16, 2006 at http://news.bbc.co.uk/1/hi/world/africa/4986904.stm

[12] The press release by Reporters Without Borders is available at http://www.rsf.org/article.php3?id_article=17715

the business of journalism. Without proper equipment, proper working conditions, good incentives and professional training, it would take time before the media acquires the desired freedom and independence. There are also other challenges that have to do with culture and the diversity of African society in which the press needs to exhibit maturity in order not to subject the society to turmoil, like the case of Isioma Daniel in Nigeria during the beauty pageant when on November 12, 2002, a report was carried by *Thisday* that was insensitive to Muslims, which resulted in the loss of lives (Tettey 2006).

The reporting of the herdsmen crisis in Nigeria is another example where the newspapers take a regional and very sentimental approach in its reporting (Abubakar 2017). In an article entitled "This thing called 'killer herdsmen'", A newspaper columnist, Mahmud Jega, states this about the approach of Nigerian newspapers in reporting the Fulani herdsmen crises:

> There is no denying what is obvious. Herdsmen have attacked rural communities in different parts of Nigeria. The attacks are often brutal; the attackers would surround a village in the dead of night, shoot indiscriminately and set fire to huts…Even though criminal killings are going on in many parts of Nigeria, newspapers shout the loudest only when some sides of the divide carry out atrocities. Otherwise there is little media interest and there is no political capital to be derived from the killings. Where the herdsmen themselves or their ethnic, regional or religious kinsmen find themselves at the receiving end, as happened in Mambilla and Numan, the dominant news media takes little interest in happenings and sees it as either a case of just deserts or, where both combatants are from the wrong ethnic and religious divides as in Zamfara, as dog-eat-dog. (Jega 2018)

A Nigerian blogger and university professor in the United States wrote about the culpability of the media in reporting the herdsmen conflict where he states that "where the Fulani are the victims of murder or any crime, their ethnic identity—and the ethnic identity of their tormentors—is often concealed, as happened in Benue recently where the murder of 7 Fulani cattle herders by Tiv militia was reported in the national media with the following headline: "Bandits kill, burn 7 travelers" (Kperogi 2018)."

As stated by Mahmud Jega (2018), crime is a crime, and should not be condoned, yet the media needs to be fair in its reporting. This character of the Nigerian press, where it takes a vehemently partisan position provides a similarity with what the local language media does in Kenya during elections by promoting ethnic and tribal sentiments as discussed in Chap. 5.

The external challenge involves restrictions and interference by the government and its security apparatus when the press carries reports unfavourable to the government. Here the press needs to be more engaging to the public and work towards economic independence. By and large journalists and media organisations will address some of the challenges they face when they accept the fact that they are responsible for their actions, and also realise their role in responding to the needs of the public. This can be done when media organisations think and engage other institutions, economic political, educational and make them part of the communication process that is desired in any developing society (M'Bayo et al. 1995; Pratt 1998).

In terms of the degree of freedom, it is difficult to say that the Nigerian press is free, because it did not completely pass the criteria proposed by Freedom House which can be used to assess the extent of media freedom as discussed above; nor is it easy to declare it as restricted press because to a large extent the press in Nigeria, especially the private ones, still maintain the tempo which was acquired even before independence by being critical and nationalistic in nature.

Conclusion

In this chapter the circumstances that gave birth to the Nigerian newspapers, and how the content of the newspapers responds to specific challenges have been discussed. The historical origin of the newspapers, the nature of ownership and the transformations undergone by the newspapers both during colonialism and after independence have been reviewed. The chapter also looked at the concept of press freedom, the various approaches to understanding the concept, the criteria for evaluating press freedom the kind of freedom enjoyed by the press in Nigeria, as well as the constitutional provisions of press freedom in the Nigerian constitution.

It is, therefore, clear that the newspapers in Nigeria have been part of the history of Nigeria as a sovereign state, and the newspaper landscape shows there is still need for improvement. The challenges before the media at the moment requires a lot of restructuring that will make it economically independent, and professionally qualified enough to meet the basic standards of the requirements in the practice of journalism, but also to realise and understand that the circumstances of its birth, and the challenges it has undergone would help in creating a media environment that would provide a platform for all Nigerians to discuss and have an input in the future direction of their country.

References

Abubakar, A. T. (2011). *Media Consumption Amid Contestation: Northern Nigerians' Engagement with BBC World Service.* PhD Thesis, University of Westminster, London.

Abubakar, S. (2017). Newspapers Coverage of Herders/Farmers Conflict in Nigeria. *International Journal of Communication, 22*(1), 213–225.

Adebanwi, W. (2004). Hegemony and Spatial Politics: The Press and the Struggle for Lagos in Colonial Nigeria. *Africa Development, XXIX*(4), 75–91.

Ado-Kurawa, I. (2005). *Nigerian Politics & the National Political Reform Conference.* Kano: Tellettes Publishing House.

Ado-Kurawa, I. (2006, 10–12 October). *Press Coverage of Islam in Nigeria.* Paper Prepared for the International Conference on Fundamentalism and the Media, Boulder.

Agbaje, A. (1990). Freedom of the Press and Party Politics in Nigeria: Precepts, Retrospect and Prospects. *African Affairs, 89*(355), 205–226.

Ahrend, R. (2002). *Press Freedom Corruption and Human Capital.* Downloaded via. www.scholar.google.com, 3 Dec 2006.

Arnold, G. (2005). *Africa: A Modern History.* London: Atlantic Books.

Azikwe, B. N. (1931). Ethics of Colonial Imperialism. *The Journal of Negro History, 16*(3), 287–1931.

Babalola, E. T. (2002). Newspapers as Instruments for Building Literate Communities. The Nigerian Experience. *Nordic Journal of African Studies, 11*(3), 403–410.

BBC News. (2006). *No Third Term for Nigerian Leader.* Available at http://news.bbc.co.uk/1/hi/world/africa/4986904.stm. Downloaded 6 Dec 2006.

Crowder, M. (1987). Whose Dream Was It Anyway? Twenty Five Years of African Independence. *African Affairs, 86*(342), 7–24.

Ette, M. (2000). Agent of Change or Stability? The Nigerian Press Undermines Democracy. *The Harvard International Journal of Press/Politics, 5*(3), 67–86.

Gunaratne, S. A. (2002). Freedom of the Press: A World System Perspective. *Gazette: The International Journal for Communication Studies, 64*(4), 343–369.

Hallin, D. C., & Mancini, P. (2004). *Comparing Media Systems: Three Models of Media and Politics.* Cambridge Cambridge University Press.

Idemili, S. O. (1978). What the West African Pilot Did in the Movement for Nigerian Nationalism Between 1937–1957. *Black American Literature Forum, 12*(3), 84–91.

Jega, M. (2018). This Thing Called 'Killer Herdsmen'. Retrieved May 15, 2018. Available at https://www.dailytrust.com.ng/this-thing-called-killer-herdsman.html

Jones, G. I. (1979). Press and Politics in Nigeria, 1880–1937. *The International Journal of African Historical Studies, 12*(3), 562–563.

Jose, A. B. (1975). Press Freedom in Africa. *African Affairs, 74*(296), 255–262.

Kperogi, F. (2011). Webs of Resistance: The Citizen Online Journalism of the Nigerian Digital Diaspora. PhD Dissertation, Georgia State University.

Kperogi, F. (2018). News Media's Cultivation of "Fulani Herdsmen" Hysteria. Retrieved May 15, 2018. Available at https://www.farooqkperogi.com/2018/02/news-medias-cultivation-of-fulani.html

M'Bayo, R., Nwokeafor, C., & Onwumechilli, C. (1995). Press Freedom and the Imperatives for Democracy: Towards Sustainable Development. *Africa Media Review, 9*(3), 32–53.

Malaolu, O. (2004). *The Effects of Militant Press on Nigeria's Democratic Evolution.* Unpublished MA Thesis Submitted to the Department of Mass Communications, University of Florida.

Nnaemeka, T. I. (1990). Cultural Influence, Modern Changes, and the Sociology of Modern African Political Communication. *Journal of Black Studies, 20*(3), 306–323.

Nossek, H., & Rinnawi, K. (2003). Censorship and Freedom of the Press Under Changing Political Regimes: Palestinian Media from Israeli Occupation to the Palestinian Authority. *Gazette: The International Journal for Communication Studies, 65*(2), 183–202.

Ogbondah, C. W. (2003). *State-Press Relations in Nigeria (1993–1998): Human Rights and Democratic Development.* Ibadan: Spectrum Books LTD.

Ogbondah, C. (2004). Democratisation and the Media in West Africa: An Analysis of Recent Constitutional and Legislative Reforms for Press Freedom in Ghana and Nigeria. *West Africa Review 6*, 1–36.

Olayiwola, R. O. (1991). Political Communications: Press and Politics in Nigeria's Second Republic. *Africa Media Review, 5*(2), 31–45.

Omu, F. I. A. (1968). The Dilemma of Press Freedom in Colonial Africa: The West African Example. *The Journal of African History, 9*(2), 279–298.

Omu, F. I. A. (1978). *Press and Politics in Nigeria* (pp. 1880–1937). London: Longman.

Oso, L. (1991). The Commercialization of the Nigerian Press: Development and Implications. *Africa Media Review, 5*(3), 41–51.

Oyovbaire, S. (2001). The Media and Democratic Process in Nigeria (1). Available at http://www.waado.org/nigerdelta/Essays/Oyovbaire.html. Downloaded 15 Aug 2006.

Perkins, M. (2002). Freedom(s) of the Press in Latin America: Reconciling Societal and Individual Rights in International Law. *Gazette: The International Journal for Communication Studies, 64*(1), 5–19.

Pratt, C. B. (1998). Responsibility and Ethical Reasoning in the Nigerian Press. *Africa Media Review, 2*(2), 46–64.

Reporters Without Borders. (2006). *Calls for Third Presidential Term Increase Pressure on News Media.* Available at http://www.rsf.org/article.php3?id_article=17715. Downloaded 06 Dec 2006.

Sahara Reporters. (2018). About Us. Retrieved May 15, 2018. Available at http://saharareporters.com/about

Sambrook, R. (2017). Stop Press: Last Words on the Future of Newspapers. Retrieved May 15, 2018. Available at https://theconversation.com/stop-press-last-words-on-the-future-of-newspapers-72027

Shettima, K. A. (1993). Structural Adjustment and Student Movement in Nigeria. *Review of African Political Economy*, *56*, 83–91.

Tettey, W. J. (2006). The Politics of Media Accountability in Africa: An Examination of Mechanism and Institutions. *The International Communications Gazette*, *68*(3), 229–248.

Tomaselli, K. G. (2003). 'Our Culture' VS 'Foreign Culture': An Essay on Ontological and Professional Issues in African Journalism. *Gazette: The International Journal for Communication Studies*, *65*(6), 427–441.

Wu, H. D. (2003). Homogeneity Around the World: Comparing the Systematic Determinants of International News Flow Between Developed and Developing Countries. *Gazette: The International Journal for Communication Studies*, *65*(1), 9–24.

Yahaya, I. Y. (1988). *Hausa a rubuce: tarihin rubuce rubuce cikin Hausa*. Zaria: Northern Nigerian Publishing Company.

CHAPTER 4

White and Black Press: Racial Parallelism in South African Journalism

Introduction

South Africa is one of the most diverse nations in Africa with a complex history that includes racial discrimination, as seen during the apartheid era. It is also a country that combines several ethnic nationalities from Europe, Asia, and Africa living within a single nation-state. As an economic giant within the African continent, a study of the media system of South Africa is important to unearth the nature of ownership, readership and to explore the relationship between media and society. This chapter examines this complexity within the media system paradigm that guides the study of this book.

As discussed in the introduction, the media reflects the society in which it operates. While it is difficult to avoid the influence of western scholarship in analysing the media system in South Africa, it is also important to understand that the media landscape in South Africa has its distinct nature, rooted in its history and political context (Wasserman 2010).

This chapter is therefore divided into the following sections. The first section studies the historical landscape of the media in South Africa during the apartheid era. An era where there was clear demarcation in terms of the character of the media between the pro-apartheid or what will be referred to in this book as the white press, and the anti-apartheid or black press.

The second section will focus on the post-apartheid press when South Africa gained independence and black majority rule was established. This period came with its own challenges. Issues such as media diversity and the

M. J. Yusha'u, *Regional Parallelism and Corruption Scandals in Nigeria*, https://doi.org/10.1007/978-3-319-96220-7_4

attempt of the government to ensure inclusivity is discussed. The media landscape was completely different with the anti-apartheid media searching for new readers, and the white press seeking to reinvent itself and maintain its hold of the elite readers. It is in this period of soul-searching by the media that a new phenomenon emerged: tabloid journalism, catering for a completely new set of audiences, the black working-class majority living in urban areas.

But how do we evaluate the media system of South Africa within the context of media systems theory suggested by Hallin and Mancini (2004), which is the subject of this book? The third section explores the media system of South Africa in general and looks at how it fits within the three models of media and politics suggested by Hallin and Mancini. The final section concludes the chapter.

Media Landscape in South Africa: White and Black Press and the Apartheid Period

Some clarification needs to be made on the use of the terms *white* and *black press* in the South African context. It would be too simplistic to use these terms literally within the South African media landscape. The *white press* refers to media organisations that support the apartheid regimes of South Africa from 1948 to 1994, when white majority rule prevailed in the country. It also refers to media organisations that are owned by the same white media moguls after independence, although the nature of the editorial content might have changed to reflect the new South African society after independence in 1994.

Black press within this context refers to the liberal media that was against the apartheid regime, although ownership might be under the control of liberal white media proprietors. It also refers to media organisations owned and operated by new black elites that emerged in post-independent South Africa.

As discussed by Tomaselli and Teer-Tomaselli (2008), the media landscape in South Africa during apartheid can be classified into those that support the ruling party, Afrikaner National Party, and those that are in opposition. What is interesting about this period in South African history is that the English press, which was the most liberal, although owned by the whites, was the one that stood against apartheid. Citing Louw (1993), Tomaselli and Teer-Tomaselli (2008: 172) state:

> The English language press in the main was well disposed to the official opposition, with a significant amount of subterranean sympathy for the banned liberation movements, particularly from those English-language newspapers servicing the needs of the urban black majority within the country. Playing on the sidelines was anti-apartheid, anticapitalist "alternative press," a disparate group of independent papers with vaguely socialist aspirations backed by Non-Governmental Organisations (NGOs) and foreign funding.

Tomaselli and Teer-Tomsaelli (2008) further added that the character of the media in South Africa was developed during the apartheid period. With the white press and its subdivisions supporting the white minority rule, and the black press, with its structural idealogical complexities, being anti-apartheid.

What is interesting within this period was the emergence of the intranational character of the South African press. The seed of racial parallelism cloaked in the political character of the news media was emerging. A study by Kotze (1986) shows that the nature of political socialisation and media consumption in South Africa reflects these parallel divisions. All English language newspaper, according to Kotze, support the liberation movements and opposition parties, while the Afrikaans-controlled newspapers maintained their support for the apartheid administration. The black press, according to Kotze, were editorially run by black journalists, but financially supported and controlled by "white interest groups" (Kotze: 420).

Therefore, throughout the apartheid period, the media was divided into either pro-nationalist, pro-apartheid, or liberal and anti-government press. Kotze (1986) summarised the situation as follows:

> This division holds strong ideological implications—it is a division concerning racial issues that extend deeper than mere political partisanship. It could apart from a pro- and anti-apartheid division, also be described as reflecting the language division—Afrikaans-speaking people nearly all support the Nationalist Party and English-speaking people predominantly support the liberal opposition parties. Exposure to the press also reflects this pattern of division.

During the apartheid era in South Africa there was a strong similarity between the concept of political parallelism suggested by Hallin and Mancini (2004) and the political character of the media. But the similarity is not conclusive. While in Europe and North America where the study by Hallin and Mancini focused more towards party politics and the reflection of views of political parties in the media, in the case of apartheid South Africa there is a major difference. Racism was a core component of media character and audience consumption. It was more a racial parallelism than simple characterisation of political parallelism. Media organisations owned by white Afrikaans reflected pro-apartheid views; media controlled by white English liberals and black liberation movements reflected anti-apartheid views.

Van der Pas, der Brug, and Vliegenthart (2017: 493) noted that while the concept of political parallelism as espoused by several scholars focuses on ideological, organisational and party affiliations, the intranational context of South Africa is different. The nature of discrimination and racial composition of the country makes media content and exposure highly influenced by racism and ethnicity.

A notable feature of the South African media system is the influence of public broadcasting since the era of apartheid. The South African Broadcasting Corporation (SABC) had been a prominent part of the historical evolution of the media.

History of broadcasting in South Africa dates back to 1923 when the first wireless transmission was made in Johannesburg. A daily programming in Afrikaans language and one hour of news transmission also in Afrikaans began in 1927. But this attempt was faced with a serious funding problem. Therefore, an investigation was launched by the prime minister, James Barry Munnik Hertzog, into all aspects of broadcasting in the country. This investigation gave birth to SABC, which was formally established in 1936. Broadcasting by SABC continued to grow in the 1950s and 1960s, and by the 1970s more programmes were launched in African local languages. Despite this development, SABC was largely seen as the mouthpiece of the apartheid regime in South Africa (Tomaselli and Teer-Tomaselli 1994; Saho 2018).

Therefore, the role of SABC during apartheid was noted by South Africans and it came under heavy criticism after independence. It was a focus of attention during the Truth and Reconciliation Commission established after independence in 1994 over its role in serving the apartheid regime from 1948 onwards.

This is important, because unlike the print media, or the press which was under private control, SABC was established as a public service broadcasting entity that should serve members of the public irrespective or race, ethnicity or religious affiliation. Yet the ideals of public service were ignored and the SABC became a propaganda tool in the hands of the apartheid regime. Tomaselli and Teer-Tomaselli (1994: 46) summarised the situation in SABC under apartheid thus:

> Ironically, the translocation of the BBC ethos to South Africa in the 1930s suited the National Party's (NP) policy of apartheid after the 1950s, as neither Reith nor the NP recognised black Africans as part of the listening/viewing audience except on white terms. Media, and especially broadcasting, thus contributed to social and economic disparities. They legitimised apartheid in empowering a small sector of the population working on behalf of the global functions of capital, at the expense of the black-driven motor of the apartheid economy. Herein lay the essential flaw of apartheid. In serving the narrow interests of the South African bourgeoisie and petty bourgeoisie.

Public service broadcasting in South Africa during apartheid highlights the imperfection of what I would like to describe as cut-and-paste journalism. The BBC which represents the hallmark of public service broadcasting in the UK receives popular support and goodwill among party politicians and the public in Britain. As stated by Humphreys (2014), the BBC is seen by the public and politicians as being impartial to a large degree, and as the champion of international journalism with roots in the UK.

In the case of South Africa, it has the opposite effect (we shall see whether the situation changes in post-apartheid South Africa). In this case SABC, with its unquestionable support of the apartheid regime has reinforced racial parallelism by supporting the racial and discriminatory policies of the apartheid regime. That is why it is important to study media systems intranationally to identify the specificities caused by local contexts rather than a wholesale application of theories that emanated elsewhere.

Post-apartheid Period: Media Diversity and Inclusion

The international campaign against apartheid and the intense pressure within South Africa from anti-apartheid activities had tremendous impact on the media landscape of the country. While there was clear difference in reporting between the liberal English language and other anti-apartheid press compared to the Afrikaans language newspapers; a new wave of reporting began to emerge. Some of the Afrikaans language media like *Vrye Weekblad* and *Beeld* began to take an anti-apartheid stand and even urged the apartheid regime to release Nelson Mandela from prison (Armoudian 2013).

A new era was emerging in South Africa, and with the release of Mandela on 11 February 1990, South Africa was entering a new page in its history. A transition to democracy and the end of apartheid had come. This had a huge impact on the transformation of South Africa, from a racist political system to a multiracial and multiparty political and economic system. The media cannot be isolated; it reflects the larger society. A new dawn had emerged that would alter the media landscape to reflect the new reality in South Africa.

The changes in the political, economic and judicial structure of South Africa was changing (Mogadime 2005) and would have significant impact on the mass media. With the establishment of a new government led by the African National Congress (ANC), disadvantaged groups were becoming powerful and new media moguls from the black and other disadvantaged communities during apartheid were emerging (Sparks 2011).

Just like during the apartheid era, South African media landscape remained diverse. The print media which was undergoing major transformation due to the new transition remained influential and controlled by the private sector. What about the broadcast media which was monopolised by the apartheid regime through SABC? We shall see soon. Leonard (2014) has extensively researched the transformation of the media landscape in South Africa after 1994. He stated that the print media was more accessible to disadvantaged communities, though there is need to expand their reach to other localities.

To avoid the experience of the apartheid era, there was a call from several spectrums of the South African Society on ensuring media diversity in the country. The government came up with several initiatives, which included the establishment of the Government Communications and Information Systems (GCIS), Multipurpose Community Centres Programme, the Universal Service Agency (USA), the Independent Communications Authority of South Africa (ICASA) and the Media Development and Diversity Agency (MDDA) among others (Skinner 2006).

The establishment of the MDDA provides several lessons on the media system in South Africa. It suggests an acknowledgment from the government that the media landscape of South Africa is not even in terms of distribution and ownership. It connotes the economic imbalance between various ethnic and racial groups. It also suggests the need to make the media landscape more inclusive so that all groups within the country would have a sense of belonging and the opportunity to participate in the political process. These are peculiar intranational issues that could not be captured by the work of Hallin and Mancini (2004).

The MDDA's 2017 report signifies how far the South African society has moved forward in promoting media diversity and inclusion across the country. The report suggests that since 2015, four major media conglomerates—known as the "Big Four"—dominate the media scene in South Africa. These firms are Media 24, which is the print arm of Naspers Group, the Independent Group, and the Media Times Group, which was previously known as Avusa and Caxton (Media Diversity and Development Agency 2017; Leonard 2014).

The progress made so far by MDDA is promoting more inclusion in terms of content and increasing media recruitment of blacks and female journalists in South African print media. The South African media landscape is becoming more representative of the ethnic and racial configuration of the country. Table 4.1 highlights some of these changes:

Like in many African countries, broadcast media play an important role in the lives of the people. It is the same thing in South Africa where majority of the population listen to radio stations. The study by MDDA suggested that when South Africa gained independence in 1994, there were only 32 licensed radio stations in both the public and the private sector with a combined audience of 19.8 million. Community radio and TV stations legally sanctioned by the state do not exist at all. The MDDA report added that "twenty years on, in 2014, there were 250 licensed radio stations with a weekly audience of 33.2 million and 16 licensed TV operators working across 170 channels with an audience of about 40 million. South Africa has therefore seen a rapid expansion of broadcast media with

Table 4.1 Print media ownership scorecard 2014

	Black ownership	*Female ownership*	*BBBEE status*
Media 24	52.94	24.95	Level 4
Caxton	17.78	6.28	Level 4
Times Media Group	58.47	18.44	Level 3
Independent newspapers	55.00%	25.30%	Level 2

Source: Media Diversity Development Agency (2017)

a plethora of channels, programmes that are available in a number of languages, and new formats appearing." (Media Diversity Development Agency 2017: 21).

Public sector broadcasting is still dominated by SABC, though it has also gone through major changes. It has become the biggest player in South Africa due to the rapid expansion of the station and a special act of government that was promulgated in 1999 called the Broadcasting Act No 4. The SABC has a monopoly with a 40% share of radio audiences and 70% in television (Media Diversity Development Agency 2017).

The biggest question with regards to SABC though is whether its expansion and increase in audience share by reaching out to more South Africans has changed anything compared to the position of the station during apartheid. Or is it simply a case of what Sparks (2011: 12) described as "elite continuity". This is one of the hottest topics of debate among media scholars and journalists alike to ensure press freedom in South Africa (Duncan 2014).

The ANC, which is now in power, has received massive support from South Africans. But the question to be asked is: Is the nature of its handling of the broadcast landscape represented by SABC any different from the monopoly exercised by the National Party during apartheid? The expectation from media scholars and journalists was that the South African media, particularly broadcast media will be more critical of government, since under apartheid, the media was operating under an authoritarian climate (Leonard 2014).

Views expressed by journalists on the state of broadcasting as represented by SABC is mixed, as stated by this journalist from one of the Big Four media conglomerates:

> SABC is a public broadcaster. 9 million people watch SABC 1, it reaches audiences that don't speak English. Radio Zulu has 17 million listeners, funded by advertising and TV license. The radio is linked to who is in power. South Africans pay license because it is a duty.
>
> At its worse—SABC was ordered to play 90% South African music and 10% international music. The stations must find the content. There was a very big race problem, no content in their language. A station was stuck because they can't get music from India. Producers were given money to make programmes.
>
> SABC at its best—When there is change of government, there is change on how they tell a story. SABC did not switch off the camera and captured

every person going in and moving out of the hotel informing the country about the transition of power. SABC covered every step in the power. (Interview)

The opinion of this journalist identifies three critical views about the role of SABC in the South African media landscape. Firstly, it has confirmed the outcome of the effort of MDDA to expand and ensure inclusiveness among South Africans when it comes to engagement with the media. It particularly shows the effort to have local languages having more influence within the media landscape.

Secondly, it shows that at its worst, SABC can simply be a tool to be manipulated by the ANC government. The point the journalist was making was the influence of appointing people to lead the SABC without proper qualifications or experience. In this case, the station was asked to broadcast 90% of locally produced music in the station. Ordinarily, this shouldn't be an issue. But it negates the rainbow nature of South Africa. A significant part of the population is still connected to their regions of origin culturally. The Indian and Pakistan community is a very good example of that. With this decision to play locally produced music only according to what the above journalist stated, stations targeting the Indian and Pakistani community found it difficult to fill slots with locally produced music that will satisfy the need of this community.

Thirdly, there are moments when the station lived up to expectation and served the public responsibility it was mandated to pursue by the act that established it. The example he cited was the party convention where the successor of Jacob Zuma will be announced by the ANC. According to this journalist, the station provided critical coverage and its cameras never left the venue of the convention even if nothing was happening. The challenge faced by SABC was summarised by Fourie (2013: 7) where he stated that "of all the problems the SABC may experience, and despite the inherent attributes and possibilities of PSB in terms of access, addressing a diversity of public needs, etc., it is government interference and assaults on the political independence of the SABC that threatens the future existence of the SABC most."

Fourie further stated that problems related to public service broadcasting (PSB) are not restricted to South Africa. They are issues faced globally by countries implementing the idea of an ideal broadcasting service based on the principles of public service that is accountable to the people rather than to politicians holding political office. According to Fourie (2013: 7), "in the new media environment, which is far more democratised than has been the case in the era of scarce frequencies and top-down approaches to audiences, government interference in the governance and management of a broadcaster has become indefensible and poses a far greater threat to a broadcaster's existence than has been the case in the past."

A major feat achieved in public service broadcasting in South Africa is the influence of MDDA in ensuring that the country moves away from the apartheid policy which sees broadcasting as a tool to reinforce racial segregation. According to Barnett (1999: 650), "television programming sharply differentiated between channels on the basis of 'race', with one channel explicitly directed at white Afrikaans- and English-speaking audiences, while another was targeted at non-white audiences."

Barnett added that an Independent Broadcasting Authority was established to regulate the broadcasting industry and commercial operators could join the broadcasting arena, which results in changes on programme formats.

Tabloidisation of Journalism

While pundits, researchers and journalists were focusing on how the media would become more inclusive and depart from the journalism of the apartheid era, there was a third force coming to the media scene that was not envisaged by media elites. The new phenomenon is tabloid journalism.

The transition from an apartheid regime has brought tremendous changes to the South African Society. One of the biggest changes, I would suggest, is turning the minority ruling Afrikaans into citizens without political authority, and at the same time bestowing political power in the hands of the black majority who have now become the masters of the polity, and even more appropriately equal citizens. In between these two groups there was some commonality though. The exchange of political power took place between white elites and their black counterparts. The black working-class citizen needs a voice. Although the ANC led by Nelson Mandela was speaking on behalf of all subjugated black and coloured South Africans, both Nelson Mandela and the comrades who fought for independence were part of a minority group of black elites with sound education and access to resources that were not available to the average working-class person.

This left a huge gap in South African journalism. The answer to it was the introduction of tabloid journalism. Tabloid journalism is a form of journalism that focuses on entertainment. At the heart of it is stories about celebrities, their lifestyles, scandals, achievements and pitfalls. It also provides stardom to ordinary citizens by helping them to rise into fame and be recognised by society (Clark 2012).

Opinion is highly divided among experts on tabloid journalism. Some see it as an example of bad journalism, an example of lack of professionalism and at worst a failure of the fourth estate that should focus on investigative reporting and public education rather than focusing on stories that lack real substance. According to Popovic and Popovic (2014: 12), tabloid journalism is

> a form of commercial media culture created for profit and distributed in the form of goods whose products are going to sell well because of their factual popularity. As part of popular journalism, tabloidisation means creating the product which attracts the maximum number of customers. The emergence of such products which shocked the world by breaking with the conventions led to the creation of a new form of media literacy, whose celebrities replaced the old values of life and way of thinking, creating new models of identification and resonant performances of style, fashion and behavior. Since profit and not ethics is the deepest motivations of tabloid journalism, some authors of tabloids do not consider them among traditional print media, rather placing them in a separate category defined as "consumerist magazines".

The word tabloid refers to both content and format of a newspaper which is normally smaller in size compared to large broadsheet newspapers associated with quality or professional journalism (Wasserman 2010). There are several opinions about the origin of the word *tabloid*. Some versions have it that the name originates from the Latin word *Tabula*, and the Greek word *eidos*. Other perspectives suggest that tabloid came from the pharmaceutical industry, while others link it to an English man called Henry Wellcome, who together with an American, Silas M Burroughs, established a pharmaceutical company in 1880 called Wellcome & Burroughs, which was registered in 1884. Afterwards, the company began to produce a painkiller called tabloid (Popovic and Popovic 2014).

Wasserman further traced the history of tabloid journalism in his work, *Tabloid Journalism in South Africa*. Citing Bird (1992), he stated that tabloid journalism traces its roots to broadside ballads in the seventeenth century in Europe and America "packed with tales of strange and wonderful happenings—murders, natural disasters, unusual births and omens." The arrival of these ballads according to Wasserman coincided with the emergence of the printing press and has benefited from materials that originated from oral traditions. The foundations of the stories were based on rumours, loose facts and gossips (Wasserman 2010: 17).

Tabloid journalism focuses more on human interest stories and pays less emphasis on analysis (Skovsgaard 2014). In other words, tabloid journalism is the unserious or non-professional version of journalism that simply responds to the emotion of the readers. Emphasis is put on what entertains the reader and creates a topic of discussion during coffee breaks or at informal gatherings of friends.

While it is true that tabloid journalism doesn't produce high quality information that interrogates the sources of stories, conducts investigative journalism and strictly adheres to journalistic values such as honesty, transparency, balancing of stories, fact checking and so on, it would be too simplistic to dismiss it completely as unworthy form of journalism particularly in the case of South Africa.

The emergence of tabloid journalism in South Africa is a powerful statement about a vacuum created by the mainstream media which neglected black working-class readers during apartheid, and the post-apartheid government of ANC couldn't quickly grasp that reality. The private sector saw an opportunity and quickly jumped in to fill the gap with the introduction of the *Daily Sun*, a tabloid newspaper mimicking the famous British Tabloid, *The Sun*.

Steenveld and Strelitz (2010) saw tabloid journalism in South Africa as a response from the commercial media to address the needs of a new reading public, the working-class black South Africans. According to them, tabloid journalism is a "hybrid bundle of texts which exists along the continuum ranging from 'trash' to 'service journalism'. Within this context we locate the *Daily Sun* as closer to the tabloid-service journalism side of the continuum." (Steenveld and Strelitz 2010: 531).

The argument here is that tabloid journalism cannot be dismissed automatically as a trash form of journalism, rather it reveals what can be described as an alternative public sphere, where commercial interest is used to drive new audiences into the mediated political discourse (Wasserman 2008).

Here it is important to highlight some of the factors that led to the emergence of tabloid newspapers like the *Daily Sun*. Expectation was very high after the elections which saw the ANC emerging as the ruling party. Several members of the black community expected to see improvement in their economic conditions. Yet it was becoming clear that their expectations were not being met by the new political reality in South Africa.

According to Steenveld and Strelitz (2010), during this period foreign funding for the alternative newspapers was withdrawn, a situation that resulted in the extinction of newspapers such as *Grassroots*, *Saamstaan*, *South*, *Vrye Weekblad* and *New Nation*. These newspapers, which normally catered for the needs of the working class, could no longer survive due to lack of interest from advertisers. It was in this circumstance that, New Africa Investment Limited (NAIL), the black economic consortium introduced the *Sowetan Sunday World* to compete with Media24's *City Press*, but due to economic pressure on *City Press* and the fact that Vusi Mona, the then editor of *City Press*, saw his paper as catering for middle-class black readers, Media24 had to seek an alternative, hence the launching of *Sunday Sun* in 2001 as the first tabloid newspaper aimed at black working-class readers. Steenveld and Strelitz (2010: 533) explains that "in 2002 Media24 launched the *Daily Sun*, aimed at first-time newspaper readers who are 'predominantly black, English literate with a minimum high school education, working class earner—the economic core of South Africa'".

This phenomenon marked the arrival of a new dawn in South Africa. A huge contingency of readers hitherto neglected have found a voice that expresses their world view. Within a short period, the paper had increased its audiences and became a household name in South Africa. Steenveld and Strelitz (2010: 533) quoted Wasserman and Du Bois (2006), referring to the publisher of the newspaper, Deon Du Plessis, saying:

> It had to target one guy: the blue-collar, skilled working-class guy who generally lived in the townships. This guy was on the move. He now owned his house, he was starting to decorate it, worrying about his kids, rather than manning the barricades. The politics of struggle were over...We started with him, the potential reader and ended with the paper: a paper to suit the skilled working-class guy in 21st century South Africa. (2006: 50)

Since its launching in 2002, the *Daily Sun* has maintained its position as the leading circulating newspaper in South Africa with circulation figures that reached 500,000 copies per day in its early years. It was so popular that it even had a second-hand market (Wasserman 2010: 1). Figures released by the Audit Bureau of Circulations (ABC) in the last quarter of

2017, shows that the newspaper has a daily circulation of 143,981 (Media24 2018; Marklives.com 2018). Although there is a decline in its sales compared to a decade ago when it was averaging a circulation between 240,000 and 280,000, it is still far ahead of the nearest circulating newspaper, *Isolezwe*, which has a circulation of 95,430 and the 3rd highest, the *Star* which has a circulation figure of 84,857, according to the 2017 ABC report.

There are several lessons to be drawn from the newspaper market in South Africa in our attempt to understand the media system of the second largest economy in Africa, but also the most advanced in terms of infrastructure and technological advancement. The first lesson is the emergence of new readership because of the changes in the political structure of the country. Political independence has brought a new dawn to the country with serious consequences for the entire political system. Unlike Hallin and Mancini's (2004) postulation about the reflection of the political views of dominant political parties in newspapers, in the case of South Africa, at least as the tabloid culture has suggested, you have a new class of readers who are not necessarily apolitical, but with a completely different need that should be reflected in journalism. The commercial media was able to understand that and fill the vacuum. What is interesting here, is that this new readership is driven by the profit interest of the media organisations rather than any political or ideological interest of the publishers.

This leads to the second lesson in our attempt to understand the media system in South Africa. That is the role of race in media ownership; the white and black issue in South African journalism. The *Daily Sun* which has been the largest circulation newspaper for way more than a decade is owned by white Afrikaans, the owners of Media24, yet serving primarily a black or coloured constituency. A form of reversed racial parallelism, where white-controlled news outlets reflect the views of black readers in newspapers that are owned and editorially controlled by white Afrikaans. According to a journalist in one of the major media conglomerates in South Africa:

> News24 is biggest online group owned by NASPERS, Afrikaans word for national press, they own DSTV. A Media that began in apartheid South Africa. It has huge circulation. They publish the biggest magazine in South Africa. Got license to broadcast throughout the continent. News24 is owned by white Afrikaans, it has young editors. Typical African-looking boy, Adriaan Basson is the editor, linked to Stellenbosch University. (Interview)

The journalist above was discussing the complicated role of race in South African journalism. In his opinion, South Africa is independent politically from apartheid, but economically, the whites remain in control, a fact that is reflected in media ownership and editorial control. According to the journalist, it is still difficult for non-whites to have senior leadership roles in media outlets controlled by the whites. That was the reason for citing an example with 'typical African-looking boy' Adriaan Basson who was appointed the editor of News24 in 2016 (Politicsweb 2018). The journalist further suggests the role of premier institutions such as Stellenbosch University, which according to him has a strong connection with News24 and the Naspers Group in terms of grooming their journalists and providing part-time teaching roles for the editors of the company, a form of intellectual parallelism. Of course, this can be interpreted in different ways. It might be due to the historical connection that starts during the apartheid era. It might also suggest some form of tradition among successful newspapers in other parts of the world that have their editors coming from the top universities of the country.

The third lesson is the role of economic and commercial interest over ideological or political interest in journalism. Of course, apartheid is gone, the pro-apartheid media can no longer serve a government in power that is racist in nature, no few minority groups that have lost the support of the political authority. It is now a game of survival. Therefore, the media conglomerates had to find new audiences which they can use to attract advertisers, hence the decision to invest in tabloid journalism. This has reinforced the position of scholars like Herman and Chomsky (2002) who were very critical of the news media that succumbs to the power of advertisers and official sources of information.

The extensive study on tabloid journalism in South Africa by Wasserman (2010) has shown how commercial interest is driving the media agenda in the country. But as he suggested, the issue of racism cannot be divorced from the media character of South Africa. In fact, after independence there was so much mistrust between the government and the media, with the former seeing the media as being too white. As he pointed out, allegations of racism in South African media even resulted in investigations by the government; the first investigation was handled by the Truth and Reconciliation Commission (TRC), while the second investigation was conducted by Human Rights Commission (HRC) "following a complaint by the Black Lawyers Association and the Association of Black Accountants of South Africa about alleged racism in the media" (2010: 5).

What this suggests is that every society has its distinct nature and a myriad of social, economic and political events that shape its media structure. In the case of South Africa, there are several factors that influence the media landscape such as apartheid, political independence and commercial and profit interest of the media. With this background in mind, where do we then locate the media system of South Africa in relation to the media system theory of Hallin and Mancini (2004). The next section will explore this issue.

Understanding South African Media System

As discussed in Chap. 1, Hallin and Mancini's (2004) seminal intervention on developing models that will explain media systems mainly concentrated on Western Europe and North America. Even so, the research was focused on economically advanced societies like the United Kingdom, France, Italy, United States and so on. These are countries with distinct histories, political orientations and strong economic systems that are not comparable to any African country. Even South Africa, being the most advanced African country in comparison with Western nations, is not at the same level as these European or North American countries. It also has a distinct history from any country in either Europe, North America or its neighbours in the African continent.

This is the first complication in applying Hallin and Mancini's models within the African context. Despite this considerable shortcoming, the Hallin and Mancini models have major strengths: they provide a framework that can guide future studies, they have elements that are clearly in consonance with what obtains in Africa, and they also have major areas of differences.

Scholars have made attempts to situate the South African media system within the Hallin and Mancini models. One such study was conducted by Hadland (2012) who tried to situate the three models of media and politics and the framework proposed by Hallin and Mancini for studying media systems within the African context, using South Africa as a case study.

Hadland suggested that the most powerful predictors of South African media are race, ethnicity and language. These are the factors that shape the media landscape in South Africa. These societal divisions according to Hadland have reached such an extent that white and black South Africans watch different television stations and read different newspapers with few exceptions. Therefore, this had profound impact on the media structure of the country.

It is important to discuss at length how Hadland (2012) sees the media in South Africa fitting within Hallin and Mancini's paradigm. He states that from the early nineteenth century to the 1940s, the English language print newspapers dominated the media scene in South Africa. These newspapers, according to Hadland, completely resemble those found in English-speaking countries like Britain where the newspapers are generally driven commercially, with underpaid reporters and a broadsheet style of journalism. The newspapers are owned by mining interests and managed by immigrant English editors; in the words of Hadland, if these newspapers and their style of journalism represent the South African context, then the media system in South Africa can be said to fall within the liberal model espoused by Hallin and Mancini (2004).

On the other hand, categorising the media in South Africa based on linguistic, ethnic and racial categorisation is too simplistic, because the media has different focuses sometimes and mixed orientation. According to Hadland, the media in South Africa tends to support certain political causes. It is either overly in support of apartheid or against it. The media had connections with political actors both during apartheid and after independence in 1994.

A recent example is how the likes of Cyril Ramaphosa, the newly elected president of South Africa, develops a strong relationship with the media and has a stake in newspaper and television stations; even during campaigns, he tried to position himself with journalists in a more favourable manner compared to his opponent, Dlamini Zuma, whose personality the media detests. In addition to this, the media in South Africa dedicated huge space to political coverage. Hadland therefore suggested that these are characteristics of the polarised pluralist model proposed by Hallin and Mancini.

Yet a different look at the media in South Africa suggests a different scenario, one that is closer to the Democratic Corporatist Model. Why is this so? South African media exhibits a degree of political parallelism and state intervention. It also has a strong civic life. Civil society activism is one of the hallmarks of South African media. These features, Hadland states, belong to the Democratic Corporatist Model. Despite these tendencies, according to Hadland, there are certain characteristics of South African media that are the opposite of this model, such as a degree of clientelism, inadequacy in mass literacy and access to the news media.

The issue of clientelism raised by Hadland is quite relevant to this book as we shall see in Chaps. 7, 8 and 9 where the Nigerian press is discussed in more detail. Particularly in relation to the reporting of corruption and political clientelism. In post-independence South Africa, media proprietors have also developed a clientelist relationship with the ANC government to the extent that editors interfere in the editorial work of journalists. One journalist from the Independent Media Group explains:

> Media ownership determines how corruption is reported. My company was the most affected by how we report. Independent media has been highly partial to the Zuma presidency, the owner attempted to use the newspaper to influence ANC elected conference. The owner is one of the most hated people in journalism. Lost so many colleagues through retrenchment, firing people because they disagree with him. (Interview)

The journalist was recounting the history of the Independent Media Group owned by Irish proprietors, but later sold to a South African entrepreneur. The new owner wanted the media to openly and blindly support the Zuma presidency and his ex-wife during the party elections. Editors who disagreed with the owner were fired, according to the journalist, and within the editorial team, he allegedly had some lackeys who were ready to toe the line and give unquestionable support to the ANC government. This tradition is not new because private media proprietors use the media as a way of receiving favours from their political associates. Hallin and Mancini (2004) explained this in more detail:

> Private business owners also will typically have political connections, which are essential to obtaining government contracts and concessions (including broadcast licenses) and in many other ways necessary for the successful operation of business. These owners will often use their media properties as a vehicle for negotiating with other elites and for intervention in the political world; indeed, in many cases this will be the primary purpose of media ownership. For these reasons political parallelism tends to be high where the tradition of clientelism is strong. (Hallin and Mancini 2004: 58)

The conclusion by Hadland (2012) is that the media in South Africa has features from the Liberal Model, the Polarised Pluralist Model and the Democratic Corporatist Model, although it tilts more towards the Polarised Pluralist Model. Yet there are certain aspects, such as the influence of language, ethnicity and race which the three models did not capture.

As suggested by Hallin and Mancini (2004), it is difficult to find a country that practises one form of media system; rather, a range of systems emerge over time to define the media character of the country. This is true for South Africa. In a major study on the South African media system within the framework of Hallin and Mancini's three models of media and politics, Hadland (2007: 69) stated that:

> Scholars have identified three traditions that have evolved semi-autonomously of one another in the South African media. These traditions have been named the English-language press, the Afrikaans press and the black press. During the colonial and apartheid eras these categories provided reasonably useful means for differentiating the varying political cultures, languages and histories that lay behind each tradition. But what was once conceptually porous has now become obsolete.

Hadland further added that:

> There are, for instance, many newspapers and magazines published in Afrikaans, but these are by no means the sole domain of the ideologues formerly known as the Afrikaans press. In fact, the largest of what used to be the Afrikaans press houses, Nasionale Pers, is now a multi-billion rand, global media empire conducting business in several languages (including English) in more than 50 countries. Neither the black press, which in fact existed only as an indigenous language press, nor the English-language press can be confined any longer to the convenient but deeply flawed apartheid era categorisations. (Hadland 2007: 69)

The statements by Hadland (2007) reveal how complex it is to situate the South African media system within the Hallin and Mancini paradigm despite the resemblance of the media traditions of the country within the three models of media and politics. This is for several reasons. The first is that the origin and approach of the research by Hallin and Mancini (2004) was written in a purely Western context, albeit with a great window to apply it with modification within other contexts. The second is the unique history of South Africa as a nation. The racial and ethnolinguistic traditions of the media are quite unique to South Africa. This uniqueness, such as the influence of apartheid which shaped the media landscape before independence may be exclusively South African.

In Sub-Saharan Africa the influence of ethnicity, regionalism (Yusha'u 2010) or what Nyamnjoh (2005) described as the politics of belonging in

Africa might be pervasive, and South Africa is not an exception; these are issues that the Hallin and Mancini model could not capture and it is therefore difficult to define within the framework of the media systems theory.

The third reason, which is also uniquely South African, is the assimilation of all the complexities of racism, ethnicity and language barriers into a commercially driven enterprise with profit-making as its goal, while the underlying issues of race and ethnicity continue to play a role behind the scenes. Even the idea of public service broadcasting as championed by SABC is commercially driven with 80% of its financial resources generated from advertising and sponsorships (Ciaglia 2017: 821). The media in South Africa has proved to be complex and therefore not easy to categorically fit fully into any of the models suggested in media systems theory.

Conclusion

This chapter has discussed the nature of the media environment in South Africa. It started by looking at the nature of the media environment during apartheid where there was clear official support for racism in the way the news media operates. The section discusses the categorisation of the press into white and black press, with the white press dominated by Afrikaans and the black press dominated by liberal English news media and some black-owned newspapers managed by mining interests.

The chapter then discussed the issue of media diversity and the effort by the South African government to establish the Media Diversity and Development Agency (MDDA). The MDDA played a crucial role in ensuring that ethnic and other minority groups have access to information without any barrier caused by language or lack of access to information outside urban areas. Following that was a discussion about the emergence of tabloid journalism, which brought a new wave of change in the media landscape of South Africa. New audiences, particularly black working classes were targeted by tabloids like the *Daily Sun*.

Interviews with journalists were used to buttress some of the points discussed in this chapter. The South African media landscape within the context of the media systems theory proposed by Hallin and Mancini was analysed. The analysis shows that the media system in South Africa has elements of the Liberal Model, the Polarised Pluralist Model and the Democratic Corporatist Model. Yet it has its distinct feature that is unique to South Africa. What this suggests is that despite the historical connection between the establishment of media organisations in Africa with those in former colonial countries such as Britain, France, Italy and so on, the media in Africa has its unique features as the South African example has shown. The Hallin and Mancini models were steps in the right direction in the effort of scholars to understand global media systems, but they are too inadequate to be generalised or applied without major modification.

Intranational contexts are very crucial in understanding media systems. The complex history of South Africa comprising native Africans, European migrants, Asian communities and a host of other nationalities has contributed in creating a unique intranational character that is reflected in the media industry. The next chapter looks at Kenya, an anglophone country in East Africa, to see how its media system operates.

References

Armoudian, M. (2013). *Media and the End of Apartheid in South Africa*. Available at http://www.truth-out.org/news/item/20679-media-and-the-end-of-apartheid-in-south-africa retrieved 13/04/18

Barnett, C. (1999). The Limits of Media Democratisation in South Africa: Politics, Private and Regulation. *Media, Culture & Society, 21*(5), 649–671.

Bird, E. (1992). *For Enquiring Minds: A Cultural Study of Supermarket Tabloids*. Knoxville: University of Tennessee Press.

Ciaglia, A. (2017). Explaining Public Service Broadcasting Entrenched Politicization: The Case of South Africa's SABC. *Journalism, 18*(7), 817–834.

Clark, S. (2012). Issues in Mass Media Writing: The Role of Tabloid Journalism. Retrieved April 18, 2018, Available at http://www.ualr.edu/saclark3/writing_samples/the%20role%20of%20tabloid%20journalism.pdf

Duncan, J. (2014). A Political Economy of Press Self-Regulation: The Case of South Africa. *Media, Culture & Society, 36*(2), 167–182.

Fourie, P. J. (2013). The Rise and Fall of Public Service Broadcasting in South Africa: A Motivation for a New Broadcasting Model (Television). *Communitas, 18*, 1–20.

Hadland, A. (2007). *The South African Print Media (1994–2004): An Application and Critique of Media Systems Theory*. Unpublished PhD Thesis, Centre for Film and Media Studies, University of Cape Town.

Hadland, A. (2012). Africanising Three Models of Media and Politics: The South African Experience. In D. C. Hallin & P. Mancini (Eds.), *Comparing Media Systems: Beyond the Western World* (pp. 96–118). Cambridge: Cambridge University Press.

Hallin, D. C., & Mancini, P. (2004). *Comparing Media Systems: Three Models of Media and Politics*. Cambridge/New York: Cambridge University Press.

Herman, E. S., & Chomsky, N. (2002). *Manufacturing Consent. The Political Economy of the Mass Media*. New York: Pantheon.

Humphreys, P. (2014, November). *A Comparative Study of Public Service Broadcasting under Pressure: Are We Seeing the Triumph of Hallin and Mancini's Liberal Model?* Paper Presented at ECREA, European Communication Conference, Lisbon. Retrieved from https://www.research.manchester.ac.uk/portal/files/33173284/FULL_TEXT.PDF 11/04/18

Kotze, H. J. (1986). Mass Media and Political Socialisation-A South African Case Study. *International Political Science Review, 7*(4), 415–434.

Leonard, L. (2014). The Network Society, Power and the Print Media in Post-apartheid South Africa. The Case of Media Contestation in Durban for Environmental Justice. *Media, Culture & Society, 36*(7), 966–981.

Louw, P. E. (Ed.). (1993). *South African Media Policy: Debates of the 1990s*. Johannesburg: Anthropos.

Marklives.com. (2018). ABC Analysis Q4 2017: The Biggest Circulating Newspapers in SA. Retrieved April 24, 2018, Available at http://www.marklives.com/2018/02/abc-analysis-q4-2017-the-biggest-circulating-newspapers-in-sa/

Media Development Diversity Agency. (2017). Impact of Media Development Diversity Agency (MDDA) on Community Media Development in South Africa. Retrieved April 15, 2018, Available at http://docs.wixstatic.com/ugd/f97c7f_979cf6a3b1f34e4880a1fa2d37041828.pdf

Media24. (2018). *Daily Sun Is the Biggest Selling Newspaper in South Africa*. Retrieved April 24, 2018, Available at http://www.media24.com/newspapers/daily-sun/

Mogadime, D. (2005). Elite Media Discourses: A Case Study of the Transformation of the Administrative Judiciary in South Africa. *Journal of Black Studies, 35*(4), 155–178.

Nyamnjoh, F. B. (2005). *Africa's Media, Democracy & the Politics of Belonging*. London: Zed Books.

Politicsweb. (2018). Adriaan Basson Appointed Editor of News24. Retrieved April 24, 2018, Available at http://www.politicsweb.co.za/news-and-analysis/adriaan-basson-appointed-editor-of-news24

Popovic, V., & Popovic, P. (2014). The Twenty-First Century, the Reign of Tabloid Journalism. *Procedia-Social and Behavioural Sciences, 163*, 12–18.

Saho. (2018). The South African Broadcasting Corporation Introduces Its First National News Service. Retrieved April 10, 2018, Available at http://www.sahistory.org.za/dated-event/south-african-broadcasting-corporation-sabc-introduces-its-first-national-news-service

Skinner, K. M. A. (2006). Untitled Masters Thesis. Retrieved April 13, 2018, Available at http://wiredspace.wits.ac.za/bitstream/handle/10539/1457/01Chapter1.pdf?sequence=1&isAllowed=y

Skovsgaard, M. (2014). A Tabloid Mind: Professional Values and Organisational Pressures as Explanations of Tabloid Journalism. *Media, Culture & Society, 36*(2), 200–218.

Sparks, C. (2011). South African Media in Comparative Perspective. *Equid Novi: African Journalism Studies, 32*(2), 5–19.

Steenveld, L., & Strelitz, L. (2010). Trash or Popular Journalism? The Case of South Africa's *Daily Sun*. *Journalism, 11*(5), 531–547.

Tomaselli, K. G., & Teer-Tomaselli, R. E. (1994). Reconstituting Public Service Broadcasting: Media and Democracy During Transition in South Africa. *Communicare: Journal for Communication Sciences in Southern Africa, 13*(2), 44–66.

Tomaselli, K. G., & Teer-Tomaselli, R. E. (2008). Exogenous and Endogenous Democracy: South African Politics and Media. *Press/Politics, 13*(2), 171–180.

Van der Pas, D. J., der Brug, W., & Vliegenthart, R. (2017). Political Parallelism in Media and Political Agenda-Setting. *Political Communication, 34*(4), 491–510.

Wasserman, H. (2008). Telling Stories: South African Tabloid and Post-apartheid Politics. *LSE Research Online*. Retrieved April 23, 2018, Available at http://eprints.lse.ac.uk/21584/1/WassermanLSE30paper(LSEROversion).pdf

Wasserman, H. (2010). *Tabloid Journalism in South Africa*. Bloomington/Indianapolis: Indiana University Press.

Wasserman, H., & Du Bois, M.-L. (2006). New Kids on the Block: 'Tabloids' Entrance into the Print Media Market. In A. Olorunnisola (Ed.), *Media in South Africa after Apartheid*. Lewiston: Edwin Mellen Press.

Yusha'u, M. J. (2010). Regional Parallelism and the Reporting of Corruption Scandals in the Nigerian Press. *Journal of African Media Studies, 2*(3), 353–369.

CHAPTER 5

Foreign Ownership, Local Dynamics: The Media System in Kenya

Introduction

In the previous chapter we saw the evolution of the media system in South Africa, the complexity of the media that combines the historical specificity of South Africa and how the media landscape changed after independence in 1994. This chapter aims to study another Sub-Saharan African country and see how its media system evolved. Kenya has a more conventional history that is closer to other African countries in the last sixty to hundred years. It was a history of colonial struggle that resulted in hard-fought approach to independence in 1963. Kenya became a one-party state, leading eventually to multiparty democracy in the 1990s. This historical reality has serious implications on the media system of Kenya. One unique feature of Kenya though, is its immunity from military intervention.

The late Ali Mazrui, one of the most distinguished African scholars, has classified African countries into two types: coup-prone countries and coup-proof countries. Coup-prone countries are those that were susceptible to military intervention in the first fifty years of African independence. Such countries include Nigeria, Sudan, Congo and Burkina Faso among others. The coup-proof countries are Tanzania, Malawi, Senegal, Morocco, Kenya and Zimbabwe (Mazrui 2004). In the case of Zimbabwe, the military intervention that ousted president Robert Mugabe in January 2018 has called into question the extent to which it can be classified as a coup-proof country. Of course the military did not takeover power directly, but they installed Mugabe's ex-deputy, Emmerson Mnangagwa, in power.

M. J. Yusha'u, *Regional Parallelism and Corruption Scandals in Nigeria*, https://doi.org/10.1007/978-3-319-96220-7_5

One of the characteristics of the coup-proof countries is a relative degree of openness. The fact that Kenya did not experience military coup could explain why media scholars and practitioners see Kenya as having one of the most developed media systems in Africa. Of course, Kenya has experienced dictatorship even under civilian regimes, but relative to other African countries that faced full-blown dictatorship whether under civilian or military rule, Kenya can be seen as having a good example of a strong and vibrant media environment.

The country had only four civilian presidents from independence to date: Jomo Kenyata, Daniel Arap Moi, Mwai Kibaki and now Uhuru Kenyata. How these personalities managed the country in the last five decades has implications on the media system of Kenya too.

This chapter, therefore, will study the media system in Kenya by highlighting its evolution and challenges from independence to the current state. A brief history of Kenya is provided. This is important because the media has played a vital role in the emergence of modern states in Africa. In some cases, it was the newspapers that supported the struggle for independence and journalists of that era ended up as the first civilian leaders of their countries.

Following that is a section on the state of the media after independence. For a long time, Kenya was governed under a one-party state led by President Jomo Kenyata, and later his successor Daniel Arap Moi. What was the media landscape under those regimes, and what role did the media play in leading Kenya to multiparty elections? The latter is the subject of the section that follows. This section will highlight the current state of the media, level of literacy among Kenyan journalists and the challenges faced by media practitioners and institutions of higher learning that provide training to journalists.

The penultimate section will focus on contextualizing Kenya within the media systems theory proposed by Hallin and Mancini (2004). Is the media tilting towards the Liberal Model, does it fit in the Polarised Pluralist Model, or is it closer to the Democratic Corporatist Model? How does the media fit into the framework of Hallin and Mancini, such as political parallelism or the degree of professionalism, and how active is the civil society in driving the Kenyan media system? These are questions the section would seek to explore. The final section would be the conclusion. The analysis in this chapter will be supported with interviews conducted with journalists in Kenya.

A Brief History of Kenya

Kenya is one of the oldest civilizations in Africa and the nature of its history could serve as a window for understanding the ethnic, regional and political composition of the country. Historical accounts have shown that the history of the country known as Kenya today dates to 2000 BC, when several ethnic nationalities speaking different languages settled in the territory that we today call Kenya. The country has around forty-two ethnic groups, mostly living in a tribal structure. These ethnic groups came from different parts of Africa. They comprised several groups, such as the Kikuyu, Akamba and Meru from West Africa; Turkanas from Ethiopia; and the Luo, Masai and Samburu from what is today known as Southern Sudan (Eklund 2010; Kenyatraveltips 2018).

The Arabs were among the first people to make contact with this territory around the year 600 and settled there, which led to facilitation of trade that opened the territory to the Arab world, India and Persia. By the sixteenth century, the Portuguese discovered the area too and tried to establish their dominance but were driven out by the Swahili States and the Omani Arabs who had consolidated their hold in the territory by the 1830s. By 1895, the British developed an interest in the region and they established the British East African Protectorate, thereby establishing their dominance over the Arabs. By 1920, the British colonialists established what they called the Crown Colony of Kenya under the administration of a colonial governor (BBC 2018).

The Swahili language, which is widely spoken in East Africa and has the status of a lingua franca in Kenya, and being the language of commerce and education represents the complex nature of Kenyan Society. This is because Swahili as a language has an etymological foundation in Bantu-speaking tribal groups as well as a huge Arabic vocabulary (Encyclopaedia Britannica 2018).

Unlike some African countries that received political independence through intense negotiations and compromises, Kenya had a different story. Independence was received from Britain after a bloody confrontation known as the Mau Mau uprising which lasted from 1952 to 1960. The Mau Mau uprising was a product of the resistance from colonial rule, the expulsion of Kikuyu from settler farms and the lack of representation of Africans in the colonial government. It was estimated that during the uprising about 200 British police and army personnel were killed, including 32 white settlers, and over 1800 civilians lost their lives. The estimated number of Mau Mau rebels killed was around 20,000, in addition to an estimated 150,000 Kikuyu held in detention camps by the British colonial government (Blackpast 2018).

Kenya African Union (KAU), a political party formed after World War II, played a vital role in the struggle for independence in Kenya. It was formed in 1944 and was largely dominated by the Kikuyu ethnic group, and Jomo Kenyatta became its leader in 1947. KAU was banned in 1953, and Jomo Kenyatta was arrested by the colonial government. But after strong agitation and a continued struggle by Kenyans, a transitional council was formed, which allowed the formation of political parties in 1960. A group of leaders, namely Tom Mboya, Oginga Odinga and James Gichuru, formed a new political party called Kenya African National Union (KANU), while Jomo Kenyatta was still in prison. Upon his release from prison, he formed an inclusive government that included other political parties like the Kenya African Democratic Union led by Ronald Ngala and Daniel Arap Moi. After elections were held in May 1963, Jomo Kenyatta assumed the presidency of Kenya on 12 December 1963 (The Commonwealth 2018; Ugboajah 1985).

The State of Kenyan Media After Independence

The independence of Kenya and the assumption of office by indigenous Africans who led the liberation struggle was good news to the ears of the continent. Several countries in Sub-Saharan Africa, such as Ghana, Nigeria, Niger and others have received political independence. The continent was beginning to taste the flavour of independence. New, vibrant leaders such as Kwame Nkurumah of Ghana, Nnamdi Azikwe and Abubakar Tafawa Balewa in Nigeria, Patrice Lumumba of Congo and Ahmed Sekou Toure of Guinea to mention but a few were elected into office.

These African leaders fought gallantly to achieve political independence and restore the confidence of the people of the continent. Expectation was high, to quote the former Nigerian military head of state, General Murtala Mohammed, "Africa has come of age." But has it really, when it comes to political freedom? The emergence of Jomo Kenyatta, a prominent leader in the liberation struggle for Kenya came with the same high hopes. But soon after independence, the political climate began to change. The following passage describes what happened in Kenya afterwards:

> Kenya became a republic in December 1964, with Kenyatta its first President. In 1966 Odinga resigned from the vice-presidency to form the Kenya People's Union (KPU). Throughout the 1960s, radical elements within KANU challenged the moderates, who were led by Mboya (assassinated

> 1969 in unclear circumstances) and Moi (who with the entire membership of the Kenya African Democratic Union had earlier joined KANU). Following a dispute, the KPU was banned and Odinga detained. Kenyatta was elected unopposed to a third presidential term in September 1974. He died in 1978, aged 82. The presidency passed to Moi. (Commonwealth 2018: 1)

Kenya was drifting into what came to characterise many African countries. The polity was tilting towards dictatorship and a one-party state. The opposition were being emasculated or absorbed within KANU. Although Ali Mazrui has characterised Kenya among coup-proof countries, which was true, but the new regime was beginning to behave like the coup-prone countries that were characterised by dictatorship. Although, many African countries have suffered from military rule which contributed greatly in suppressing media freedom, the difference with countries that were under military rule was simply the military uniform.

Daniel Arap Moi, who succeeded Jomo Kenyatta, was no different; he continued the path of Jomo Kenyatta in terms of maintaining the absolute control of KANU on Kenyan politics. According to Wanyande (1995), Kenya was drifting into a one-party state. While the Kenyan independent constitution has provision for a multiparty system, the new government after independence took the path of a one-party state. In the words of Wanyande, "while initially no law was passed to this effect, the country operated as a de-facto one-party state between 1964 and 1966, and later between 1969 and 1982. In 1982, parliament passed a law making it illegal to form another political party other than the ruling party, KANU…the restriction of political activity during the one-party rule was soon extended to organisations within civil society such as the mass media, women's organisations, and ethnic welfare associations." (Wanyande 1995: 57).

One of the arguments advanced for the suppression of the media by the government, especially under the one-party state, was that the media was unpatriotic, and was serving foreign interest rather than national interest (Wanyande 1995). This line of argument was not unique to Kenya; the idea of development journalism has been promoted to many countries in the developing world. The idea is that the media should serve development purposes by focusing on agriculture, education, health and other challenges that newly independent states were facing. As discussed by Odhiambo (1991) the idea of development journalism is intended to depart from Western mass media system that is critical of governments.

Therefore, the news media was an instrument of socio-economic development. Odhiambo cited an example with a policy paper published by the government of Kenya entitled, "Sessional Paper No 1 on African Socialism and its Application to Planning in Kenya" in 1965. This paper made it clear that the government would not condone political radicalism and was interested in promoting the participation of the private sector in the economy and promoting investment in health, education and rural infrastructure. The mass media was expected to rally behind this initiative (Odhiambo 1991: 22).

While the notion of development journalism that pays significant attention to the immediate priorities of African countries in transition is not without substance, a major shortcoming of development journalism is that it became a tool in the hands of autocratic regimes to suppress the media. A clear example of how political authorities suppress the media was discussed by Ogbondah (1994), where the editors of *Society* and *Finance* Magazine in Kenya were critical of the government by criticizing its mismanagement of resources. The editors of the magazine had to go into hiding when the government used its security apparatus to close the media houses. Ogbondah added:

> In Kenya, within six days of Daniel Arap Moi's election victory in 1993, government security agents impounded several magazines and newspapers, including *Society*, *Finance*, *Economic Review*, *The Nairobi Weekly Observer* and *The People*. Security forces also raided the printing firm of Fotoform and destroyed the printing press which printed the country's independent press. (Ogbondah 1994: 14)

This is the climate under which the media thrived in Kenya. Despite these challenges, there are several media organizations established in Kenya, some of which have been mentioned in Chap. 2, that were privately owned and have tried to live up to the watchdog role of the media, while others were simply after promoting some political, ethnic or commercial interests. Wanyande (1995) suggested that under a one-party system that Kenya found itself, especially under the leadership of Daniel Arap Moi, the media tilts more towards authoritarian system which champions the government's hegemonic interest, and at the same time turning a blind eye to its excesses. Media proprietors at the same time have their own interest, which can either be political, commercial or a combination of the two.

But one unique characteristic of the media system in post-independent Kenya, which is quite different from countries like Nigeria is the dominance of foreign ownership of the media. This phenomenon is not new; it has been a central feature of media ownership in post-independent Kenya. One of the early studies on media ownership in Kenya in the 1960s was conducted by Carter (1968). His study found that the media in Kenya is dominated by two foreign conglomerates. The two companies control English news dailies and *Swahili* newspapers. The only papers that were owned by Kenyans at the time were the *Sunday Post* and *Gujerati Weekly Africa Samachar*. Carter suggested that the oldest newspaper group in Kenya, the Standard Group, was acquired by Lonrho Group, a British based company in London with strong business interests in Africa. It was quite interesting because the business interests of the company is in several sectors such as hospitals, infrastructure and agriculture, yet it went on to become a key player in media ownership in East Africa.

The second largest conglomerate in the 1960s according to Carter was the East African Newspapers, which later became the Nation Group owned by the Aga Khan. These two companies have monopolised media ownership in Kenya since independence. What is clear from this was that the media system in Kenya has, right from independence, developed three key characteristics that distinguished it from South Africa. The first characteristic is authoritarianism due to the nature one party state that characterised the leadership of the country from independence to the 1990s. The second feature of the media system in Kenya is foreign ownership since the major media conglomerates are owned by the British or Indians. And a third feature is commercial interest since all the conglomerates are owned by private interests.

Although communication scholars and media analysts see Kenya as an example of the vibrant media landscape in Africa, the three features also show a clear case of monopoly, which perhaps explains one of the reasons for a one-party state to last for a long time under Jomo Kenyatta and Daniel Arap Moi. Media scholars have expressed concern about monopoly by few conglomerates. Such studies include Herman and Chomsky (2002), Badgikan (2004) and Compaine and Gomery (2000). Barnett (2010) in his study on what's wrong with media monopoly suggested that concentration of media ownership in the hands of few companies or individuals is against the tenets of democracy. This is because once you have monopoly of ownership, certain voices in the society will be controlled, which leads to the suppression of public opinion. "The fewer owners or gatekeepers, goes the argument, the fewer the number of voices and the more damaging the consequences for diversity of expression. Not only will fewer interests be represented but there will be fewer opportunities for elites to be held properly to account: less opportunity to 'tell truth to power'" (Barnett 2010: 4).

Even the Nations Media Group took some time to have its footprint in the Kenyan media landscape in the 1960s due to the monopoly enjoyed by the Standard Group. Carter (1968) suggested the monopoly enjoyed by the Nations Media Group and the Standard Media Group had made it very difficult for individual and other independent media groups to survive. This was the case in the 1960s and 1970s, but has the situation changed in contemporary Kenya? This is what a journalist with an in-depth understanding of the Kenyan media system suggested:

> The structure of media holdings in Kenya undermines pluralism. As much as 90 percent of media space is controlled by three companies i.e. Nation Media Group, Standard Group and Royal Media Services. The remaining 10 percent is largely controlled by Radio Africa Group, while People's Daily plays with whatever remains. It gets interesting with the names behind the holdings: – Nation Media Group – HRH the Aga Khan; Standard Group – Former President Daniel Arap Moi & family; – Royal Media Services – S.K Macharia (Kikuyu kingpin); – Radio Africa Group – William Pike & Patrick Quarcoo (Sold controlling stake to Times S.A around 2014;- People Daily/K24 – President Uhuru Kenyatta & family) (Interview).

The opinion of this journalist confirms that the two major conglomerates, The Nations Media Group and Standard Group are still the dominant forces controlling the media business in Kenya since the 1960s. A third force has entered the scene which is the Royal Media Services. What is interesting though is the involvement of politicians in media ownership with such high-profile names like Daniel Arap Moi under whose watch Kenya was turned into a one-party state before becoming a multiparty democracy, and the present head of state, Uhuru Kenyatta. It also suggests how tribal groups delve into the media landscape. This is quite interesting in the light of the work of Hallin and Mancini (2004), where some of these characteristics belong to the liberal model of commercial ownership of the media, and at the same time show elements of the polarised pluralist model. It is also interesting about the similarities emerging in this book between the South African media system which was discussed in the previous chapter, and the Nigerian media system which we shall elaborate on in Chap. 8 in the discussion on regional parallelism. In the three countries, an interesting convergence is the involvement of politicians in media ownership.

The evolution of the media in Kenya has seen several permutations and reflections of the Kenyan society itself. Tully and Tuwei (2016) suggested that the media in Kenya is tied to its political history and was a tool in the hands of government under various regimes. According to them, it was clear that media owners were aligning themselves with certain political personalities. But a major feature of the Kenyan media system, according to Tully and Twei, is the role of ethnicity, whereby politicians use ethnic incentives to mobilise voters during elections.

This could explain some of the reasons for violence during elections in Kenya as we shall discuss in the next section.

Kenyan Media After Transition to Multiparty Elections

So far, Daniel arap Moi has been the longest serving president in the history of Kenya after taking over from Jomo Kenyatta. It is apt to say that he, more than any other leader, has shaped the political and media landscape of Kenya. Daniel arap Moi served under the one-party state, KANU. At the same time he has served as president during the period of pluralism. In both cases he has contributed in shaping the political future of Kenya. As discussed by Wanyande (1995), pressure started to mount on Daniel arap Moi to move away from the one-party state and embrace pluralism through multiparty elections. The internal pressure was coming from civil society organisations, and other ethnic and tribal groups who see him as a minority holding tightly to political authority. The external pressure was coming from the international community, particularly from the Bretton Woods institutions, the IMF and World Bank who were vehement on imposing structural adjustments in developing countries.

During this period according to Wanyande, the media landscape was divided, each segment taking a particular stand on the debate about the future of Kenya. Newspapers like the *Daily Nation* and the *East African Standard* began to be critical of government, while the KANU-owned *Kenya Times* took side with the government of Daniel arap Moi. While other newspapers like *Weekend Mail* and Magazines such as *Finance* sided with the opposition. The campaign launched by the media and civil society against the government of Daniel arap Moi became so intense that the then minister of education called for the banning of newspapers like the *Nation* and *East African Standard*.

Heath (1992) described the situation in Kenya in the 1980s as presidential authoritarianism due to the excessive power exercised by President Daniel arap Moi, to the extent that no major decision on government activities or anything to do with the political process takes place in the country without some form of interference from the presidency. As a means of survival, newspapers had to devise a means of satisfying the government. Newspaper owners like the Lornho Group, owners of Standard Media Group in the 1970s and 1980s, decided to appoint people with close ties to the government to serve as chairmen for the Group (Ugangu 2012). This was with a view to appeasing the government or at least to avoid attracting sanctions from the administration of Daniel arap Moi.

The 1980s was a difficult time for journalism in Kenya. Several journalists were detained, channels of debate about the future the country were closed, and several publications were seized. People who criticised the government and its policies were silenced and ridiculed. There was a clear effort by those in authority to remain in power by hook or crook (Wanyande 1995; Heath 1992). According to Ugangu (2012: 144):

> Henceforth, through the 1980s, the government did not hesitate to punish any journalist who attempted to criticise it. In 1987, for instance, Paul Amina (a local Kenyan journalist) was arrested and detained for following up on a story that was considered an embarrassment to the government. Odero (2000: 19) writes that although Amina's disappearance was known to the local media, the local dailies did not report about it; apparently being careful not to publish any news that would have been considered offensive to the government. Before Amina's detention, three other journalists and tens of other Kenyans had been accused of being part of a clandestine opposition movement, Mwakenya, and had been subsequently jailed under the Preservation of Public Security Act.

Siebert, Peterson, and Schram (1956) led the argument about the nature of media systems in different societies, and they identified an authoritarian media system as one in which the state has absolute control and is the moral force of the society. Under such a system, the media has little leeway except to pursue the line of thinking approved by the government and those in authority. They argued that under an authoritarian system, the state has the highest authority over any group or organization. The state has power over the individual because of the proposition that the individual cannot function without the power of the state. The state has full authority in the development of the man.

Of course, the authoritarian theory was developed in sixteenth- and seventeenth-century Britain, but its features have become the hallmark of several societies. There have been several criticisms of the authoritarian theory, including this book, which sees the theory as lacking in evidence and over-generalised. Yet, despite these criticisms, the way the media was handled in some African countries, as we have seen here in the case of Kenya and during military rule in several African countries, suggests that some elements of the theory were valid in Kenya during the one-party rule.

Despite the authoritarian tendency of the one-party state in Kenya, the civil society, the media and other groups continued to put pressure on the government to be more flexible and move from one party state to a plural society defined by multiparty elections. The pressure came from such institutions like the National Council of Churches (NCCK), Law Society of Kenya and Amnesty International (Heath 1992).

Eventually, Daniel arap Moi caved into pressure and started a transition programme that would lead to multiparty elections in the country. Although he still used the tactics of the one-party state, such as ethnic favouritism and marginalization of the opposition forces (Steeves 2006). Irrespective of the negative tactics of the government, the new transition provided some relief to the media and a new era was beginning to unfold. Press freedom began to flourish and the relationship between the media and the government improved. The professional and national media platforms played a vital role in this period, though not free from challenges because of evidence of ethnic and biased reporting that sets one part of the society against another began to emerge, especially among ethnic and local media organisations (Andreassen and Barasa 2011).

One of the key outcomes of the transition to civil rule in the late 1980s and early 1990s in Kenya was the deregulation of broadcasting. The government officially established the Kenya Broadcasting Corporation (KBC). Minister of information Waruru Kanja told the Kenyan parliament that the aim of creating KBC was to remove financial and human constraints. Newspapers such as the *Kenya Times* even followed with a supportive editorial calling for the purchase of more transmitters and strengthening the KBC (Heath 1992). It is quite notable that such supportive editorial was coming from newspapers like the *Kenya Times*, which was owned by the ruling party, KANU. This signified several possibilities. Either the government was succumbing to pressure, or as discussed by Heath (1992), the Moi government was employing new tactics that would attract sympathy from the Kenyan population and international organisations that were paying attention to the political situation in Kenya.

Wanyande (1995) suggested that from a media perspective there is a mixed results as Kenya moves toward a multiparty system. Some of the positive results according to him were the ease of establishing newspapers, magazines and radio stations. New outlets such as *Weekend Mail*, the *People* and *Patriot* were established. On the negative side, newly established KTN did not show much improvement as the station continued to behave like a government mouthpiece as explained by Wanyande.

For every opportunity there is a challenge. In the case of the media system in Kenya, the new pluralism has opened a window of opportunity. People can express themselves. News media can play its watchdog role much easier than before. There was a possibility for government to be more measured in its response to the media and the citizens at large. But Kenya is a diverse country with several regions, ethnic groups and languages spoken. While freedom of the press is an integral part of progressive societies, it also comes with a responsibility. The degree of training among journalists remains an issue. Divorcing the practice of journalism from sentiment is required if Kenya is to succeed in its effort to become a successful country and a role model for other African countries that were equally passing through transition. Yet as discussed by Wanyande (1995), lack of training and fact-checking remains an issue in Kenya. in several newspapers and media organisations, journalists were recruited on their ability to write rather than for sound professional training.

Kenya went into multiparty elections in 1992, which was won by President Moi and he continued to win the elections until 2002, albeit controversially. The real test came after the 2002 elections when Kenyans would vote for a president for the first time after independence without either Jomo Kenyatta or Daniel Arap Moi on the ballot. The real test of multiparty elections was at stake. One unique feature of Kenya from colonial times to the post-independence period was the potential for electoral violence. This has been a feature from the Mau Mau uprising up to the 2017 elections between Raila Odinga and Uhuru Kenyatta.

But the real test for the media and Kenya as a society was during the 2007 elections. A historical opportunity to transfer political power from an incumbent to another candidate, whether from the ruling party or to the opposition had arrived. On 30 December 2007 the Kenyan electoral commission declared Mwai Kibaki as the winner of the elections despite unofficial reports suggesting that the opposition candidate Raila Odinga was ahead. The country broke out into chaos, which was unprecedented in post-colonial Kenya. The violence attracted global attention as was seen from newspaper headlines around the world. The UK Guardian (2007) said, "Kenyan riots as Kibaki declared poll winner", "Kibaki 'stole' Kenyan election through vote-rigging and fraud" said the UK *Independent* (2007), and the *Washington Post* (2007) stated "Incumbent declared winner in Kenya's disputed election".

Although this was the perspective of the international media, which could have its own biases in reporting stories about Africa, the unanimity in framing the story against Mwai Kibaki who had some goodwill in the international media when he was opposition candidate in the 2002 elections suggest that something was wrong in Kenya. The big question is, what role did the media play in the 2007 elections? This could help us to understand the psychology and the character of the media in this East African giant.

Ogenga (2008) studied the role of Kenyan media in the controversial 2007 election. One of the key observations made in the study was the ability of politicians to purchase air time and dominate political discourse. Beyond that, the media dedicated enough space to the coverage of the elections and was constantly providing updates to the electorates about the unofficial results that were released at various polling units. "One reason for the contested presidential election was that the media carried extensive coverage of the voting process and released unofficial results in which Kenyans believed" (Ogenga 2008: 128).

The problem according to Ogenga started when the official results announced by the electoral commission differed from the unofficial results announced by the media during the voting process. Immediately after the government of Mwai Kibaki was sworn in for second term, it banned all broadcasting. Human Rights activists blamed the media for being silent in the face of violence, tribal clashes and what some pundits described as ethnic cleansing. However, major media organisations took steps to call for peace and tried to unify the country.

Be that as it may, the media was not fully absorbed from blame. Some pundits argued that the media was in possession of almost the entire results of the election, and they could have played their watchdog role by ensuring that proper results were announced, given the faith that Kenyans have in the media as well as the obvious shortcomings of the Kenyan electoral commission. In fact, during the voting process, major news organisations like the *Daily Nation* and *Kenya Television Network* published the results of the election on their websites which shows that Rail Odinga was ahead by securing 4.5 million votes ahead of Mwai Kibaki's 4.2 million, yet the media withdrew the figures from their websites (Ogenga 2008).

This situation raised several questions about the role of the media in society during the elections in Kenya. First, it raises questions about the level of independence of the media. It shows that no matter the level of pluralism, and the improvement in freedom of the press, there are question marks about media autonomy. The second issue is government interference with media, and forcing it to play to the gallery, and thirdly, the media prioritising its commercial interests and connections with the political authority over national interests. There are more questions that can be raised from this situation. Did the predominant ownership of the media by foreigners play a role in the reporting of the election violence? Would the reporting and the level of interference with the media be different if Kenyans were majority owners and shareholders in the media industry? These are questions that demand answers. This is one journalist's position on media autonomy in Kenya:

> Hence, media houses that dominate the Kenyan space are nowhere near independent. They are quasi-independent at best, for the following reasons, which I don't need to explain in the case of Standard Group and People's Daily. Meanwhile the Aga Khan, whose Nation Media is the largest in the region, puts business first and his expansive empire across east Africa is heavily dependent on state concessions. While there are attempts at independent and critical reporting, it's well-known that his executives never hesitate to pull a story deemed uncomfortable by governing regimes from Kenya to Uganda and Tanzania. For Samuel Kamau Macharia of Royal Media Services, his loyalty has always been with his tribe – the dominant Kikuyu from central Kenya. He hinted on support for the opposition's Raila Odinga in the last election but nobody really bought that. Meanwhile Radio Africa's William Pike and Patrick Quarcoo started their journey in Uganda where the former founded the New Vision newspaper, a government mouthpiece and ran it for over two decades. They founded their first radio station, Capital FM there too, before venturing in Kenya. In short, Pike is a man always eager to please the establishment. (Interview)

The opinion of the above journalist about the media being more focused on its business interests rather than playing a watchdog role in the society might have some weight. Happenings during the 2017 elections between Uhuru Kenyatta and Raila Odinga showed that the media played a game with audiences by publishing stories purely for commercial reasons. A study by Yusha'u (2018) found that "on 6 August 2017, the *Standard* newspaper produced three different editions with different headlines on the same day. Each headline looked at opinion polls and came up with a caption that supported the candidate with the highest support in the region where each edition was sold. In the regions where voters were undecided, a more neutral headline was presented. One edition says "Uhuru smells victory", another edition says "Raila smells victory", while another headline had the caption "The choice is yours"" (Yusha'u 2018: 478).

Abdi and Deane (2008) conducted another study that focused mainly on the role of other local language media in Kenya. This is quite important because the majority of Kenyans speak local languages other than English and Swahili. The majority of the newspapers and broadcast media that we have discussed in this chapter use English as the medium of communication. The study by Abdi and Deane was more implicating because it established a direct link between the coverage provided by the local language media and the promotion of hatred and violence in Kenya.

Liberalisation has contributed greatly in the establishment of local radio stations with the first FM station in English language established in 1996, called Capital FM. Following that, several local English FM stations were established. But a major breakthrough for local languages was the launching of the Kikuyu language FM station, *Kameme* in the year 2000. By 2004, several communities such as the Kikuyus in the Central province, the Luos in Western Kenya, the Kambas in the Southeast, the Kalenjins in Northwest and Kisiis in the Southeast had the opportunity to establish FM stations. These stations were able to start talk shows that were very popular with the local communities, including radio programmes like "Baraza", which means informal assembly, by Lake Victoria FM; Luo station's Lake Victoria FM's talk show, 'Just Say It', and *Kameme* FM's talk show, 'Wake Up'. These stations gave a voice to the voiceless people that were hitherto silenced, and the shows became a platform for expressing the anger of the people. Unfortunately, these new local language stations became a platform that was used to set people against each other. This problem was compounded by lack of training and professionalism from the hosts and commentators (Abdi and Deane 2008: 322).

The study by Abdi and Deane shows that during the 2007 elections, these stations simply promoted violence and set one ethnic group over the other due to the nature of their reporting. It went to the extent that comparison was made with Radio Milles Collines of Rwanda, which had promoted the genocide between Hutus and Tutsis in 1994, with one commentator saying, "We did not reach the Radio Milles Collines level, but we are not far from it". Some of these FM stations were also owned by politicians who benefited from inflaming the crisis. Of course, not all stations contributed, but certainly a lot of them were happy to promote the violence (Abdi and Deane 2008: 324).

Kenya in the Context of Media Systems Theory

One of the lessons from the above discussion is the applicability of a Western model of media system in an African context. From the discussion above, there are several elements of the media system in Kenya that fits into one of the three models of media and politics suggested by Hallin and Mancini (2004), and there are those that are remarkably different and quite unique to Kenya. The three models identified by Hallin and Mancini are the Polarised Pluralist Model, the Democratic Corporatist Model and the Liberal Model. They studied these models using the following criteria. The development of newspaper industry and mass circulation press, the degree of political parallelism, the development of professionalization and the role of the state in a media system.

Let us take the models one by one and analyse them within the available information on the media system in Kenya. The Polarised Pluralist Model is characterised by an elite oriented press, but newspaper circulation is small. The commercial media as well as the development of press freedom generally came late within the historical development of the country. There is a high degree of political parallelism as well advocacy journalism. The level of professionalisation of journalism is weak. There is strong relationship between business owners and politicians and the state plays a major role as an owner and regulator in the media system. One of the features of the Polarised Pluralist Model according to Hallin and Mancini is the transition from a state controlled to a commercial broadcasting system. There, the state maintains influence, clientelist relationship continues and there is a weak development of legal–rational authority.

An in-depth look at the Polarised Pluralist Model suggests that the Kenyan media has a lot of these elements. Kenya has an elite oriented press right from colonial times to the post-independence period down to the multiparty era. According to Ireri (2016), the development of the press in Kenya can be classified into three types: the press in the colonial era (1895–1962), the press in post-independence era (1963–1990), and the press in the era of multipartism (1991–present). What is interesting though is that in the colonial period the press was divided into three different categories according to Ireri: the European press, the Indian press, and the

African press. The focus of the European press was to provide information to missionaries and settlers from England, while the African press was very political in its orientation, particularly the fight for independence.

The similarity here with the Polarised Pluralist Model is the elitist orientation of the press. The newspapers were published in English language and were targeting educated and literate or semi-literate readers. They were also serving the larger interest of the British colonial government. What is different though is foreign ownership of the media and strong interest in maintaining the hegemony of the external forces that own the media that the Polarised Pluralist Model of Hallin and Mancini could not capture, because the model was essentially explaining a European system.

Another similarity of the Polarised Pluralist Model with the media system in Kenya is the late development of press freedom. From the discussion earlier in this chapter, it is clear that press freedom in Kenya evolved gradually. This can also be classified into three periods. In the colonial era, when Kenya was a colony under British control, the confrontation between the liberation movements which later resulted in the Mau Mau uprising suggests the level of lack of freedom of expression and to a larger degree the absence of press freedom in Kenya. The second period could be classified as the era of the one-party state under the auspices of KANU led by Jomo Kenyatta and later Daniel arap Moi. Under this period, the media in Kenya faced a lot of harassment from the government. The idea of development journalism, which sees the media as an extension of the state by promoting development programmes in agriculture and industrialisation, suggests the kind of dilemma the media was in. The third period in the development of press freedom was the era of multiparty elections, when the Kenyan media environment was liberalised, and more newspapers and broadcast stations were established. In this case the Kenyan media system has a strong similarity with the Polarised Pluralist Model. Yet despite these similarities, there is an area of difference, because the media in Kenya and the newspapers particularly were commercially orientated even if they succumb to the pressure of the state.

Political Parallelism is one of the strong features of Polarised Pluralist Model. In the case of Kenya, this is slightly mixed. Under colonial rule, one can argue that the colonial newspapers promote a degree of political parallelism by championing the interest of the colonial government. The establishment of newspapers like *Kenya Times*, which was owned by KANU, the ruling party from independence to the 1990s also suggests a degree of political parallelism. Yet, it is difficult to generalise this because

Kenya spent a large part of its history under a one-party system, unlike in other European countries where several political parties own or have relationship with newspapers that basically promote the interest of these political parties.

Yet, Kenya has its own form of parallelism which is similar or closer to what Yusha'u (2010) found in the study of Nigerian media system, what he terms "regional parallelism", a situation where the media reflects ethnic and regional bias in the reporting of issues (see Chaps. 7 and 8 for details).

Ireri (2017a) found that the media in Kenya pay significant attention to stories about politicians from dominant tribes. He found an evidence of bias in favour of these major tribes, a factor he said contributed to the 2007 election violence. Ireri states that:

> The five major tribes also are the predominant inhabitants of Rift Valley, Western, Central, Nyanza, and Eastern provinces – the reason why 87 percent of the Kenyan journalists originate from these regions. Though the Kalenjin community largely inhabits Rift Valley, Kikuyus are the second largest tribe in the province's population. Westernis, a Luhya-dominated region, the same as Central province – dominated by the Kikuyus. The Kambas occupy the lower part of Eastern province, while Luos are the most populous ethnic group in Luo-Nyanza part of the Nyanza province. Therefore, the same way the Kenyan journalists are likely to show bias in covering politicians from their tribes; they also might be biased when reporting on issues affecting the regions where they come from (Ireri 2017a: 254).

Under the Polarised Pluralist Model, the degree of professionalisation is weak. In the case of Kenya there is a similarity here. The media system in Kenya is more vibrant compared to many African countries, yet the degree of professionalism is not very strong. Even the former chairman of the Media Council of Kenya, Absalom Mutere, expressed concern about the degree of professionalism of the media in Kenya. Some of the training schools, according to him, were operating from top casinos and bars (Mulama 2006 in Ireri 2017b). The consistent violence that followed the elections in the era of multiparty elections from 1992 to 2017 in which the media was accused of playing a role suggests the degree of weak professionalism, particularly among the local language media organisations. In line with the Polarised Pluralist Model, there is a strong relationship between business owners and the managers of the state as we discussed earlier; the likes of the Aga Khan and media ownership by current or former politicians such as former president Daniel arap Moi and Uhuru Kenyatta suggests the strong relationship between state actors, politicians and business interests. The deregulation of the media with the emergence of more commercially oriented broadcast systems in the 1990s suggests a gradual development of from a state controlled to a commercially oriented broadcasting system, which is another feature of the polarized pluralist model.

The next model espoused by Hallin and Mancini (2004) is the North/Central or Democratic Corporatist Model. The features of this model include early development of press freedom along with the development of the newspaper industry. There is a strong tradition of newspapers owned by political parties and the media is connected to organised social groups. Political parallelism is high though it diminishes gradually and gives way to commentary-oriented journalism. In contrast to the Polarised Pluralist Model, journalistic professionalism is high in the Democratic Corporatist Model and the level of press freedom is linked to the support of the state. There is an autonomous broadcasting system and the development of the commercial press is quite high. The Democratic Corporatist Model is normally found in places where there is strong welfare state.

The media system in Kenya has little similarity with the Democratic Corporatist Model. Press freedom in Kenya was achieved after a lot of struggle by media campaigners and human right activists. The confrontation between the colonial government and indigenous Kenyans as well as the emasculation of the media under the one party-state suggests the challenges of achieving press freedom in Kenya. Even in the era of multiparty elections, where there is a much higher degree of press freedom, subtle interference by the state is not completely ruled out. The degree of political parallelism is different from what occurs in Western countries, but as discussed under the Polarised Pluralist Model, there is a degree of ethnic and regional bias in reporting. This means the media is more likely to reflect the views of ethnic, regional and tribal interests of those of political parties to the extent that the media was accused of promoting hate speech and violence as discussed by Somerville (2011). According to this journalist:

> The tribal nature of Kenyan politics means ethnic considerations influence journalism. You will often find that newsroom profiles are similar to the ruling structure in government and this impacts objectivity. Religious sectarianism is also a factor with the perceived persecution of Muslims. (Interview)

But there is a reason behind the ethnic and regional bias of the Kenyan media. In a survey of 504 journalists, Ireri (2017a: 250) found that 24.9% of Kenyan journalists belong to the Kikuyu ethnic group, 20% are from Luhya tribe and 13.3% percent from Luo, while Kalenjin constitute 10% and Kamba 6%. The study also found that 21.4% are from Rift Valley province, the country's biggest administrative region, while 19.5% of journalists came from the Western province, and the Central and Eastern provinces have 15.5% and 15% each.

A semblance of similarity with the Democratic Corporatist Model is the development of what Ireri (2017b) described as the advocacy–protest tradition in Kenya. The tradition of advocacy which can be found in the traditional media in Kenya is now being shifted to the social media. Although the study by Hallin and Mancini (2004) did not cover the social media, the role of social media cannot be ignored, especially when we look at the opportunity it provides to citizen journalists to provide commentary on issues and put pressure on government and draw attention to issues that affect the society. This trend was seen particularly during the 2007 post-election violence. A study by Makinen and Kuira (2008) suggests that when Mwai Kibaki was declared the winner of the 2007 elections, traditional media, which had already published some of the results, replaced them with new ones and then went silent due to the five-day ban imposed by the government. This provided an opportunity for citizen journalists to make commentary and people who have access to the Internet followed the commentary on social media. But this development has to be seen with some level of caution because of lack of professionalism by citizen journalists, and the tendency of the social media to spread fake news in recent years.

As discussed earlier the degree of professionalism is not very strong compared to the ideal type proposed by Hallin and Mancini (2004) in the Democratic Corporatist Model. Yet a study by Ireri (2017b) on journalism training and education in Kenya found that Kenyan journalists rate themselves very highly when it comes to journalism training and education. However, Ireri suggested that this should be viewed with caution because the same respondents who had had favourable views of the journalism training also identified major challenges with the institutions that provide the training, such as lack of training facilities and other challenges facing institutions of learning in Africa.

An important clarification needs to be made here. In comparison with other African countries, Kenya has a strong media environment and a good degree of professionalism; the presence of Kenyan journalists working in several international media organisations, such as the BBC and CNN, points to the degree of professionalism that is available in Kenya. A lot of these journalists, such as Joseph Warungu, former head of BBC Africa News and Current Affairs, Solomon Mugera, the current editor of BBC Africa Region or Zain Verjee, formerly with CNN International, had developed their training in Kenyan media institutions like Kenya Broadcasting Corporation and Kenya Television Network before joining these international media organisations. Yet in comparison to the ideal type proposed by Hallin and Mancini, there is a need for major improvement in the degree of professionalism in the Kenyan media system.

The third model proposed by Hallin and Mancini (2004) is the North Atlantic or Liberal Model. Under this model the development of mass circulation press and the degree of press freedom is not as advanced as in the Democratic Corporatist Model. There is predominance of commercial newspapers and political parallelism is low. It has internal pluralism and professionalisation of journalism is relatively strong. There is high degree of commercial pressure which determines journalistic autonomy. This model is commonly found in Britain, United States and Canada. Under this model, there is regulation on public broadcasting and insulation from political control.

The discussion at the beginning of this chapter and the analysis that follows suggest that there are similarities between the Kenyan media system and the Liberal Model proposed by Hallin and Mancini. One can even argue that the media system in Kenya sits between the Polarised Pluralist Model and the Liberal Model. Because right from inception, the Kenyan media system is commercially oriented. There is strong commercial ownership since the establishment of the Nation Group by the Aga Khan or the Standard Group. The degree of press freedom under the one-party system, and even after the multiparty elections, is not as strong as it is in countries that fall into the Democratic Corporatist Model. According to Ireri (2016: 167) "the commercial media are the majority in the country—a reflection of the profit motive behind their establishment and existence. The Kenyan media has thrived in this commercial front in the last few years due to the country's good economic performance."

Recent events in the country suggests that commercialism is getting stronger. The example cited earlier about the *Standard* newspaper featuring three different editions of the headline for different regions based on opinion falls shows how aggressive the newspapers are becoming in order to make a profit.

The media environment in Kenya suffers from challenges that other media systems in Africa face, such as low pay, allegations of corruption and in the words of Ireri (2017a: 255), "manipulation by powerful elites who offer them wide range of favours".

While there are similarities with the Hallin and Mancini models in Kenya, especially the Polarised Pluralist Model and the Liberal Model, there are several elements that are quite distinct to Kenya. At least two characteristics can be distinguished. The influence of foreign ownership of the media is quite unique. It started from colonial times, continued during the one-party era under Jomo Kenyatta and Daniel arap Moi, and persists after multiparty elections. The second feature of Kenyan media is the influence of ethnicity and tribalism. The presence of local language media in broadcasting and print has contributed greatly to the violence that greeted elections in Kenya in the multiparty era.

Close attention should be paid to these two features in an intranational comparative study of the media system in Kenya. What are the issues that attract foreign-owned media over locally-owned ones? How are questions about national interest handled by the media? Is the foreign-owned media more obsessed with profit making over peaceful coexistence as was seen in the coverage of the 2017 elections, where the media was more interested in profit making despite the possibility of their coverage setting the society against each other? Are the tribal and local language media more interested in ethnic and regional politics to the extent of putting the country in turmoil during elections? Several questions need answers which can be explored through an intranational comparative research.

Conclusion

There is no doubt that Kenya has one of the most vibrant media landscapes in Africa. The media system in the country is evolving right from independence to date. In this chapter, we have examined the historical evolution of the media in Kenya from colonial times to the present. A brief history of Kenya was provided to identify how the political system of the country contributed in shaping its media system. The state of Kenyan media after independence was discussed, and also the development of the media landscape after multiparty elections.

This helped in providing the context to analyse the media system of Kenya within the framework of the Hallin and Mancini Models. From the discussion so far, it is clear that the media system in Kenya is closer to the Polarised Pluralist Model as evident from the literature reviewed and the interviews conducted with journalists. The Kenyan media also has core elements of the Liberal Model, but certainly the features are closer to the Polarised Pluralist Model.

This is not surprising because the countries that belong to the Polarised Pluralist Model are closer to developing countries. Recent studies also have shown consistently that developing economies are closer to the Polarised Pluralist Model. For instance, Ghana, which is in a way similar to Nigeria and Kenya in English-speaking Africa, has a media system that is closer to the Polarised Pluralist Model according to a study by Diedong (2018). Yet just like in Kenya, Ghana also has a thriving commercial media which is closer to the Liberal Model.

What this suggests is that there is still need for further research in Africa to determine clearly the media system that exists. While the Hallin and Mancini models remained a remarkable improvement and a pathfinder in political communication research, the studies in Kenya, South Africa and Nigeria as we shall see in subsequent chapters, shows that current studies almost end up with the conclusion that the media system in these countries falls between one or two of the three models. Of course, the study by Hallin and Mancini also highlights that the eighteen countries studied do not fit into models without some adjustment from one model to the other, but the characteristics and data used originated from Europe and North America; therefore, it is easier to make informed generalisations about the media system in the Western world using the Hallin and Mancini models.

References

Abdi, J., & Deane, J. (2008). The 2007 General Elections in Kenya and Its Aftermath: The Role of Local Language Media. *Press/Politics, 13*(3), 319–327.

Andreassen, B. A., & Barasa, T. (2011). *Political Transition, Governance and Human Rights in Kenya: Political Context Study.* RIPOCA Research Notes. Norwegian Centre for Human Rights, Oslo. Retrieved May 11, 2018, Available at https://www.jus.uio.no/smr/english/research/projects/ripoca/rn/6-2011.pdf

Badgikan, B. (2004). *The New Media Monopoly.* Boston: Beacon Press.

Barnett, S. (2010). *What's Wrong with Media Monopolies? Lesson from History and a New Approach to Media Ownership Policy.* In R. Mansell & B. Cammaerts (Eds.), Media@LSE Electronic Working Papers. Retrieved May 9, 2018, Available at http://www.lse.ac.uk/media-and-communications/assets/documents/research/working-paper-series/EWP18.pdf

BBC. (2018). Kenya Profile-Timeline. Retrieved May 7, 2018, Available at http://www.bbc.com/news/world-africa-13682176

Blackpast. (2018). Mau Mau (1952–1960). Online Encylopedia. Retrieved May 7, 2018, Available at http://www.blackpast.org/gah/mau-mau-1952-1960
Carter, F. (1968). The Press in Kenya. *International Communication Gazette, 14*(2), 85–88.
Compaine, B. M., & Gomery, D. (2000). *Who Owns the Media? Competition and Concentration in the Mass Media* (3rd ed.). London: Routledge.
Diedong Africanus, L. (2018). Political Communication in Ghana: Exploring Evolving Trends and Their Implications for National Development. In B. Mutsvairo & B. Karam (Eds.), *Perspectives on Political Communication in Africa* (pp. 255–268). Cham: Palgrave Macmillan.
Eklund, D. (2010). Kenyan Conflict, Post-colonial Media. Department of Political Science, Lund University. Retrieved May 8, 2018, Available at http://lup.lub.lu.se/luur/download?func=downloadFile&recordOId=1607637&fileOId=1607653
Encyclopaedia Britannica. (2018). Swahili Language. Retrieved May 7, 2018, Available at https://www.britannica.com/topic/Swahili-language
Hallin, D. C., & Mancini, P. (2004). *Comparing Media Systems: Three Models of Media and Politics.* Cambridge/New York: Cambridge University Press.
Heath, C. W. (1992). Structural Changes in Kenya's Broadcasting System: A Manifestation of Presidential Authoritarianism. *Gazette, 37*, 37–51.
Herman, E. S., & Chomsky, N. (2002). *Manufacturing Consent. The Political Economy of the Mass Media.* New York: Pantheon.
Independent. (2007). Kibaki 'Stole' Kenyan Election Through Vote-Rigging and Fraud. Retrieved May 11, 2018, Available at https://www.independent.co.uk/news/world/africa/kibaki-stole-kenyan-election-through-vote-rigging-and-fraud-772349.html
Ireri, K. (2016). High Job Satisfaction Despite Low Income: A National Study of Kenyan Journalists. *Journalism & Mass Communication Quarterly, 93*(1), 164–186.
Ireri, K. (2017a). A National Survey of Demographics Composition of Kenyan Journalists. *Journalism, 18*(2), 241–261.
Ireri, K. (2017b). Exploring Journalism and Mass Communication Training in Kenya: A National Survey. *Journalism & Mass Communication Educator*, 1–15.
KenyaTravelTips. (2018). History of Kenya from Colonial Period to Today. Retrieved May 7, 2018, Available at https://www.kenyatraveltips.com/history-of-kenya/
Makinen, M., & Kuira, M. W. (2008). Social Media and Postelection Crisis in Kenya. *Press/Politics, 13*(3), 328–335.
Mulama, J. (2006, May 2). World Press Freedom Day: Of Information Bills, and Schools Onbars. Inter Press Service. Retrieved from http://www.ipsnews.net/2006/05/world-pressfreedom-day-of-information-bills-and-schools-on-bars/
Mazrui, A. A. (2004, July 12). *The Ethics of Africa's Governance: Rights, Rules and Relativism.* Inaugural Lecture on Human Rights. Africa Legal Aid, Ghana.

Retrieved May 1, 2018, Available at http://www.africalegalaid.com/download/afla_lecture_series/The_Ethics_of_Africa's_Governance_Rights_Rules_and_Relativism.pdf

Odero, M. (2000). Press in Kenya: An Overview. In *Media, and Performance in Kenya*. Nairobi: FES.

Odhiambo, L. O. (1991). Development Journalism in Africa: Capitulation of the Fourth Estate. *Africa Media Review, 5*(2), 17–30.

Ogbondah, C. W. (1994). Press Freedom and Political Development in Africa. *Africa Media Review, 8*(3), 1–39.

Ogenga, F. (2008). The Role of Media Kenyan Media in the 2007 Elections. *Journal of African Elections, 7*(2 (1)), 124–134.

Siebert, F. S., Peterson, T., & Schramm, W. (1956). *Four Theories of the Press. The Authoritarian, Libertarian, Social Responsibility and Soviet Communist Concepts of What the Press Should Be and Should Do.* Urbana/Chicago: University of Illinois Press.

Somerville, K. (2011). Violence, Hate Speech and Inflammatory Broadcasting in Kenya: The Problems of Definition and Identification. *Ecquid Novi: African Journalism Studies, 32*(1), 82–101.

Steeves, J. (2006). Presidential Succession in Kenya. The Transition from Moi to Kibaki. *Commonwealth and Comparative Politics, 44*(2), 211–233.

The Commonwealth. (2018). Kenya-History. Retrieved May 7, 2018, Available at http://thecommonwealth.org/our-member-countries/kenya/history

The Guardian. (2007). *Kenyans Riot as Kibaki Declared Poll Winner.* Retrieved May 11, 2018, Available at https://www.theguardian.com/world/2007/dec/31/kenya.topstories3

Tully, M., & Tuwei, D. (2016). We Are One Kenya: Representations of the Nation, Leadership, and De-ethnicised Identity on Reality TV. *Media, Culture and Society, 38*(8), 1119–1135.

Ugangu, W. (2012). *Normative Media Theory and Rethinking of the Role of the Kenyan Media in Changing Social Economic Context.* PhD Thesis, University of South Africa.

Ugboajah, F. O. (1985). Media Habits of Rural and Semi-Rural (Slum) Kenya. *Gazette, 36*, 155–174.

Wanyande, P. (1995). Mass Media-State Relations in Post-Colonial Kenya. *Africa Media Review, 9*(3), 54–75.

Washington Post. (2007). *Incumbent Declared Winner in Kenya's Disputed Election.* Retrieved May, 11, 2018, Available at http://www.washingtonpost.com/wpdyn/content/article/2007/12/30/AR2007123002506.html

Yusha'u, M. J. (2010). Regional Parallelism and the Reporting of Corruption in the Nigerian Press. *Journal of African Media Studies, 2*(3), 353–369.

Yusha'u, M. J. (2018). For the Attention of African Media Scholars: An Introduction to Critical Discourse Analysis. In B. Mutsvairo (Ed.), *The Palgrave Handbook of Media and Communication Research in Africa* (pp. 465–482). Cham: Palgrave Macmillan.

CHAPTER 6

Corruption Without Borders: PTDF and Former Governors' Scandals in the Nigerian Press

Introduction

The Petroleum Technology Development Fund (PTDF) scandal and the former governors' scandal, which this book studies, were the first high profile cases of corruption in the history of Nigeria where the president, the vice president and more than 31 out of the 36 regional governors were accused of corruption at the same period. The investigations were led by an institution established by the same government, the Economic and Financial crimes Commission (EFCC). The constitution of Nigeria has a provision that provides immunity to executives while they are in office. Yet the EFCC was able to launch a massive investigation on these allegations of corruption. It was important to select these cases because they involved Northerners and Southerners, Muslims and Christians at the same time.

Some of the accused governors, like James Ibori, have already served prison terms (Ibori served in Britain). Other cases are still ongoing in the courts almost ten years after the alleged culprits have left office. Of course, there are other high-profile cases of corruption like the ongoing investigations against former national security adviser, Sambo Dasuki, who allegedly embezzled US $2 billion for the purchase of arms to fight the violent extremist group, Boko Haram, and former petroleum minister Diezani Alison-Madueke under whose watch US $20 billion that was supposed to be remitted to the Federation account in 2013 allegedly went missing.

M. J. Yusha'u, *Regional Parallelism and Corruption Scandals in Nigeria*, https://doi.org/10.1007/978-3-319-96220-7_6

In the PTDF scandal, former president Olusegun Obasanjo was accused of diverting resources meant for the fund to other projects against the law. Former vice president Atiku Abubakar was also accused of diverting resources from the PTDF to the accounts of his associates. The Nigerian senate established a committee to investigate the scandal. The committee indicted both the president and the vice president. The vice president was accused of diverting US$125 million and US$20 million. The vice president alleged that the president, Obasanjo, had diverted 10 billion Nigerian Naira from the fund to support his bid to change the Nigerian constitution so that he could qualify to serve additional terms in office (Ojeifo 2006; Wikileaks 2006).

The former governors' scandal refers to the series of investigations carried by the EFCC against several Nigerian state governors who served a term of office from 1999 to 2007. They were accused of diverting or directly taking money from the treasury to serve personal interest. The allegations involved personalities from every section and religious affiliation in Nigeria.

The newspapers that will be studied are the *Daily Trust* and the *Punch*, the former located in the north of the country and the latter located in the south of the country. This is to test the framework suggested in Chap. 1, which looks inward by conducting comparative research intranationally.

These two newspapers represent the north/south dichotomy in Nigeria in terms of their readership and editorial direction, such that other newspapers from the region can perhaps fit within the direction of these two newspapers. They both pay equally significant attention to stories about the scandals under study.

The focus of the chapter will be on the social use of language, which critical discourse analysis (CDA) seeks to uphold.

CDA is a method of study that is interested in finding out the structures used in communicating messages, whether verbal, textual or conversational. It is interested in finding out the relationship between dominance, power and ideology, and seeks to uncover how the use of language contributes to an understanding of social inequality. The aim of CDA is to understand and study social issues (Van Dijk 1993).

In his discussion on the principles of CDA, citing Norman Fairclough, Van Dijk (1993) suggests that it is "a true multidisciplinary, and an account of intricate relationships between text, talk, social cognition, power, society and culture" (p. 253). It is an analysis that looks at the intertextual nature of the text (Yusha'u 2018: 467).

By concentrating on the social aspect of language, issues that may influence the selection of words and phrases and the circumstances that shape the story will be used in the analysis.

According to Richardson (2008) "the form, function and politics of the language of journalism have attracted scholars from a wide range of academic disciplines, including linguistics, discourse studies, media studies, sociology and others. It goes without saying that such work has developed sophisticated and intricate analytic tools in order to describe the form and content of the news and has produced detailed and frequently astute readings of the products of journalism" (p. 152).

The interest shown by scholars, as stated by Richardson, makes it imperative for researchers to further study the use of language in journalism, as that will avail them with the opportunity to look beyond the surface of news by looking deeper into the social, historical, cultural, political and environmental factors that shape the nature of journalism and influence our understanding of media output.

Different scholars have provided insight into areas of discourse that the researcher should pay special attention to, especially in the study of newspapers. One such scholar is Carvalho (2008) who states that "the analyst should pay close attention to headlines and the first one or two paragraphs of all the articles that constitute the corpus" (p. 166). For this reason, this chapter will concentrate on the use of language in the headlines of the newspapers under study and, as Carvalho suggested, also look at some texts from the stories. Although the focus of this chapter is based on qualitative analysis, some element of quantitative analysis will be used to find the frequencies and charts that will further explain the qualitative data. This approach has been used by other scholars like Canel and Sanders (2006), Richardson (2007) and Stenvall (2008). The quantitative element was carried out using the Statistics Package for Social Scientists (SPSS). A total of 157 stories have been coded, 40 from the *Daily Trust*, and 117 from the *Punch*[1] (Table 6.1)

[1] Since this study is interested in the differences in the nature of coverage between northern and southern newspapers, the difference between *Daily Trust* and the *Punch* in terms of the quantitative aspect has clearly shown that the *Punch,* a southern newspaper, has more stories on the cases under study than *Daily Trust*, which is from the north. This could perhaps be explained for a number of reasons. The *Punch* dedicates more pages on news stories and opinion articles compared to *Daily Trust*; it also has more pages than *Daily Trust.* It has also shown the kind of interest the paper has on stories about corruption scandals. As indicated in the interviews conducted which were analysed in earlier chapters, that corruption is universal, as such this may indicate the strong interest shown by the *Punch.*

Table 6.1 Total number of stories coded from *Daily Trust* and the *Punch*

	Newspaper	*Frequency*	*Percentage*	*Valid percentage*	*Cumulative percentage*
Valid	*Daily Trust*	40	25.5	25.5	25.5
	Punch	117	74.5	74.5	100.0
	Total	157	100.0	100.0	

The chapter is divided into different sections, each section will focus on a newspaper, and then analyse the discourses that emerge from the headlines according to the categories. It should be noted that some of the categories do appear in some scandals or newspapers but may not in others, for instance, "Satire", and as such this is the reason for not using all categories in all the analysis of the scandals.

Daily Trust: PTDF Scandal

Ideas are communicated through language. This may be one of the reasons why editors choose certain words to convey stories to the audience. Language carries different meanings and can be interpreted in different ways. As suggested by Fairclough (2003) "language defines a certain potential, certain possibilities, and excludes others" (p. 24). This, therefore, could be interpreted to mean that editors do select certain words and exclude others deliberately for various reasons which may include competition, political or regional interest, fear of flak, and so on. As such, it is important to study carefully the kind of linguistic categories, phrases and the lexical structure of the sentences used in reporting the cases of corruption scandals in the Nigerian press.

The analysis of headlines is very important because it is the gateway to a story. It is also the first contact between the reader and the story. Previous studies such as Van Dijk (1988), Richardson (2007) and Taiwo (2007) have focused on the analysis of headlines.

Metaphor and Description

It is evident that the newspapers used metaphor in their headlines, as can be seen from the examples below:

"PTDF: No soft landing for Obasanjo, Atiku, says senate committee"
—front page news, March 13th 2007

"No soft landing" is used by the paper here to describe the position of the senate committee investigating the allegation of wrongdoing involving former president Olusegun Obasanjo, and former vice president Atiku Abubakar. Human beings do work on the surface of the earth; therefore, no one expects a human being to land like, say, an aeroplane. But an aeroplane or a missile that is thrown will be expected to land on the ground. However, such landing may come with a risk, it can either land safely, or it may crash. As such, certain mechanisms are set to ensure that the landing takes place without harming either the environment or the people living in the environment.

So, when the headline says "no soft landing" for both individuals, it could have different meanings. Editorially it may suggest that the paper's position is that both men should not be treated mildly because they hold important positions; rather, they should be investigated like any other individual. The second meaning that could be read from the headline is that the newspaper is giving prominence to the position of the senate committee, indicating that they will not be biased in their investigation. This is because on many occasions, allegations of bias and even bribery trails the work of the senate (Fig. 6.1).

Consider the next headline:

Senate *C'ttee: Atiku diverted $145 PTDF funds...say Obasanjo breached the law; it is hatchet job-VP*
—lead story, February 28, 2007

The choice of description here is ***divert***. In English language to divert means to redirect, to switch, to go in a different direction. And the word preceding the description was the proper name of the accused, ***Atiku***, and the figure allegedly diverted followed the description immediately. However, the entire headline was a rider to *Senate Committee*, which suggests that the paper is directly linking the story to the investigation of the senate committee. The understanding of this headline could be different if the newspaper said *Atiku diverted $145m PTDF funds*—senate committee. The source of the story therefore influences the headline. ***Atiku diverted $145m*** would have conformed more to the sentence structure of subject+verb+object. So, what this headline did was to use a description to

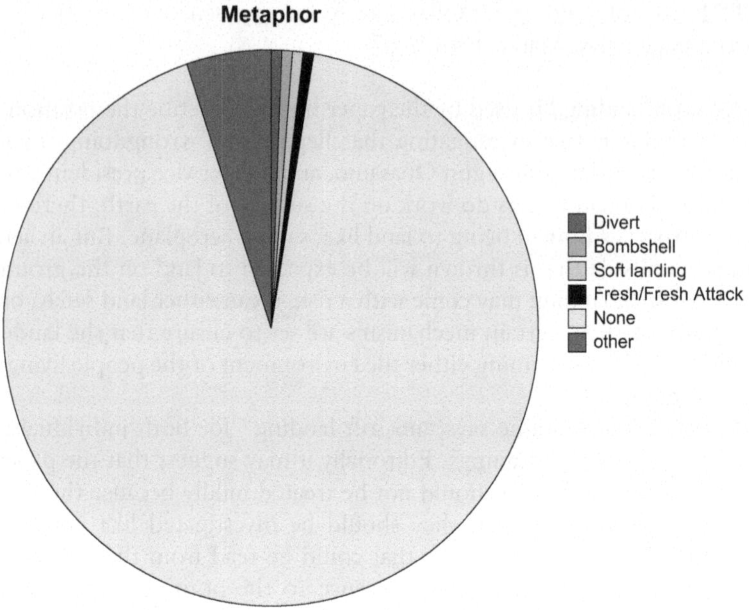

Fig. 6.1 Chart explaining the occurrence of metaphor in the newspapers

express the position of the senate committee on the investigation, but also the newspaper used the headline to reveal the quantity of the amount, as well as to further expose the gravity of the wrongdoing. That is why Fairclough (2003) said "language defines certain potentials" and "certain possibilities" (p. 24).

But to have a better understanding of the report, it would be helpful to quote from the text of the story:

> Vice president Atiku Abubakar diverted $145 million Petroleum Technology Development Fund (PTDF), a senate investigation said yesterday. It also said President Olusegun Obasanjo "breached" laws governing the Fund. The Panel said Atiku should be sanctioned, but that Obasanjo should be advised to adhere strictly to the provisions of the laws establishing the PTDF. In a swift reaction, vice president Atiku Abubakar described the report as "a hatchet job."

One of the meanings that can be derived from the discourse in the above text is the issue of power, which is one of the key aspects of critical discourse analysis. As stated by Wodak (2001), "power is about relations of difference, and particularly about the effect of differences in social structures—language indexes power, expresses power, is involved where there is contention over and challenge to power" (p. 11).

What is at play in the story about the diversion of $145 million suggests the struggle for power between the former president Olusegun Obasanjo and the former vice president Atiku Abubakar. The media in this case provides the platform for exercising the power. From journalistic perspective, it might look like the paper was trying to balance the story by quoting both sides—this is called balancing. But a critical examination of the content indicates how each of the two sides carefully used language to draw attention to their own perspective of the story, especially the Atiku side which calls it a "hatchet job", suggesting that there is more to the story than what the legislators were alleging.

Another meaning that can be derived from the headlines—which also reoccurs several times in other headlines—is how the names of the accused are used. In the two previous examples, both Obasanjo and Atiku were addressed without the title of the office they were holding, that is, the president and the vice president. This is very important in critical discourse analysis. According to Richardson (2007):

> The way people are named in news discourse can have significant impact on the way in which they are viewed. We all simultaneously possess a range of identities, roles and characteristics, that could be used to describe us equally accurately but not with the same meaning. The manner in which social actors are named identifies not only the group(s) that they are associated with (or at least the groups that the speaker/writer wants them to be associated with) it can also signal the relationship between the namer and the named. (p. 49)

Let us look at the segments of the headlines where the names of the president and the vice president appeared:

(a) No soft landing for Obasanjo, Atiku
(b) Say Obasanjo breached law
(c) Atiku diverted $145m PTDF funds
(d) It is a hatchet job, VP

In all the four cases above, both Obasanjo and Atiku were mentioned by their proper names, except in (d) where it says *it is a hatchet job, VP*, and that was perhaps used in order to avoid tautology by repeating Atiku once again. What this could suggest is that the newspaper decided to strip the title of the offices they occupy so that they can be seen as ordinary citizens whose behaviour shouldn't be above the law. It can also be the house style of the newspaper. The meaning of the headlines could have changed if they were written as:

(a) No soft landing for President Obasanjo, Vice President Atiku
(b) President Obasanjo breached law
(c) Vice President Atiku diverted $145m PTDF funds

Therefore, even the way names are used can have a meaning and influence the way we consume the news. In this case, Richardson (2007) could be right when he suggests that "journalists have to provide names for the people in the events they report, and this naming always involves choice. And logically, by choosing one social category over another, they include them within a category and exclude them from other different categories—or perhaps, choose to foreground one social category over other equally accurate alternatives" (p. 49) (Table 6.2).

Table 6.2 Reference made to the accused in the newspapers under study

Reference to the accused	*Frequency*	*Percentage*	*Valid percentage*	*Cumulative percentage*
James Ibori	17	10.8	10.8	10.8
Saminu Turaki	6	3.8	3.8	14.6
Joshua Dariye	3	1.9	1.9	16.6
Orji Uzo Kalu	6	3.8	3.8	20.4
Olusegun Obasanjo	15	9.6	9.6	29.9
Atiku Abubakar	10	6.4	6.4	36.3
Chimaroke Nnamani	4	2.5	2.5	38.9
Jolly Nyame	1	.6	.6	39.5
Ayo Fayose	1	.6	.6	40.1
Two or more	33	21.0	21.0	61.1
None	47	29.9	29.9	91.1
Other	14	8.9	8.9	100.0
Total	157	100.0	100.0	

Legal Terms

The headlines represent different types of discourses that explain the kind of transition the reporting of the scandals make. Some of those discourses include the use of words that lexically imply a legal process or associated with punitive measures. Here is an example from a lead story carried by the *Daily Trust* on March 22nd, 2007:

PTDF: Committee recommends Obasanjo, Atiku for trial—I did nothing illegal, Obasanjo-president must be punished—AC.

There are three headlines in one, with sections of the headline as a rider to the lead headline. Let us dissect the headlines and see the words signifying the legal aspect (Table 6.3).

(a) PTDF: Committee recommends Obasanjo, Atiku for trial
(b) I did nothing illegal, Obasanjo
(c) President must be punished—AC

Table 6.3 Explaining the frequency of some of the legal terms used in the stories

	Legal terms	*Frequency*	*Percentage*	*Valid percentage*	*Cumulative percentage*
Valid	Charge	2	1.3	1.3	1.3
	Probe	2	1.3	1.3	2.5
	Remand	6	3.8	3.8	6.4
	Trial	11	7.0	7.0	13.4
	Arraign	2	1.3	1.3	14.6
	Testimony	1	.6	.6	15.3
	Culprit	1	.6	.6	15.9
	Bail	1	.6	.6	16.6
	Defer	1	.6	.6	17.2
	Dock	2	1.3	1.3	18.5
	Court/court order	2	1.3	1.3	19.7
	Prosecution	1	.6	.6	20.4
	None	122	77.7	77.7	98.1
	Other	3	1.9	1.9	100.0
	Total	157	100.0	100.0	

As suggested by Fairclough (1995) language as a text helps in constituting social relations and system of knowledge and cultural identity. A surface reading above shows that certain journalistic principles have been applied in the reporting of the senate committee on PTDF. The work of the committee is to investigate whether there is any form of wrongdoing between the president and the vice president. The committee recommends that both Obasanjo and Atiku should be tried. The first duty of the journalist as a gatekeeper is to report information, which in this case has been done. But the journalist or the media organisation also has a responsibility to balance its reporting by giving a fair chance to the parties involved to explain their own side of the story. The paper did that by quoting Obasanjo saying that he had done nothing illegal. But in the last aspect of the story, the Action Congress (AC), which was the party formed with the backing of former vice president Atiku Abubakar, under whose platform he contested for the 2007 presidential election, the AC was quoted saying that the president must be punished. Critical discourse analysis (CDA) is interested in what is stated and what is omitted (see Fairclough 1995), and in this case what is omitted is that rather than quoting Atiku explaining his own side of the story, the *Daily Trust* decided to quote his party, AC, calling for the president to be punished. This suggests some form of sympathy towards Atiku Abubakar and bias against Olusegun Obasanjo. Critics of the paper might see this as a regional bias for the paper to call for the punishment of Obasanjo and remain silent about punishing Atiku, at least from the headline. The text of the story provides additional insight:

> The senate committee reviewing allegations of corruption and embezzlement in the Petroleum Technology Development Fund (PTDF) recommended that President Olusegun Obasanjo and Vice President Atiku Abubakar face trial by the Code of Conduct Bureau. However, the presidency in a reaction faulted the Senate Review Committee's Report. The Special Assistant to the President on Public Affairs, Mallam Uba Sani, disagreed that the funds approved by the president from the organisation's accounts were for projects outside the mandate of the funds. Also yesterday, the Action Congress (AC) called for the immediate publication of the report of the Senate special review committee on PTDF. In a press statement issued last night the party said: "We cannot have one set of rules for some and another set of rules for others in a country governed by the rule of law."

The text of the story revealed the intertextuality that takes place in newspaper discourse. The first sentence in the text shows that despite the attention given by the mass media on the scandal, it is still at the level of allegation. The senate committee does not have the power to make prosecution; it can only make investigations and recommendations. So, the discourse in the text as expressed by the senate makes a transition by recommending a trial by the Code of Conduct Bureau. The next thing that followed was a conversation about the interplay of power between the presidency and the camp of the vice president, each using language that will portray the other in a negative light. This further suggests that language plays a vital role in the way discourses about power are shaped. Although it is one story, it was expressed in at least three stages: allegation, recommendation, and denial.

This is one of the advantages of critical discourse: it helps in looking at a story beyond the surface meaning. The language used in the story shows how politicians can utilise the media in the struggle for power, and language becomes the instrument for exercising such power. According to Fairclough (1995):

> Connections between the use of language and the exercise of power are often not clear to people, yet appear on closer examination to be vitally important to the working of power. For instance, ways in which a conventional consultation between a doctor and a patient is organised, or a conventional interview between a reporter and a politician, take for granted a whole range of ideologically potent assumptions about rights, relationships, knowledge and identities. For example the assumptions that doctor has the source of medically legitimate knowledge about illness, or that it is legitimate for the reporter—as one who "speaks for" the public to challenge the politician. Such practices are shaped, with their common sense assumptions, according to prevailing relationships of power between groups of people. (p. 54)

What this suggests is the limitation of control over certain things, and the tendency of human beings to concede those things they see beyond their power to a body or individual who supposedly possesses that knowledge or power. So, when the headline states that the *committee recommends Obasanjo, Atiku for trial*, it was suggesting that the senate does not have the power to exercise any form of authority on the accused. Therefore, its work is a mere recommendation, but a body vested with that power, the judiciary, should be the one to exercise such power, should the recommendation be taken. And when the paper quoted Obasanjo saying he did

Table 6.4 Prominence given to the stories under study

	Prominence	*Frequency*	*Percent*	*Valid percent*	*Cumulative percentage*
Valid	Front page	10	6.4	6.4	6.4
	Front page/lead	33	21.0	21.0	27.4
	Inside page	110	70.1	70.1	97.5
	Back page	2	1.3	1.3	98.7
	Other	2	1.3	1.3	100.0
	Total	157	100.0	100.0	

nothing illegal, it implies that he is communicating to the body that has the power to prosecute him that he is innocent. The statement by the Action Congress that the *president should be punished,* even without mentioning the court, can be seen as communicating to the body that does the execution to take necessary action. Let us look at another headline:

PTDF: I didn't call for Obasanjo, FEC's trial
—Sen Ogunwale, March 30, 2007 (Table 6.4).

This story appeared on page 13 of *Daily Trust*. The prominence given to a story in a newspaper is determined by its location: a story that appears on the front page is considered more important than the one that is buried inside the pages. Because the story that appears on the front page is unlikely to escape the attention of the reader. What does this signify in relation to the headline above? The senator was denying ever calling for the trial of Obasanjo. But why is the view of Senator Ogunwale important? This is not something we can easily understand from the headline. But an extract from the story reveals why senator Ogunwale was denying the story:

> Ogunwale, an ardent supporter of president Obasanjo said the argument he advanced in the interview was that it would amount to no meaning should the senate seeks to try Obasanjo over an allegation that did not establish the president as corrupt. According to him "the review committee of the PTDF was to look into the recommendation of the Senator Edoma-Egba committee which had called for witnesses. The outcome of calling for witnesses was however that Obasanjo and Atiku be tried. It was on the basis of this that I reminded them that if Obasanjo should be tried, will it also amount to trying the entire FEC which empowered Obasanjo and that will such not turn out to be meaningless? But I was surprised to have read that I called for Obasanjo's trial".

The extract from the story has revealed who senator Ogunwale is: *an ardent supporter of Obasanjo* trying to be by the side of his friend. As such the newspaper decided to publish the story in page 13, perhaps not to give too much prominence to those who may wish to support the former president. But an additional meaning that can be derived from the story is the elitist nature of the news media. According to Stenvall (2008) quoting Galtung and Ruge (1965), the news is centred on elites.

The entire conversation within the headlines so far analysed sounds like an interplay of power between elites. The stories revolved round the president, the vice president and the senators. But the people who might be affected by the real impact of the scandal, the ordinary citizens, have been left out in the story. Indeed, in almost all the headlines, the word scandal is completely absent. The headlines most of the time start with PTDF followed by a colon. If we look at the PTDF scandal, it fulfils the entire criteria that qualifies a story to become a scandal as discussed in detail in Chap. 1.

Punishment

Among the themes that emerged from the texts under study are words signifying the need to punish those that allegedly perform the scandal. Let's look at this story of March 14, 2007, in the *Daily Trust.*

PTDF: Culprits must be punished—Nnamani.

The text of the story reads:

> The Senate President Chief Ken Nnamani said anyone indicted in the report of the senate ad hoc committee that investigated allegation of corruption in the petroleum Technology Development Fund (PTDF) must be sanctioned.

The headline suggests that those involved in the PTDF scandal, if found guilty, they should be punished. Carvalho (2008) suggested that in critical discourse analysis, we should look beyond the text, but try to analyse the issue under study from a broader perspective. That is why she suggested two forms of analysis: "comparative–synchronic analysis" and "historical–diachronic analysis". Comparative–synchronic analysis seeks to compare the story either with other stories or texts or analyse different ways in which the issue is represented. Historical–diachronic analysis pays attention to the circumstances surrounding the story, be they political, or economic and so on. It also "involves looking at the sequence of discursive constructions of an issue and assessing its significance. How did representations of reality impact on the subsequent ones?" (pp. 171–172). Carvalho's idea of having a broader approach by looking at social factors in news production becomes relevant in the case of the above headline because the person quoted to be calling for the punishment of the culprits is Ken Nnamani, the former senate president.

Ken Nnamani was a member of the ruling People's Democratic Party, which provided the platform for both Obasanjo and Atiku to serve as president and vice president, though Atiku later decamped to the Action Congress. When Ken Nnamani was the senate president, he led the effort to throw out the attempt by former president Obasanjo to amend the constitution so that he could run for third term. The third term bid by Obasanjo was highly unpopular in Nigeria, and by throwing out the bid, senator Nnamani became a hero. His name became associated with integrity.

When the *Daily Trust* quoted him in that headline calling for the culprits to be punished, the newspaper was not quoting an ordinary floor member of the national assembly, but it was quoting a senator whose words are valued because of the integrity associated with it. As such, the suggestion by Meyer (2001) that "discourses take place within society, and can only be understood in the interplay of social situation, action, actor and societal structures" (p. 21) becomes very relevant in our analysis of text, rather than simply paying attention to grammatical construction only.

As stated earlier, one of the features of the headlines under study is the omission of the word *scandal.* Consider the next headline, for instance, which features as the lead story on March 21, 2007:

PTDF: senate review committee members resign.

Let us borrow from Carvalho (2008), who emphasised the need to pay attention to the first of two headlines of the story when analysing headlines: the first paragraph of the story states the following:

> A whiff of scandal enveloped the senate late yesterday when all seven members of the committee set up to review the earlier report of the Petroleum Technology Development Fund (PTDF) resigned their posts on the review committee. Committee Chairman Senator Umar Tsauri said they were resigning to protest against the demands by the Senate leadership to see the report before it was officially presented to the senate.

Looking at the attention the PTDF story attracts, and the decision of all the committee members to quit their positions makes it more imperative for this headline to contain what may appropriately be termed *PTDF scandal.* This is for a number of reasons, especially if we refer to the criteria that qualify a story to be a scandal as discussed in Chap. 1. The story has attracted enough attention from the mass media, as it was making front page headlines, and those investigating the story, because of the perceived intrusion from the leadership of the national assembly who decided to resign in protest—which is another feature of stories about scandal: people resign either because they want to avoid being party to the mess, or because they are involved in the wrongdoing. In fact, the very first sentence in the first paragraph of the story from the newspaper itself lends support to the argument this story should take the label *scandal.* It says: "A whiff of scandal enveloped the senate late yesterday."

The next headline differs from the previous ones because it is based on an opinion article. The article was published by the *Daily Trust* on March 20, 2007.

PTDF probe: between sanction and advice.

Newspapers have a tendency to publish opinion articles related to stories making the news. It is also a way of maintaining a connection between the audience and the news media. This is one of the reasons why having clear and simple headline is important. The headline above does not convey any meaningful understanding at first reading. This brings us to another aspect of critical discourse analysis which scholars use in sociolinguistic analysis, and that is called nominalisation. "Nominalisation is a type of grammatical metaphor which represents processes as entities by transforming clauses (including verbs) into a type of noun" (Fairclough 2003: 220), "nominalisation involves abstraction from the diversity of processes going on, no specification of who or what is changing, a backgrounding of the processes of change themselves, and a foregrounding of their effect" (Fairclough 2000). See also Richardson (2007) and Fowler (1991). If you remove *PTDF probe*, the headline will simply read, *between sanction and advice,* which makes it even more vague and negates one of the journalistic principles that wants to draw the attention of the reader at first glance (Table 6.5).

Table 6.5 Frequency of the type of article according to the scandal and the newspaper

	Type of article	*News story*	*Opinion*	*Editorial*	*Other*
Former governors	*Daily Trust*	17			1
	Punch	43	14	1	4
PTDF	*Daily Trust*	13	3	1	5
	Punch	40	5		9
Other	*Punch*		1		

Sympathy

As discussed earlier in Chap. 1, Hallin and Mancini (2004) argued that no one should assume that the news media is value neutral; rather, it has an interest, and therefore it can be sympathetic to a particular course. This course could be ideological, political, religious or even environmental as discussed earlier in the framework of this research in Chap. 1, the press in Nigeria is regionally divided. It would be interesting to see if there is an element of sympathy in the way headlines are cast. The following headline which appeared on March 28th in the *Daily Trust* provides an example.

PTDF: Finance Minister confirms Atiku innocence-Campaign Organisation.

According to the text of the story:

> The Atiku Campaign Organisation on Tuesday thanked the Minister of Finance, Mrs Nenadi Usman for confirming that the vice president did not engage in any secret deal over the placement of PTDF's £20m in TIB. In a reaction to the statement issued by the minister on Monday on the subject, the Campaign Organisation said Usman has unwittingly confirmed the contention of the vice president that the placement of the $20m followed due process. The group said by admitting that the Ministry of Finance authenticated the release of the money, Usman has unwittingly confirmed that the vice president did not carry out a secret transaction on the PTDF fund.

The impression the above headline will likely make in the mind of the reader is that a minister in the government that is fighting with the former vice president has exonerated him from the alleged wrongdoing of diverting money inappropriately. But reading through the story it will be clear to the reader that the story is a public relations effort by the Atiku

Campaign Organisation. This can be confirmed by looking at some of the phrases used to frame the story. Consider the following:

(a) *confirming* that the vice president *did not engage in any secret deal* over the placement of PTDF's $20m in TIB
(b) the Campaign Organisation said Usman has *unwittingly confirmed* the contention of the vice president that the placement of the $20m *followed due process*
(c) by admitting that the *Ministry of Finance authenticated the release of the money*, Usman has *unwittingly confirmed* that the vice president *did not carry out a secret transaction* on the PTDF fund.

Although vocabularies are used to communicate an idea, that does not mean that words are innocent; literal words may maintain their everyday meaning, but their lexical mapping can be used to protect or communicate a particular political or ideological stand. Fowler (1991) has dealt with this exhaustively in his work on *language in the news: discourse and ideology in the press.* According to him "vocabulary or lexis is a major determinant of ideational structure", therefore "each term crystallises and normalises the essentially artificial slices which are cut out of the cake of the world. It is an elementary, but fundamental, task for the critical discourse analyst to note, in the discourse s/he is studying—clusters of related terms are found to mark out distinct kinds of preoccupation and topic" (pp. 80–82).

What this suggests is that by looking at the words and phrases selected to frame the story—namely confirm, due process, authenticate, not engaged in secret deal—are carefully selected to exonerate the former vice president, and the headline of the story: *PTDF: Finance Minister confirms Atiku innocence*, simply finished the work of the campaign organisation. Another thing to point out from this story is the complete absence of a second opinion, whether that of the minister or her spokesperson, which goes against the journalistic principles of fairness and balancing in a news story.

Some of the respondents interviewed in this research (see Chap. 7) stated that the Atiku Campaign Organisation is "good" in issuing press releases in a format that can simply be published by the news media which makes the work of the journalist easy. There could also be economic reasons for publishing the story as they are: consider the following headline for instance which appeared on March 26th, 2007.

How Obasanjo authorised $20 million PTDF investment—Atiku

The headline was about an advertorial placed by the Atiku Campaign Organisation. This type of full-page advertorial cost a lot of money, which brings revenue for the survival of the newspaper. And if the Atiku Campaign Organisation advertises in newspapers, it can easily be understood why its press releases will find a place in the pages of the newspapers without paying much attention to editorial issues like balancing of reports.[2]

The following two headlines, also from the *Daily Trust*, are no different from the previous ones.

PTDF: Atiku Abubakar did no wrong

The above headline is an opinion article published on March 26, 2007. It is simply strengthening the effort of Atiku Abubakar to clear his name in order to fulfil his ambition of becoming the successor of President Olusegun Obasanjo. The headline reveals a lot of things which might shed light on the removal of the word scandal from the lexis of the story. If the headline had suggested a scandal, then it may have constantly reminded the reader to ask questions when an attempt is made to portray the former vice president in a positive light. But also consider the simplicity of the headline. *Atiku Abubakar* did no wrong. The subject of the headline was made very visible; it was much clearer than saying *the vice president* did no wrong.

Just three days before the opinion article above, on March 23, 2007, an advertorial was featured in the *Daily Trust* with the following headline:

My Story of the $20 million PTDF investment—Atiku

This is an example of how spin doctors can use phrases and words in order to shape our understanding of the issue at stake. Study the headline carefully, at the beginning of the headline, the story was personalised, *My Story*, and PTDF was described as an *investment*. What this headline did was to completely overturn the story by taking away the allegation and branding the headline to portray a positive image of the former vice president. If the headline was not an advertorial, if it were an interview, the

[2] For more on the influence of advertising, see Herman and Chomsky (2002), specifically the chapter on the propaganda model.

headline could have made a front page lead story that would be read as *My story of the $20 million PTDF scandal.* This reaffirms the argument made earlier that the newspaper should have made an editorial decision to always refer to the PTDF stories as PTDF scandal.

As suggested by some of the respondents in the interviews (see Chap. 7), the *Daily Trust* tried to be as professional as possible, which according to them was one of the reasons for the survival of the newspaper. However, even though from the headlines described above it did not take a highly partisan position, the kind of caution exhibited by the paper in the way it reports the PTDF scandal suggests that other factors, like the region of the vice president being the same as the location of the paper, might have influenced the way the story was covered (see Chap. 8 for a discussion on the factors that determine regional parallelism, like location and the interest of the elite). This may not be surprising as some of the people managing the Atiku campaign organisation are themselves former journalists who have a network of friends not only among northern journalists, but also among the southern journalists (see Chaps. 7 and 8 for a discussion of clientelism).

This is one of the advantages of qualitative analysis by means of critical discourse analysis in that it allows the researcher to look beyond the surface of the argument, but also to study other historical and social factors associated with the production of news. The meanings that can be derived from these analyses is firstly, the way the PTDF scandal was reported fits the research framework of this book (discussed in Chap. 1), in terms of the clientelist relationship between journalists and news sources; and secondly, the findings remain relevant in terms of the differences in reporting between northern and southern press. In the case of *Daily Trust* here, there are reasons to suggest some sympathy towards Atiku Abubakar, possibly due to both regionalism and clientelism.

Daily Trust: Former Governors' Scandal

The stories of the former governors who served between 1999 and 2007 made a lot of headlines in Nigerian newspapers, especially after the formation of the Economic and Financial Crimes Commission (EFCC) under the chairmanship of Nuhu Ribadu. In one of his appearances before the Nigerian senate, Mr. Ribadu stated that he has evidence that 31 out of the 36 state governors in Nigeria are corrupt:

> Almost all of Nigeria's state governors are being investigated for corruption, the anti-graft agency head has said. Nuhu Ribadu told the Nigerian Senate that 31 of the 36 governors were being investigated and that 15 of them would be charged in the coming weeks. He also said that the world's biggest thief was Nigerian but was prevented from naming him. Critics of President Olusegun Obasanjo say the fight against corruption is being used as a political tool. But Mr Ribadu denies these charges. Nigeria's governors enjoy immunity from prosecution while in office and the country is regularly ranked as one of the world's most corrupt countries. The president and vice-president have also swapped corruption accusations in recent weeks. (BBC News 2006: 1)

One of the reasons that prevented the prosecution of the former governors as stated in the story, was the immunity they enjoy in the Nigerian constitution which protects them from facing legal charges. Immediately after they left office on May 29, 2007, the EFCC under Nuhu Ribadu began hunting them. The governors were not arrested at the same time: some were arrested individually, and others were arrested in group. The arrests of the former governors under study took place in the months of March, July and December 2007. So how does the *Daily Trust* frame the stories of the former governors, seeing that they cut across the regions? Here are some examples.

Metaphor and Description

One of the headlines by the *Daily Trust* which attracted attention was this headline which appeared on July 30, 2007, as the lead story:

Ex-govs live cosy life in prison.

A prison is not a place for enjoyment. It is meant for punishment, and no matter the luxury available in the prison it remains a prison. What does it signify when the newspaper described the ex-governors as living a cosy life? Critical discourse analysts believe that language is communicated by incorporating other texts and social practices in order to make a meaning. This is what they call intertexuality. According to Richardson (2007), "The concept of intertexuality is founded on the notion that texts cannot be viewed or studied in isolation since texts are not produced or consumed in isolation: all texts exist, and therefore must be understood, in relation to other texts…texts are only intelligible—when contextualised and 'read' in relation to other texts and other social practices" (p. 100).

Let us explain the possible reasons why the paper decided to cast the headline in this format, since, as argued by Richardson, texts can best be understood when they are contextualised. The term ex-governors are used here as a stereotype. According to Fowler (1991) in his discussion of stereotypes, "news values, then, are to be regarded as intersubjective mental categories in determining the significance of events, the papers and their readers make reference, explicit or more usually implicit…a stereotype is a socially-constructed mental pigeon-hole into which events and individuals can be sorted thereby making such events and individuals comprehensible" (p. 17).

As such, the entire former governors that found themselves in custody were grouped as ex-governors. The use of the terms may be derogatory in that the way they were behaving while in office portrays them as people who are overwhelmed by the political power they were holding. They decide who to appoint in any position within their states, but also influence the appointment of others at the federal level. Ministers from their state who show an interest in contesting for governorship election face a lot of opposition from them, sometimes even losing their ministerial appointments because the governors in most cases make the nomination to the federal government. Some of the former governors became so powerful that they relocated from the government house, where they should officially conduct the administration of the state, to their private residences. Commissioners and permanent secretaries had to report to them in their own homes. When the paper decided to call them ex-governors, it was indirectly expressing the fact that no condition is permanent: you can be a governor today and tomorrow you will be an ex-governor. The newspaper did not stop there; it described their conditions in the prison as a *cosy life*. This is to draw attention to the fact that they are finding it difficult to adjust to normal life because of their former lifestyle as governors.

Richardson (2007) and Fowler (1991) emphasised the importance of intertexuality in critical discourse analysis; the words contained in a sentence represent different social and discursive practices which should be understood in order to unravel the meaning behind a text. According to the text of the first paragraph of the story:

> A relaxed life of social visits, reading of books and newspapers, prayer sessions, conversations under leafy trees and receiving streams of visitors is the lot of four former governors, now cooling their heels at Abuja's Kuje prison, *Daily Trust* learnt yesterday.

The text of the story further reveals the kind of life these former governors were used to and were extending even while they were in prison. Some points of interest to a critical discourse analyst are the list of activities which these governors were reported to be doing in the prison. Social visits, and reading books and newspapers as well as prayer sessions. This is where the understanding of culture becomes relevant. As discussed in Chap. 1, the meaning of political culture is that political behaviour has to be seen in cultural context; what the text of the story suggests is the cultural and political behaviour of the Nigerian politician. Someone who presents himself in public as learned, caring and religious even if his actions contradict that. Another point of interest here is that irrespective if region and religion, the politicians have the same traits in their attitude.

Legal Terms

One of the key moments in the former governors' scandal was the time they appeared before the court. Prior to that, some newspaper reports suggested some doubts, thinking that the former chairman of EFCC, Nuhu Ribadu, was simply making empty threats. Although Nuhu Ribadu's EFCC had arrested powerful people, including his former boss, the former Inspector General of Police Tafa Balogun, and former managing director of Bank of the North, Mr. Mohammed Bulama, some people thought some of the governors were too powerful to be tried before a court of law. Even though some among the 31 former governors have been arrested and presented before the court, the happenings that resulted in the removal of Nuhu Ribadu from the commission, and his demotion from Assistant Inspector General of Police to Deputy Commissioner of Police, may add weight to those doubts. In an analysis by the *Daily Trust* on the removal of Nuhu Ribadu, the paper stated that:

> The announcement last week by the Inspector General of Police, Mr. Mike Ehindero, that Chairman of the Economic and Financial Crimes Commission, EFCC, Malam Nuhu Ribadu, is to proceed to National Institute for Policy and Strategic Studies (NIPSS) Kuru, near Jos, *signalled the end of a*

> *fierce battle to unseat headship of one agency that has become a terror to the club of past governors accused of being corrupt.* (Reef 2007, emphasis mine)

Ribadu himself indicated how powerful these former governors could be, and even suggested that one of the former governors orchestrated his removal.[3] This therefore makes it understandable why newspapers gave a lot of prominence to the stories of the ex-governor's trial. Some of the headlines read as follows:

EFCC arraigns Ibori Today, front page news December 13, 2007
Court remands Ibori in prison, lead story December, 14, 2007
Court remands Nyame, Dariye in prison, lead story July 20th 2007
EFCC may charge Saminu, Kalu to Court, front page July 13th, 2007.
Why we detain Saminu, Kalu-EFCC, lead story July 12th 2007.

At least three things can be identified from these headlines.

(1) The use of short sentences
(2) The words used like *arraign*, *remand*, *charge* and *detain* signify a legal process.
(3) Each of the headlines is either the lead story, or at least appears on the front page of the paper.

These three issues show the significance of the story and the kind of public attention it generates. Short sentences were used in order to make the story as simple as possible to enable the reader to grasp the message at a glance. The use of the words signifying the commencement of a legal process should not be seen as simply reporting the presentation of the accused in court, but also representing the *type* of people that are charged in court. There are lots of criminals charged before various courts and tribunals daily. But they hardly attract front-page attention or even become

[3] Nuhu Ribadu stated this in an interview with Washington post. He further stated that "One was a governor of a state called the Delta state, Nigeria's oil state. And we saw this guy who was rich with probably $700 million. And I brought him to justice. He gave me money—this gives you the picture of the problem of the country. He gave me $15 million, in physical raw cash, to stop the investigation. Of course, he did not succeed. We took the money and charged him for it." See http://www.washingtonpost.com/wp-dyn/content/article/2009/05/22/AR2009052202025.html

the lead story; perhaps the story will not even be published in any newspaper. What is different here is that a scandal is involved (see Chap. 1 for more detail on the definition of scandal). It will not be out of place, therefore, to once again differentiate between scandal and corruption. According to Lull and Hinerman (1997), "unlike corruption and bribery, which can exist (and often do exist) when others do not know about them, scandal is always to some extent a "public" affair" (p. 43).

This might be one of the reasons why it became imperative for the headlines to be cast in that manner; short, concise and straight to the point without any attempt to nominalise them. Another meaning that can be derived from the headlines and the attention they were given is because it involves people, whom the public expect to behave in a particular manner and so when their behaviour negates that expectation, it becomes a public issue. This is what Lull and Hinerman called "star scandal". This type of scandal "erupts when the mass media reveal an instance of how the desires of famous people overrule social expectations, norms, and practices. The private behaviour of a public persona enters the public arena under circumstances that are outside the star's control. The behaviour then becomes evaluated according to the dominant moral code. Stars are in a paradoxical position. They may be given more moral leeway in expectations about their social behaviour, but at the same time they endure closer scrutiny than other people" (p. 21).

Newspaper editors select their headlines carefully; they find the words that will convey the intended message, because they know that stories about scandals will sell. According to Bird (1997), "no matter how often media scholars and columnists scold them for it, people like scandal. Scandal sells newspapers and tabloids, keeps people in front of their televisions, and provides endless opportunities for conversation". The media therefore becomes "the story teller or town crier, but the scandal gains its momentum from the audience" (p. 99–105).

Just as in some of the headlines analysed earlier, no title was used in the headlines to signify the position of the accused, they were all addressed as Ibori, Nyame, Kalu and Turaki, which may indicate the fact that the court should see them as ordinary Nigerians irrespective of the position they held. One important thing to note about the headlines, especially after reading through the core of the story, is that the stories were either from the EFCC or simply a report from the court where the trials began. But investigative journalism is completely absent. At least from this sample, it can be said that what is reported in the newspapers about scandals conforms with the views of some of the journalists who stated in Chap. 7 that investigative journalism is not practised in Nigeria; rather, the journalists rely either on the handouts given to them in terms of press releases or the notes they have taken from routine news reporting.

Punishment

Apart from the headlines that signify the use of legal terms that set the legal process, some of the headlines also point at some form of punishment. Consider the following two headlines:

Ibori, Fayose to spend Xmas in jail
— front page story, December 18, 2007
Court sends Saminu, Kalu to prison; Dariye remanded in EFCC, custody
—lead story July 17th, 2007

The former governors mentioned in these two headlines are among the ones that attracted the highest attention in the former governors' scandal for a number of reasons. Newspaper reports across the country indicated that James Ibori, the former governor of Delta State, was the powerful governor who pledged to see the end of Nuhu Ribadu as the head of the Economic and Financial Crimes Commission. Apart from that, newspaper reports have indicated that he was one of the highest donors to the 2007 Yar'Adua presidential campaign and therefore so close to the former president, that whatever he wanted from the president or the federal government, his wishes would certainly be fulfilled. As such, it became a front-page story that such a powerful person could not celebrate Christmas at home with his family, but he would do so in jail. The text of the story reads:

> This year's yuletide season promises to be bleak for former Delta governor James Onanefe Ibori and his former Ekiti State counterpart Mr Ayo Fayose, both of whom were yesterday remanded in prison custody by different courts until early next year. While Ibori, who is standing trial before the Federal High Court was remanded until January 11, when his case will come up, Fayose was remanded by a Federal High Court in Lagos until January 10, when his own case will be heard again.

The first sentence of the story explains the kind of interest the stories about former governors generate. The phrases used in the sentence, *yuletide season* and *promises to be bleak*, tell a lot about the editorial position of the *Daily Trust*. The yuletide season refers to the Christmas period. It is a joyous moment for the Christian community, and political leaders use the time to receive special courtesy calls and organise parties. For the rest of the country, it is a public holiday. Yet this very *yuletide* period for James Ibori and Ayo Fayose *promises to be bleak* in the sense that they will celebrate it in jail, when just a year earlier they were among those politicians who receive courtesy calls from the people in their respective states.

That is not the only point of the story. The story started as an analysis rather than a normal news story. If we are to go by the principle of the 5Ws and H format (referring to who, what, when, where, why and how, which journalists are expected to answer in writing news stories), the story will simply state that *former governors James Ibori and Ayo Fayose have been remanded in prison until early next year.* Instead, the paper decided to start by expressing an opinion.

Perhaps the reason why the newspaper decided to take that line might be understood when compared with the text of the story in the second headline about Saminu Turaki and Orji Uzo Kalu. The text stated:

> With his wives and a brother offering comforting words, former Jigawa State governor, Alhaji Ibrahim Saminu Turaki shed a tear yesterday when Abuja federal High Court judge Justice Binta Murtala Nyako remanded him in prison custody until Monday next week, when his bail application would be heard. Also remanded in prison custody was former Abia State governor and PPA presidential candidate Dr Orji Uzo Kalu, standing for trial alongside Turaki for alleged money laundering.

Just like the James Ibori and Ayo Fayose stories, the text started with an explanation rather than the key story; what, however, defers is that the case of Saminu Turaki was framed sympathetically. *With his wives and a brother offering comforting words.* The reader was taken emotionally: when we talk about brothers and wives, these are people we have a lot of compassion for, they are people who bring love to us, and we will like to share our moments together. So unlike James Ibori, whose *yuletide season promises to be bleak*, Saminu Turaki has his *wives and brothers comforting him.* This story may also suggest that the *Daily Trust* here was more sympathetic to Saminu Turaki, who is from the north, than James Ibori, who is from the south-south (see Chaps. 7 and 8 for more on the views journalists expressed about northerners being their brothers' keeper, such that you don't celebrate your brothers' predicaments).

Punch: PTDF Scandal

Metaphor and Description

The *Punch* used a number of metaphors in reporting the PTDF scandal, even more than the *Daily Trust*. For example, in a news story carried on page 8 of the paper on March 3, 2007, the headline simply reads as:

PTDF: Atiku picks holes in senate panel's report

This story was a response to the recommendation by the senate committee investigating the PTDF scandal in which the report of the committee led by Senator Ndoma-Egba accused the former vice president of aiding in diverting $145 million. The Atiku campaign organisation therefore issued a press release which was published as a news story by the *Punch*. The headline of the story carefully selected a metaphor that would discredit the report and create doubt in the mind of the reader, *Atiku picks holes*. But there are more issues that can be discerned from the text of the story:

> Vice President Atiku Abubakar on Friday picked holes in the report of the Senate ad hoc panel on the Petroleum Technology Development Fund. He said the report ought to have indicted President Olusegun Obasanjo, his aides and chieftains of the People's Democratic Party for abuse of office and diversion of public fund...the vice president said in statement issued by his campaign organisation and made available to the *Punch* by email that the report failed to address pertinent issues he raised in his testimony to the committee.

The kind of metaphor used in this story, that is, *holes*, can be understood when the political atmosphere in the country at the time of the story was explained. The story was published in early March 2007, and that was less than a month before the April 2007 presidential election which Atiku Abubakar was contesting under the platform of the Action Congress. It was at that time that the investigation of the PTDF scandal reached its peak. Some even criticised President Obasanjo of masterminding the outcome of the report at that time in order to curtail Atiku Abubakar's presidential ambition. The entire story as published by the *Punch*, which the paper also claimed was sent to it by email, was a public relations effort by the Atiku Campaign Organisation to respond to any attempt aimed at stopping the presidential ambition of Atiku Abubakar. So, when the headline says Atiku *picks holes*, in plural, it is suggesting that the former vice president picked holes in the attempt by his former friend Olusegun Obasanjo to use the PTDF report to stop his presidential ambition.

Another meaning that can be understood from the story is the similarity between *Daily Trust*, a northern newspaper, and the *Punch*, a southern newspaper, in publishing press releases from the Atiku campaign organisation as they are without balancing the story by hearing from the other side. The story as published by the *Punch* was nearly half a page, yet the entire text of the story was quoting the Atiku Campaign Organisation, which further proves that it was a press release. So, is the *Punch* trying to avoid taking a regional stand in the crises between Obasanjo and Atiku? The answer to this question has perhaps been explained by one of the editors from the *Guardian*, quoted in Chap. 7, who said that Atiku was simply "financing it". If Atiku was paying for it, then this further reveals one of the challenges facing the Nigerian media, which was explained in Chap. 8 as corruption within the Nigerian press. This does not mean that the *Punch* doesn't always balance its stories; in one of the headlines on March 24, 2007, the paper said:

Fresh PTDF bombshell: How Obasanjo authorised $20 million PTDF investment—Atiku—it is a lie—presidency.

Although the paper reported the side of the presidency, but the text of the story was largely from the Atiku Campaign Organisation.

Other headlines also used different types of metaphor like the following:

Senate raises fresh panel to review PTDF report
—news story March 7, 2007
Corruption: no sacred cow now—Nnamani
—news story March 6, 2007

The metaphor used in the two headlines *fresh panel* and *no sacred cow* signifies at least two things:

1. The senate was trying to save face from allegations that the executive branch had influenced the outcome of the report of the ad hoc committee. So, the senate president made this statement that *no sacred cow*, when it comes to the issue of corruption—the statement

is almost similar to the headline quoted earlier in the *Daily Trust* by Nnamani—that culprits must be punished.

2. Following that is the formation of another panel to review the PTDF scandal, as such by describing the panel as *fresh*, it is suggesting that the existing panel is not affected by the political wrangling that pervaded the previous one, because it is *fresh* and therefore it will be unbiased.

Some of the metaphors also used in the *Punch* indicate a face-to-face struggle between the National Assembly and the Public. Consider this headline for instance.

PTDF: Senate battles to redeem image
—news/politics March 24, 2007

Context is equally important in the analysis of the headline above, which critical discourse analysis, because of its multidisciplinary nature, always pay attention to. Why should the senate battle to redeem its image? The answer is because of the public perception of the senate being a conglomerate of individuals who are after their personal interest, and being representative of the people who are elected to serve their constituency, the public have strong interest in how they conduct their affairs.[4] Since 1999, when Nigeria returned to a civilian administration, the credibility of the legislator has been questioned. They are seen as the rubber stamp of the executive who manipulate them any time they wish. This is not unconnected with the fact that during the presidency of Olusegun Obasanjo, he allegedly masterminded the removal of any senate president who disagreed with him. So during his eight years in office, the senate had five senate presidents: Evans Enwerem, Dr. Chuba Okadigbo, Anyim Pius Anyim, Dr. Adolphus Wabara and Ken Nnamani. So, when the *Punch* in its news analysis captioned the headline as senate *battles* to redeem image, it is referring to a *battle* with public opinion which questions the integrity of the senate. Such scepticism about the credibility of the senate can be seen

[4] Members of the public and the media pay attention to the activities of legislators, especially from those who are sceptical about their credibility. This is not peculiar to Nigeria, as in the United Kingdom the Members of Parliament expenses scandal drew a lot of attention from the media. See for instance http://news.bbc.co.uk/1/hi/uk/8041232.stm downloaded 27th/05/09, for a story on the MPs scandal.

in some of the opinion articles in the newspapers as exemplified by the headline of this article which featured in the *Punch* on March 24, 2007: *Senate on trial.*

One of the interesting things to learn about the headlines under study is what Fairclough (1995) calls "official discourses", referring to the way newspapers use the words expressed directly by official sources in reporting events. This can be seen in some of the similarities between the headlines in both *Daily Trust* and the *Punch*. It was evident in the story which says that Atiku *picks holes* in the PTDF report. The headline was just a summary of the first paragraph of the story which used similar metaphor.

Legal Terms

The *Punch* also used terms that can be described as signifying a legal process. The newspaper frequently use the word *trial* in reporting the PTDF scandal. The following headline is another example.

PTDF: Atiku should face trial—Presidency
—news March 2, 2007

While in the analysis of some of the previous headlines it was suggested that the *Punch* also published stories from the Atiku Campaign Organisation without balancing them on many occasions with the Obasanjo side, on the surface, the above headline might suggest that the *Punch* is using a language that is against Atiku, and pro-Obasanjo. The language was simple, that *Atiku should face trial.* But the text of the story differed from the text of previous stories which quoted Atiku's side only. In the case of this story, statements by the presidency, which obviously represented Obasanjo, were for the most part the story, followed by Atiku's response. Here is an excerpt:

> The presidency on Thursday advised the senate to recommend the prosecution of vice president Atiku Abubakar for allegedly mismanaging the accounts of the Petroleum Technology Development Fund.
>
> The advice came barely 24 hours after the senate ad hoc committee on the management of PTDF.
>
> The vice president, however, said it was president Olusegun Obasanjo, who had something to worry about.

When compared with some of the stories analysed in this chapter where Atiku's line of argument find a space without paying attention to that of Obasanjo, the way this story gave Atiku Abubakar a fair chance to air his view show clearly the bias of the *Punch* in favouring Atiku Abubakar over Obasanjo. If that is the case, then this has created a paradox. How can a southern newspaper be more favourable to a northerner, Atiku Abubakar? There might be two reasons.

First, when Olusegun Obasanjo was released from prison in 1998, and decided to run for the presidency, the south-west, which is also the predominant location of Nigerian newspapers as explained by Oyovbaire (2001), were not in support of his candidature. Therefore, to borrow the suggestion by Carvalho (2008) of using "historical-diachronic analysis", regionally and historically Obasanjo had an issue with the south-west elite, who saw him as a northern stooge, both at the time he was the military head of state in the 1970s, and in 1998 when he decided to join partisan politics and was eventually elected president in 1999. The south-western press and its elite never hide their disdain for Olusegun Obasanjo. However, after he was elected president, Obasanjo decided to incorporate a clique of the south-western mainstream politicians, like chief Bola Ige. Chief Bola Ige made it clear that he has agreed to serve in Obasanjo's government because Obasanjo had agreed to implement Afenifere[5] agenda (Haruna 2007). So, the south-western press changed their stance, from opposing Obasanjo to becoming his defender (see Chaps. 7 and 8 for more on regionalism and ethnicity in the Nigerian press). However, as suggested by one of the editors interviewed for this research, Obasanjo became highly unpopular when the south-west saw that there was little his administration could show in terms of concrete achievements, and also his attempt to change the constitution and have a third term was not popular with the media either, and the press in the south-west therefore changed its position once more and returned to its opposition against Obasanjo. This perhaps might explain one of the reasons why the *Punch* was not too supportive of him.

Second, Atiku Abubakar was becoming popular with the media for opposing Obasanjo's third term bid. Atiku was opposed to third term because he saw himself as the natural successor to Obasanjo, being his deputy, so when he had disagreement with Obasanjo, he left the party and

[5] Afenifere is the Yoruba sociocultural organisation and claims to be speaking on behalf of the south-west politicians.

fought against the attempt to change the constitution. Most of the verdicts of the supreme court between Obasanjo and Atiku favoured the latter, and so that contributed in making Atiku popular with the Nigerian press. However, the issue of using his financial muscle to get favourable coverage in the media should not be divorced from the reasons why he tends to have a better coverage in the southern press compared to Obasanjo.

Punishment

Just like the *Daily Trust*, the *Punch* carried a number of headlines which lexically imply punishment. A couple of these headlines will be illustrative:

PTDF: Panel blames Obasanjo, indicts Atiku; Fasawe to refund N1.55bn, presidency, VP react
—lead story February 28, 2007
Nnamani seeks stiff penalty for indicted officials
—news story, March 14, 2007
Prosecute PTDF scandal culprits
—March 23, 2007
Senate review panel indicts Obasanjo, Atiku; presidency faults report, Atiku praises committee,
.... We have no hidden agenda, says Nnamani
—lead story, March 22, 2007.

The similarities in the above headlines are the kinds of phrases used in framing the stories (Table 6.6).

Blames Obasanjo
Indicts Atiku
Stiff penalty
Prosecute PTDF scandal culprits

The phrases used to describe the allegation of wrongdoing in these headlines occurred on different dates. Yet they suggest almost the same thing. This brings to attention the limit of the newspapers in terms of what gets reported and the language to be used in describing the reported event. Fowler (1991) in his explanation of discourse and the reader, states:

Table 6.6 Frequency of words related to punishment theme

	Punishment	*Frequency*	*Percent*	*Valid percent*	*Cumulative percentage*
Valid	Resign	3	1.9	1.9	1.9
	Indict	5	3.2	3.2	5.1
	Blame	1	.6	.6	5.7
	Detain	1	.6	.6	6.4
	Arrest	9	5.7	5.7	12.1
	Penalty	1	.6	.6	12.7
	Sanction	2	1.3	1.3	14.0
	None	122	77.7	77.7	91.7
	Other	13	8.3	8.3	100.0
	Total	157	100.0	100.0	

> It should be clear that linguistically constructed representation is by no means a deliberate process, entirely under the control of the newspaper. The newspaper does not select events to be reported and then consciously wrap them in value-laden language which the reader passively absorbs, ideology and all. Such a 'conspiracy theory' would give the newspaper too much, and the reader too little, power—the practices of news selection and presentation are habitual and conventional as much as they are deliberate and controlled. And as for value-laden language, the crucial point is that values are in the language already. (p. 41)

What this highlights is that although editors cast the headlines, the language can give more meaning when analysed than the journalist might have intended. Linking this to Carvalho's suggestion of "comparative-synchronic analysis" and "historical-diachronic analysis", the relevance of context and multidisciplinary approach to critical discourse analysis will help unearth some of the behind the scene issues, as well as the historical, journalistic and sociological issues that will add meaning to our understanding of media discourse. As such, despite the effort by both former president Olusegun Obasanjo, and former vice president Atiku Abubakar to show themselves in a positive light, by criticising the other or exposing his shortcomings, a careful analysis of the language used in reporting the scandals will reveal that both may have questions to answer. No matter the spin contained in the text of the stories, the lexical mapping of the headlines tells the reader that something is wrong somewhere.

Sympathy

There are group of headlines also in the PTDF scandal as reported by the *Punch* which on the surface might sound sympathetic. Such headlines include:

Presidency commends senate committee
—February 28, 2007
PTDF report: senate panel exonerates Adenuga
—Globacom March 1, 2007
--------PPA seeks report's rejection---------------report vindicates Obasanjo
Why we didn't indict Obasanjo-Senator Ndoma Egba
—March 4, 2007
We do not regret our PTDF report
— senate ad hoc committee member, March 4, 2007.

The key words used in the headlines under this category may sound sympathetic especially to Obasanjo, compared to the headlines in the previous themes. Presidency *commends senate*, senate panel *exonerates* Adenuga, report *vindicates* Obasanjo, why *we didn't indict* Obasanjo, we *do not regret* our PTDF report. If you group some of the italicised words, *commendation, exoneration, vindication*, what easily comes to mind is the absence of wrongdoing.

But one basic thing that is common about these headlines, and which will help us in understanding the tone of the headlines, were the sources of the stories.

In the first headline, the story was developed from statements made on media by Mrs. Remi Oyo, senior special assistant to president Obasanjo. The second story was an extract from the ad hoc committee, while the third story was developed from an interview with senator Ndoma-Egba, who chaired the ad hoc committee investigating the PTDF scandal. As such, it is clear why the reports took such a sympathetic tone. That is why it is important in critical discourse analysis to understand what Van Dijk (2001) calls "local context" which he defines as "the immediate, interactional situation in which communicative event takes place. Some properties such as a situation are its overall domain (politics, business), an overall action (legislation, propaganda, participants in various communicative and social roles—as well as their intentions and goals, knowledge, norms and other beliefs. Such contexts are said to constrain the properties of text and talk. That is what we say and how we say it depends on who is speaking to whom, and when and where, and with what purposes" (p. 108).

By applying Van Dijk's idea, we can understand that the source of the story has influenced the content because of the "local context", and their goal was to communicate a positive side of their argument to the reader. This approach corresponds with that of Fowler (1991), who questions the assumption that newspapers have total control over what they write, rather than as suggested by Van Dijk; there are other factors like politics, and actions like legislation which play a role in shaping the language of news.

Punch: Former Governors

Metaphor and Description

The former governors' scandal received a lot of coverage from the *Punch*. Different linguistic categories emerged just like in the *Daily Trust*. As suggested by Fairclough (2000) metaphors have a social significance, because the qualities of other creatures or objects are transferred to human beings. Here are few examples of metaphors used in the *Punch* in its reporting of the former governors' scandal.

How governor nailed Kalu
—July 29th 2007
Ibori's journey to EFCC's net
—December 13, 2007

The first story on Kalu was a reference to his successor, who the report alleged was the one who reported Kalu to the EFCC in 2006, stating that he is aware of every penny that was spent in the government. Perhaps the *Punch* decided to use this metaphor, *nail*, because his successor, Theodore, Ahamefule, Orji, was formally the Chief of Staff to Orji Uzo Kalu. This can be further understood when we relate this to the nature of Nigerian politics, where godfathers play an important role, especially with regard to their successors. This is because the governors wanted to choose their successors, and many of them did not trust their deputies. Orji Uzo Kalu supported his chief of staff, a position normally held by a loyalist, yet it turned out, according to the story, that he was the one who reported his predecessor to the EFCC. Therefore, Orjo Uzo Kalu was *nailed* politically by his successor. When something is nailed, it means it is fixed to a particular position so that even if you remove it, it will leave a mark that will be difficult to erase.

Concerning the second headline, as explained earlier, James Ibori was seen as one of the most powerful governors, whose arrest seems unlikely despite the pledge made by Nuhu Ribadu, the former EFCC chairman. Yet less than a year after he left office, he was arrested and detained by the EFCC. So, it is like a fisherman who spreads his net in a river: although some of the fishes might try to escape, but with patience, the fisherman can capture them, and once in the net, it is difficult to escape. So that might explain the choice of this metaphor; Ibori's journey to EFCC's net. The EFCC symbolises the net, and Ibori was the fish that was eventually captured.

Legal Terms

The *Punch* has also carried stories which signify the beginning of a legal process or the trial of the ex-governors as can be seen from these headlines:

S'East speakers back trial of Kalu, others
—front page lead, July, 22nd, 2007
Buhari supports trial of ex-governors
—news story, July 19 2007
Ex-governor Turaki looted N17bn in one day: Judge remands him, Kalu in Custody-EFCC
—front page, lead, July 17, 2007.
How governors indicted kalu
—front page lead, July 29, 2007.
Ibori's trial begins: How EFCC arrested former Delta Governor
—front page lead, December 13, 2007.

Some of the words used in the headlines, just as in the *Daily Trust* include, *trial*, *indicted*, *remands* and *custody*. The selection of these words further adds momentum to the proposition by Fowler (1991) that the newspapers are sometimes passive in their selection of words because they have to report events as they come to them; this may explain why the lexical choices in both *Daily Trust* and the *Punch* were almost similar.

However, there is a headline which requires further analysis in the *Punch*. The need for comparison here is because we have seen how the *Daily Trust* framed the story of former governor Turaki. The first sentence in the second headline under this category states that *Ex-governor Turaki looted N17bn in one day*. The headline was as clear and as vivid as possible: that Turaki had looted N17 bn. If the headline had stopped there, it would certainly have attracted attention, and may still have sounded unthinkable for someone to loot that amount. But the paper provided additional detail by saying *in one day*, which revealed the extent to which he allegedly did the looting. The text of the story also went straight to the point. So, this brings us back to the issue of regional divide in the newspapers and how that sometimes determines how the newspapers report events. To illustrate this further, the point made by one of the correspondents from the *Guardian*, which will be discussed in Chap. 7, is very relevant:

> *If the issue of corruption involves someone from the north, the southern newspapers will announce it gleefully and be very thorough in their investigation while the northerners will manage it in such a way as not make their son look bad.*

In the interviews, respondents express their subjective opinion, but what becomes apparent in the way the story of Saminu Turaki was reported between the *Daily Trust* and the *Punch* confirms the view of the journalist. The *Daily Trust* was mild in its approach, while the *Punch*, to quote the correspondent, "announce[s] it gleefully".

Punishment

One of the common things in the reporting of the PTDF and former governors' scandal by both *Daily Trust* and the *Punch* was that the newspapers remained consistent in following the stories. But the main shortcoming as stated earlier was the absence of investigative journalism. As such, in this category, the *Punch* also carried the stories of the former governors as shown by the following headlines under the punishment category:

Kalu, Turaki: Increased security vigilance at Kuje prisons
—July 19 2007
Inside Kuje prison: Kalu, Others shun prison food
—July 21, 2007
Fayose, Ibori to spend Xmas, New year in prison

—December 18, 2007
Life in prison: Ibori buys generator, air conditioner, Fayose in Solitary Confinement for using GSM phone
—December 22, 2007

These headlines paid attention to the conditions of the former governors while they were in prison. One of the meanings that can be derived from the headlines is what Scollon (2001) calls the "chain of mediated actions". This is because critical discourse analysis is interested in actions which are produced by a chain of mediated events, and the events are represented in the text using language. What this means is that the former governors under investigation did not find themselves in this situation overnight, but there are chains of activities that led up to it. They contested for elections, they became governors, they allegedly looted or embezzled public funds, they were investigated, and then brought before the courts, detained in the prisons, which they found unbearable, so they had to buy generators, air conditioners and so on. Therefore, the entire headlines were no more than a text that describes these chains of events using language. Scollon added further that "our actions are frequently accompanied by language and, conversely, much of what we say is accompanied by action" (p. 140).

Satire

The *Punch* also carried headlines that involve satire. Study the following headlines carefully:

Ibori, His Excellency behind bars
—December 25, 2007
Hello, your former Excellencies
—July 27 2007
Their Excellencies in the dock
—July 16, 2007

As many critical discourse analysts would argue, language is not innocent and can be manipulated to suit the intended purpose. Apart from the first headline which mentioned the name of Ibori, the remaining two were both nominalised. The nominalisation here is not to hide their identity or kill the story, but to show the transition from their *Excellencies* to ***non-Excellencies***. Because they no longer live in the prestigious government houses or their personal mansions, nor are they free to engage in foreign trips or receive courtesy calls; rather, they are ***behind bars*** or ***in the dock***.

Conclusion

This chapter examined the cases under study by means of critical discourse analysis. The key differences in the two papers are in the use of language when reporting some of the former governors. Particularly former governor Saminu Turaki, where the *Daily Trust* was mild in reporting his arrest, while the *Punch* was more critical. This has exposed the regional dimension of the newspapers, which is an essential element of the study in this book.

One point to note is that the *Punch* did not sound too regionally inclined. This might be so because in the period under study, there is only one governor from the south-west, Ayo Fayose, and he did not attract much attention compared to James Ibori or even Orji Uzo Kalu both of whom were from the south-east and south-south (see Chap. 9 for analysis on the bias of south-western press on the reported allegation of certificate forgery against former governor of Lagos State, Bola Tinubu). This is also one of the criticisms against the anti-corruption war, which the EFCC led under the administration of former president Olusegun Obasanjo. That the EFCC paid more attention to governors from regions other than the south-west where the president came from, and incidentally the heart of the Nigerian press.

It is not easy to make generalisations on the level of partisanship of the newspapers because of the amount of the sample under study, and as expressed by the interviewees in subsequent chapters, corruption is something that almost everyone frowns upon; so the newspapers might be influenced, though not always, more by a patriotic and professional desire to report cases of corruption than by regional or ethnic bias, and as the literature has shown, stories about scandals sell. This chapter has provided an indication into the social, historical, environmental and political factors that shape the language that is used in the discourse of the newspapers. It has also suggested how regional and clientelist sentiments can influence the use of language in reporting. In the next chapter, the views of the journalists interview for this book are explored.

References

BBC News. (2006). Nigeria Governors in Graft Probe. Available at http://news.bbc.co.uk/1/hi/world/africa/5387814.stm. Downloaded 25 May 2009.

BBC News. (2009). *Fresh MP Expenses Claims Published.* Available at http://news.bbc.co.uk/1/hi/uk/8041232.stm. Downloaded 27 May 2009.

Bird, E. S. (1997). What a Story! Understanding the Audience for Scandal. In J. Lull & S. Hinerman (Eds.), *Media Scandals, Morality and Desire in the Popular Culture Market Place* (pp. 99–121). New York: Columbia University Press.

Canel, M. J., & Sanders, K. (2006). *Morality Tales: Political Scandals in Britain and Spain in the 1990s.* Cresskill. Hampton Press.

Carvalho, A. (2008). Media(ted) Discourse and Society: Rethinking the Framework of Critical Discourse Analysis. *Journalism Studies, 9*(2), 161–177.

Fairclough, N. (1995). *Media Discourse.* London: Arnold.

Fairclough, N. (2000). *New Labour New Language.* London: Routledge.

Fairclough, N. (2003). *Analysing Discourse: Textual Analysis for Social Research.* London/New York: Routledge.

Fowler, R. (1991). *Language in the News: Discourse and Ideology in the Press.* London: Routledge.

Galtung, J., & Ruge, M. (1965). The Structure of Foreign News: The Presentation of the Congo, Cuba and Cyprus Crisis in Four Norwegian Newspapers. *Journal of International Peace Research, 1*, 64–91.

Hallin, D. C., & Mancini, P. (2004). *Comparing Media Systems: Three Models of Media and Politics.* Cambridge. Cambridge University Press.

Haruna, M. (2007). *Nigeria: Tribune, Yar'Adua and the Minister of Abuja.* Available at http://allafrica.com/stories/200709050266.html. Downloaded 27 May 2009.

Herman, E. S., & Chomsky, N. (2002). *Manufacturing Consent. The Political Economy of the Mass Media.* New York: Pantheon.

Lull, J., & Hinerman, S. (1997). The Search for Scandal. In J. Lull & S. Hinerman (Eds.), *Media Scandals: Morality and Desire in the Popular Culture Marketplace* (pp. 1–33). Cambridge: Polity Press.

Meyer, M. (2001). Between Theory, Method, and Politics: Positioning of the Approaches to CDA. In R. Wodak & M. Meyer (Eds.), *Methods of Critical Discourse Analysis* (pp. 15–31). London: Sage Publications.

Ojeifo, S. (2006). Atiku – Obasanjo Took N10 billion PTDF Money for 3rd Term. Retrieved May, 16, 2018, Available at http://allafrica.com/stories/200612190209.html

Oyovbaire, S. (2001). *The Media and Democratic Process in Nigeria* (1). Available at http://www.waado.org/nigerdelta/Essays/Oyovbaire.html. Downloaded 15 August 2006.

Reef, M. S. (2007). *Nigeria: The Coup against Nuhu Ribadu*. Available at http://allafrica.com/stories/200712300016.html. Downloaded 25 May 2009.
Richardson, J. E. (2007). *Analysing Newspapers. An Approach from Critical Discourse Analysis*. New York: Palgrave Macmillan.
Richardson, J. (2008). Language and Journalism: An Expanding Research Agenda. *Journalism Studies, 9*(2), 152–160.
Scollon, R. (2001). Action and Text: Towards an Integrated Understanding of the Place of Text in Social (Inter)action, Mediated Discourse Analysis and the Problem of Social Action. In R. Wodak & M. Meyer (Eds.), *Methods of Critical Discourse Analysis* (pp. 139–183). London: Sage Publications.
Stenvall, M. (2008). Unnamed Sources as Rhetorical Constructs in News Agency Reports. *Journalism Studies, 9*(2), 229–243.
Taiwo, R. (2007). Language, Ideology and Power Relations in Nigerian Newspaper Headlines. Available at http://www.iiav.nl/ezines/web/Nebula/2008/No3/nobleworld/Taiwo2.pdf. Accessed 07 Oct 2007.
Van Dijk, T. (1988). How "They" Hit the Headlines: Ethnic Minorities in the Press. In G. Smitherman & T. Van Dijk (Eds.), *Discourse and Discrimination* (pp. 221–228). Detroit: Wayne State University Press.
Van Dijk, T. A. (1993). Principles of Critical Discourse Analysis. *Discourse and Society, 4*(2), 249–283.
Van Dijk, T. A. (2001). Multidisciplinary CDA: A Plea for Diversity. In R. Wodak & M. Meyer (Eds.), *Methods of Critical Discourse Analysis* (pp. 95–120). London: Sage Publications.
Wikileaks. (2006). Nigeria: President and VP Volley Allegations. Retrieved May 16, 2018, Available at https://wikileaks.org/plusd/cables/06ABUJA2773_a.html
Wodak, R. (2001). What CDA Is about-A Summary of Its history, Important Concepts and Its Developments. In R. Wodak & M. Meyer (Eds.), *Methods of Critical Discourse Analysis* (pp. 1–13). London: Sage Publications.
Yusha'u, M. J. (2018). For the Attention of African Media Scholars: An Introduction to Critical Discourse Analysis. In B. Mutsvairo (Ed.), *The Palgrave Handbook of Media and Communication Research in Africa* (pp. 465–482). Cham: Palgrave Macmillan.

CHAPTER 7

Reporting Corruption Scandals in Nigeria: Perspectives from Journalists

Introduction

In this chapter the results of the interviews conducted with journalists in Nigeria will be presented. A total of twenty-four interviews were conducted with journalists for this book. The journalists cut across the northern and southern newspapers, and others from South Africa and Kenya. Kenya and South Africa were studied in this book in order to test the applicability of the media system theory proposed by Hallin and Mancini (2004) in a wider African context (see Chaps. 4 and 5). This chapter compares how newspapers from the two regions of Nigeria cover the cases of corruption scandal. The questions asked during the interviews stem from the context of the research already discussed in Chap. 1. Most of the journalists interviewed are editors, political correspondents and columnists. The respondents were selected by means of snowball sampling, where respondents are recommended based on their knowledge of the subject matter. The majority of the interviewees have been in the profession for more than fifteen to twenty years. Because of the complexity of Nigerian society, the respondents cut across different sections of the divide. There are Muslims, Christians, southerners, northerners and women from different sections of the country.

The discussion is grouped into five themes, corruption/scandal, journalism and political culture, fourth estate role of the media, investigative journalism and suggestions and recommendations. In the first theme, the journalists were asked about their views on how newspapers from northern

M. J. Yusha'u, *Regional Parallelism and Corruption Scandals in Nigeria*, https://doi.org/10.1007/978-3-319-96220-7_7

and Southern Nigeria cover cases of corruption, whether they consider the coverage to be adequate, and if they consider the newspapers from one section to be biased against politicians from another section.

The second theme asked questions on whether the cultural background of the journalists influences the way they practise journalism, whether ethnic and regional considerations are given preference over professional ethics, and if there is a difference in political orientation between the journalists from the north and the south?

The third theme looked at the fourth estate role of the media by asking the journalists whether they are satisfied with the watchdog role of Nigerian newspapers, if the watchdog role contributes in reducing corruption, whether the watchdog role is soft or active, and whether what is reported in the newspapers is determined by the nature of ownership of the newspapers.

The fourth theme concentrated on investigative journalism. The journalists were asked what they understood by investigative journalism, if Nigerian journalists practice investigative journalism, whether corruption within the media militates against the practice of investigative journalism, if the passing of the freedom of information bill will help the journalists in practising investigative journalism, the challenges facing journalists in Nigeria, and the ways for improvement. The last theme asked for suggestions and recommendations from the journalists.

In this chapter therefore, the responses provided in each of the five themes used in the interviews will be studied, and categories that define the conceptions and descriptions of the interviewees will be itemised for analysis. This will create a better picture as to how the journalists interviewed for this book have different perspectives on how the press in Nigeria reports stories about corruption scandals in relation to the framework of the research discussed in Chap. 1.

As we shall discus in Chap. 8, the views expressed by the journalists could help us understand the nature of the Nigerian media system within the context of the media systems theory suggested by Hallin and Mancini (2004) (Table 7.1).

Table 7.1 Table on respondents, media organisations and portfolios

Newspaper/ownership/interviewees	*Region*	*Location*	*The respondents*
Trust newspapers/private	North	Abuja	Five 1. Editor/daily 2. Editor/*Aminiya* 3. Chairman, editorial board 4. Senate correspondent 5. Editor/Sunday
Thisday/private	South	Lagos	Two 1. Abuja bureau chief 2. Senate correspondent
Guardian/private	South	Lagos	Two 1. Abuja bureau chief 2. Deputy political editor
Daily Times/government-private	South	Lagos	One 1. State house correspondent
Punch/private	South	Lagos	One 1. Correspondent
The Sun/private	South	Lagos	One 1. Abuja bureau chief
The Nation/private	South	Lagos	Two 1. Chairman, editorial board 2. Abuja bureau chief
New Nigerian/government	North	Kaduna	One 1. Former editor
Independent/private	South	Lagos	One 1. State house correspondent
Columnists/former journalists	North		Five 1. Former managing director, *New Nigerian* newspaper 2. Former editor, *Triumph* newspaper 3. Former president, Nigeria Union of Journalists 4. Former editor, *This Era* 5. Former editor, *Leadership*
Anti-corruption official		Abuja	One 1. Former chairman, Economic and Financial Crimes Commission
Former correspondent	Nairobi	Kenya	Bloomberg
Journalist	South Africa	South Africa	Independent media group

First Theme: Corruption/Scandal

In this theme, corruption/scandal, various experiences and understandings have been discerned from the respondents on how Nigerian newspapers report corruption scandals. These experiences and conceptions as described by the journalists can be grouped into five categories. The first is consensus, which explains how the journalists agree that there is no difference in the way corruption scandals are reported and therefore could not see any difference between northern and southern newspapers. The second is regionalism, where the journalists see an apparent bias towards the region of the newspaper. The third is clientelism, in which personal or corporate considerations determine what is reported rather than professional ethics. The fourth is adequacy of reports, which looks at the views of the journalists on whether the amount of coverage given to a corruption scandal is adequate. The fifth category focuses on the unevenness in newspaper ownership between the south and the north. Each of the five categories under this theme will be discussed. The description of conception among journalists may not be the same in terms of their understanding of corruption scandals; the theme will therefore look at the diversity of views expressed by the respondents and analyse them accordingly.

Consensus

Many of the respondents agree that when it comes to the coverage of corruption scandals there isn't much difference between the northern and southern newspapers. This view was held by several respondents who look at the attention the front pages of many newspapers give to the coverage of stories related to corruption. According to this young editor working for a weekend newspaper in Northern Nigeria:

> *I think to a great extent, newspapers in Nigeria are doing well in terms of coverage of political corruption in Nigeria in both the Northern and Southern newspapers.*

The kind of coverage given to stories about corruption could be due to a number of reasons; the establishment of the Economic and Financial Crimes Commission (EFCC) and the Independent Corrupt Practices Commission (ICPC) has attracted the attention of the media. No newspaper would like to be out-marketed by another in its coverage. It can also be due to the tradition of Nigerian newspapers to unite on anything that is of national importance as confirmed by this woman editor:

> *And when it comes to issue of national concern I think we give it adequate coverage. I can almost say there is enough attention to issues of political corruption in both the Northern and Southern newspapers.*

Nigerian newspapers have a history of consistency, by going beyond ethnic and regional sentiments when it comes to issues of national survival. This has been exemplified from the onset of the newspaper industry. The press worked together to challenge the colonial government until independence was achieved in 1960 (see Chap. 3). The newspapers also have a history of standing together at various times to ensure that the country returns to civilian rule. Harsh economic policies like the Structural Adjustment Programme (SAP) of the 1980s was vehemently opposed by Nigerian journalists. Attempts by various leaders, military and civilian, to elongate their tenure and remain in office never received favourable coverage in Nigerian newspapers. In fact, according to one of the respondents, the Nigerian press has performed better than the national assembly since the country returned to civilian administration in 1999.

According to this journalist who reports for the *Daily Trust*:

> *They have done tremendously well in reporting such cases. Even though there are lapses here and there. Typical among this is the issue of governors who have been picked recently by the EFCC. I believe that it is apparent and very obvious that the Nigerian dailies have been in the heat of reportage of all these vices allegedly committed by these ex-governors while in office.*

The journalist is referring to the arrest of some former governors by the EFCC. The former governors are Orji Uzo Kalu, Ibrahim Saminu Turaki and Chimaroke Nnamani, allegedly for stealing public funds and enriching themselves. All the national dailies carried this report.[1] The chairman of

[1] Orji Uzo Kalu was the former governor of Abia State, Saminu Turaki was the former governor of Jigawa State, and Chimaroke Nnamani was the former governor of Enugu State. All three governors served between 1999 and 2007. Kalu and Nnamani were members of the ruling People's Democratic Party, while Turaki was a member of All Nigeria People's Party (ANPP) which is the main opposition party, but he switched to the PDP before the 2007 elections.

the EFCC, Nuhu Ribadu, vowed to arrest all governors who were corrupt after they had left office, when they would be stripped of the constitutional immunity they had previously enjoyed. According to Nuhu Ribadu:

> Our jurisdiction does not go beyond the boundaries of Nigeria, so if these people manage to run away from the country, it will be difficult to get to them...But we do enjoy very cordial working relationship with the law enforcement agencies of some countries and those of the UK and the US, for instance, have been very helpful in this regard. (BBC News 2007)

The arrest of the former governors was one of the promises Nigerians were waiting to see fulfilled,[2] seeing that majority of the governors arrested were from the ruling People's Democratic Party, whose president, Olusegun Obasanjo, had appointed Nuhu Ribadu as the Chairman of the EFCC.

Other journalists have a different perspective on the reasons why the newspapers were competing in reporting the allegations of corruption scandals against public office holders. According to this senior journalist working with the *Sun Newspaper*, a leading tabloid following the style of the *Sun* in London:

> *You see I think that the evolution of the media over a period of time now has broken down that barrier north-south as far as I know. Because a Minister was caught for the ID card scam Sunday Afolabi and Shata it was covered...There is a new Nigeria evolving where corrupt practices are not condoned. If you don't publish it you will not sell.*

From the account of the journalist above, he identified at least two reasons why he thinks there are no differences in the way the newspapers cover the cases of corruption. The first is the "*evolution of the media over a period of time*", which means that the media could be concentrated in a particular location, but the increase of the number of newspapers has reduced the likelihood of being unnecessarily biased when it comes to the issue of corruption. The second point is that *"there is a new Nigeria evolving where corrupt practices are not condoned"*, meaning that though there could be regional and tribal differences in the past, at the moment

[2] See Olayinka, Abiodun (2008): *EFCC: Before we all fall victim*, as a sample of an opinion article in the tribune newspaper on the views of Nigerians regarding the arrest of the former governors.

Nigerians cannot condone the act of taking the resources of the state for personal use, and this includes the journalists themselves who reflect that on the pages of newspapers. A leading columnist from Northern Nigeria, who has been practising journalism since the 1970s, also agrees that there is a degree of balancing in the way newspapers report stories about corruption in Nigeria, though there might be some differences:

> *I think it will be risky for one to make a generalised statement because some of them have been fairly balanced and some not so well balanced depending on who the proprietors are.*

Regionalism

It is interesting to note that while many of the respondents agreed that there isn't much difference in the reporting of corruption between northern and southern newspapers, when the interview becomes in-depth, the same journalists bring examples to show that Nigerian newspapers can tilt towards the region they belong and favour it in their report. This may suggest how different section of the country can utilise the media for regional, ethnic or religious purposes as perceived by this senior editor from *Thisday* newspaper:

> *The southwest group of this country know how to use the media to the extent that a Yoruba agenda is put on centre stage to become a national agenda. So, they make much noise out of it, that the media is the place for public opinion where you can buy and sell whatever it is. So, the media depending on which side of the divide, whether of the northern divide or the southern divide would naturally take sides on issues like this.*

Although the media tries to portray itself as national in content and outlook, it is difficult to divorce the regional divide, because as discussed in the Chap. 3 on the historical landscape of Nigerian newspapers, the historical origin of Nigeria is influenced by the regional divide. The above point suggests that the views expressed by each of the individual journalists is first of all a reflection of the diversity of views regarding the practice of journalism, and second, while the respondents try to portray a national outlook, when the interview becomes more in-depth, that is when they express their real mindset and perception of issues. The journalists do not necessarily express different points on the same issue because they want to be hypocritical but because that is how Nigeria operates as a country. The federal government, which is at the centre of the country's administration, has people from different background and ethnic nationalities, and government policies attempt to have a national approach, but once you come down to the regions, states and local governments, people become much more concerned about their immediate needs and make little pretention about being national in nature.

In fact, as confirmed by the experience of the journalist below, what might be seen as a story in newspapers belonging to one section of the country may not be seen in the same light in newspapers published in another section of the country.

> *The practice of journalism in Nigeria I must confess if I am to be sincere is just around that level of interpretation. For example, what* Daily Trust *will see as news probably we in the south west will not see it as news. And it has nothing to do with hating* Daily Trust *or anything. It just has to do with the location of the paper and its audience.*

The journalist above has highlighted a seemingly relevant issue in what determines the news. The geographical location of a newspaper in relation to whether it is northern or southern contributes in determining the news it carries. So according to this example, there could be stories which might be of more interest to the *Daily Trust*, which is published in the north, but may not be as interesting to a newspaper published in the south. For instance, an editor from the *Nation* newspaper based in Lagos stated during the interview that there are stories, for instance, about Hajj or about emirs from the north which they will not bother to publish, when similar stories can make the front page in the north. Similarly, the activities of the traditional institutions in the south may not receive much attention in northern newspapers, unless the issues have national significance. One of the respondents mentioned that if you want to see the interest of readers, you can find out from the culture sections of the newspapers: southern newspapers review the home videos produced in Lagos, and northern newspapers review the home videos produced in Kano. So, it is clear that the description of experiences from the journalists shows the presence of the regional divide.[3]

[3]The home video industry is booming in Nigeria, majority of the films, popularly known as *Nollywood* are produced in the south, the films are mostly in English and marketed across the world. But in the north also the home video industry exists, but the language used is Hausa, and Kano is the centre of the production, and the films produced there are called

A clearer example about the perception of the regional divide as understood by the journalists was given by this respondent, who was an editor in several newspapers and magazines. According to her:

> *Let me come to the most daring case "the June 12". The reporting of June 12, that singular incident on its own upturned the underbelly. It revealed the underbelly of Nigerian journalists. As soon as the event happened, all of us were democrats or pretended to be democrats at heart. Abiola got more votes in the north than he did in the south. But there is that perspective of the Northerner as somebody who wants to 'lord' it over others. And that affects the reporting of political successes even of Northern politicians.*

"June 12" was the election that took place on that date in 1993. The two contestants were Mashood Abiola and Bashir Tofa, the former from the south and the latter from the north. At the beginning of the contest the southern newspapers framed Abiola as a northern stooge, because of his friendship with previous military rulers and other members of the Nigerian elites from the north. The criticism was also because Abiola was a member of the National Party of Nigeria (NPN)[4] in the late 1970s and early 1980s, and he used his wealth to establish the *Concord* newspapers which became a rival to the main newspapers in the southwest, and the presidential candidate from the region, Chief Obafemi Awolowo. The military decided to annul the election, and immediately after that, the newspapers from the south turned around and began to support Chief Abiola, claiming that the election was annulled because Abiola was a southerner. Seeing that, journalists from Northern Nigeria who were also supporting Abiola reconsidered their support, and the regional divide in reporting became more apparent. According to Haruna (2008)

> Whereas the editorial of the *Nigerian Tribune* in question reduced June 12 to a purely Yoruba affair, an earlier editorial in The *Guardian* of June 23 had cautioned against doing just that. Titled "Arresting the drift", the editorial

Kannywood. For more details on both *Nollywood* and *Kannywood*, see Okome, Onookome (2007): "Nollywood: Audience, Spectatorship and the Sites of Consumption". *Postcolonial text*. Vol 3 No 2 pp. 1–21, and Adamu, Abdalla Uba (2007): *Transglobal Media Flows and African Popular Culture: Revolution and Reaction in Muslim Hausa Popular Culture*. Kano-Nigeria. Gidan Dabino Publishers.

[4] NPN was the political party that won the 1979 election and was in power until December 1983 when the civilian administration was overthrown by the military. Though the party was the most national in outlook at the time, it was seen as party with a strong northern base because some of its key members where from the Northern People's Congress, the dominant political party in Northern Nigeria in the 1950s and 1960s.

> argued that the struggle for June 12 was not just between Abiola and Tofa or between the North and the South or between Islam and Christianity. Rather, it was, as the newspaper said quite correctly, a struggle "between the democratic political current nationally constituted…and the anti-democratic current, also nationally constituted." Unfortunately, the *Guardian's* exhortation was ignored by the "June Twelvers" and, in time, by even the newspaper itself.

It will be apt to suggest that the annulment of the June 12 presidential election refreshed the regional memory of Nigerian newspapers. As indicated above, the newspapers drew a regional line, though it will be difficult to make a generalised statement about the extent of regionalism in the press, because there were few newspapers from the north that can balance the fecundity of the southern press, but there was hardly a newspaper from the south that did not take the regional tone, even if it was against the candidature of Abiola ab initio.

An interesting point from Haruna's assessment above was the position of the *Guardian* newspaper, which from the example quoted by Haruna, the paper tried to act professionally by cautioning Nigerians against taking a regional line of thinking. It can be said that the paper was interested in getting rid of the military so that a civilian administration can be instituted after ten years of military rule (at that time), but the fact that the *Guardian* itself later took the regional line, may be a pointer to the fact that political events can override professional considerations. And that can give room to more partisanship, or in this case regionalism (see Chap. 8 on regional parallelism). This point corresponds to Hallin and Mancini's (2004) view that no news media organisation is politically neutral.

Some of the respondents indicated that the existence of regionalism can also be found in their working relationship. A young journalist from the *Daily Trust* who has been reporting for less than three years, stated the following:

> *I have realised that this colouration exists even among the most junior among reporters. You understand that someone who is covering a story for Punch will not oblige to give that story to someone who is coming from Daily Trust willingly. He will first of all look for his 'kith and kin' from maybe ThisDay, Vanguard or Guardian. Some newspapers have a kind of a gang up, a clique a cabal sort of thing in terms of getting information. So that really exists. The fact that some people say that most of these newspapers what they practice is the*

same, yes, I will say most of what they practice is the same in the sense that when that issue is general or is national; that is when they come to meet together. But when issues touch on regional or other inclinations they really tend to exhibit those traits and characteristics.

The statement above could mean a lot of things in journalistic practice. It might suggest that cultural proximity plays a role among journalists to the extent that they feel more comfortable with colleagues who come from the same area. It could also indicate the level of competition between newspapers from different regions.

During the period of military rule, it was common in Nigerian newspapers to read stories about corruption being directly linked to the region of the individual involved, and because majority of the heads of state during the military era were from the north, the reports tend to portray northerners as corrupt and incompetent. But with the emergence of Olusegun Obasanjo as the president in 1999, there are reports about corruption with regional tone, but not as much as it was before Obasanjo as was suggested by this editor:

There is always this assumption that the country was governed by Northerners for so long that was why things went bad and that maybe they were incompetent, corrupt and so on. But you know after all the corruption, people have seen under the Obasanjo administration. I think I am not sure if I have noted that regional change in the coverage of political corruption.

Another journalist, who is the chairman of the editorial board of one of the newspapers being published in Lagos, also confirms the existence of this regional dichotomy among Nigerian newspapers:

Yes. That is a matter of fact. You see papers that are seen as south-west papers, papers that are seen as Niger-Delta papers; you get papers that are seen as northern newspapers. So there is ethnic and regional bias in newspapers.

But the question to be asked is whether the journalists see the dichotomy as something positive or as something that undermines the success of journalism as a profession. This view may signify the fact that there are journalists who believe that the existence of the regional and ethnic division is part and parcel of Nigerian journalism. With regards to the above journalist in particular, he received his education in the post-independence and post-civil war period, when the regional and ethnic rivalry was more apparent because of the existence of regions[5] at that time, perhaps it might suggest that journalists who were product of that era might have stronger views about the regional leaning of the newspapers than those who came later. It will also be interesting to know whether the regional bias is promoted because the readers like sensational stories. According to this journalist:

> *There is more of that principal divide that has existed between the two angles of the media ownership. And I will frankly say that it is not good for journalism in particular in the country.*

This experience is a lamentation of the situation, meaning that some of the journalists are not happy about it. But they can't help it, since the foundation of the country itself was based on the regional dichotomy. They may not be happy about it because for those who see journalism as a profession, and would like to uphold the principles and values of journalism, resorting to regionalism will undermine their effort. However, there is little they can do, because they are working as employees, and they lack the capital to establish media organisations that will try to uphold the principles they cherish.

As discussed earlier in the chapter on the historical landscape of Nigerian newspapers, the location of newspapers within a section of Nigeria is historical, which might also help in understanding the reason for the regional dichotomy; it starts with the arrival of Christian missionaries and later colonialists. This historical fact gave the south-western part of Nigeria an edge over the rest in terms of ownership of newspapers, but also because from the early stage of Nigerian history Lagos became both an administrative and commercial capital. This according to this respondent who has worked in both in northern and southern part of Nigeria is the reason why newspapers from south-western Nigeria control the thinking and shaping of government policies ahead of other regions.

[5] Between 1960 and 1966 Nigeria was operating the Westminster parliamentary system. The country comprises of three independent regions then; Northern Region, Western Region and Eastern Region, and later the Midwestern Region. Each of these regions had a premier who governs the region independent of the federal government. But after the military took over in 1966, the regions were abolished and substituted by states. The civil war took place between 1967 and 1970. See Chap. 1 for a brief history of Nigeria.

Why I said it is more structured is because the Yoruba have their mainstream politicians, the Afenifere group, this is the mainstream political machinery of the Yorubas. Now they have their industrialists, these are people who do not participate in politics they just run industries; they also have their own media that complement these groups. Now let me try to provide the linkages between these groups. A newspaper like the Punch which reflects the thinking of people from that part of the country especially their elite, its reporter goes out to interview professionals about government policies.

This shows that there are certain factors that contribute in the survival of the media in the south-western part of Nigeria because the region has a historical advantage in terms of the economy, professionals and other factors that are needed for the survival of newspapers.

Some of the respondents interviewed also confirmed that the location of the newspaper, the nature of its readership, and the interest of the proprietor can influence reporting as stated by this journalist:

Let me give you a typical example. The Nation is located in Lagos and the Sun is also located in Lagos. Daily Trust *is in Abuja, the north; Leadership is also in the north. Now if the former governor of Abia state was accused of corruption and corrupt practices. I wouldn't expect the* Sun *for example to take the story from the angle of Orji Kalu being corrupt, because I know the relationship of Orji Kalu with the* Sun. *If for example somebody in the north like Turaki in Jigawa was also accused of corrupt practices. Unless on exceptional cases when they are in court; the normal practice is that* Daily Trust *will pick the story from the angle the man said he used the money for third term. They might not just see it as corruption and I think it is just in our system.*[6]

This view corresponds with nature of reporting by *Daily Trust and Punch* as discussed in Chap. 6, where the stories on PTDF and former governors' scandals were analysed by means of critical discourse analysis.

If the south-western part of the country has the advantage of industries that provide advertising revenue for the survival of newspapers, the professionals that support the newspapers morally and intellectually, the banks that help maintain a business environment, then it is easier to understand why the media is concentrated in the southwest. Because the media

[6] Third term refers to the attempt by former president Olusegun Obasanjo to get the constitution amended to allow him to have a third term in office instead of the two terms stipulated in the constitution.

cannot survive in isolation, it needs some social factors to drive it. However, this may come with a price. Therefore, its content might reflect the interest of the environment that helps it to thrive. So, the newspapers that come from other regions may likely reflect the interest of the environment that will help them remain in the market. This might help in understanding the dichotomy that exists between different regions in Nigeria such that, according to this senior journalist, when there are cases of corruption against somebody the newspapers look at the region where a person comes from rather than the actual wrongdoing.

> *I think the common problem is that you find newspapers taking side not on the basis of the merit of the case but on the basis of those involved where they come from.*

Once the newspapers report the cases of corruption on the basis of the area a person comes from, then the reporting can take a different dimension, each section trying to reveal the atrocities of the other as explained by this journalist from the *Guardian* newspaper:

> *If the issue of corruption involves someone from the north, the Southern newspapers will announce it gleefully and be very thorough in their investigation while the northerners will manage it in such a way as not make their son look bad, vice versa. … the southerners have the same thing except the Yoruba's, and that is determined essentially by your political affiliation. If you are seen as an Awoist, and you are involved in corruption. (Awoist means a follower of Chief Obafemi Awolowo), the southern press on first contact with the story will want to protect the person believing that he is related to Awolowo, so he must always fight for the people, and that may be wrong.*

The statement above brought to light some issues involved in Nigerian journalism. First, it has brought to light the existence of the north/south dichotomy in Nigerian journalism, which to a large extent plays a role in reporting. It has also brought to light some form of self-censorship in which the prominence, reporting or otherwise of a news item might be dictated in a way by the region of the person affected in the story, and lastly the existence of certain stories that might be termed as taboo stories because the political leaning of the individual involved has provided a shield for him. This attitude towards reporting was stressed by a journalist from the north and a former editor of some newspapers who stated that:

> *I will give you this case; that I really discovered to my shock, a few years ago I attended the conference of Nigerian Bureau of Editors somewhere in Osun state, and there one of the editors, she is a woman[ ] she said there was a time, the late Bola Ige [allegedly] had an illegitimate child and she got the story and she was so excited about it[ ] she investigated, she got the story, she wanted to publish it, the publisher said that is a taboo, the story was not published in spite of the fact that the story was a scandal.*

While this journalist has pointed one of the areas that might be considered as taboo, or at least might receive a mild treatment in the hand of editors in southern newspapers, another journalist from a southern newspaper also pointed an area which he thinks might not receive prominence in a northern newspaper:

> *I wrote an article in 1994 in the* Guardian, *and in that article, I recall vividly that I posited that the northern newspapers were trying most the time to shield their corrupt men [ ] The culture of the people in the north restricts them from talking extensively, about traditional rulers, about elders, about political leaders, not that they don't, but they hardly talk about them. For example they hardly talk about people who entrench poverty in the north.*

Clientelism

Clientelism as described by Hallin and Mancini (2004), and Hallin and Papathanassopoulos (2002) is a form of social organisation in which access to resources and loyalty to other considerations are more important than professional values of objectivity and so on. In the case of the media, journalists and politicians or people interested in certain favours establish a relationship which promotes this sense of clientelism. The description of the experiences of the journalists is a pointer to that. According to this journalist who is the editor of a Sunday newspaper:

> *Obviously there are differences you know because some of the papers have certain links with the some of the accused persons, I mean some of those accused of corrupt enrichment. There are some of these newspapers that are somehow connected with some of these personalities and where some of the cases concern the personalities you hardly see those papers mention anything about those cases.*

What the editor above is describing is a new trend in Nigerian journalism in which serving state governors establish newspapers (see Chap. 3 for a classification of Nigerian newspapers by ownership). They employ journalists who have been in the profession for a long time. The papers carry stories like any other newspaper, except when it affects their proprietor. Then the newspapers either become silent, or treat the story mildly, and this is the point Hallin and Mancini (2004) and Hallin and Papathanassopoulos (2002) were trying to make in their discussion of media and clientelism. These relationships serve to control and oversee what gets into the pages of newspapers. One of the respondents, who is also a senior figure of the Economic and Financial Crimes Commission (EFCC) confirmed this clientelist relationship during the interview:

> *But the interesting thing is while it is going on we saw process of crime getting into the media. So much money that public officers steal is getting into the Nigerian media and is owned by them. For example, if I show you this paper [he pointed at the* Sun *newspaper] is a product of corruption.*

The above respondent made this comment in the middle of the interview, he confirmed that some newspapers, and he picked some of them from his table; the *Sun* linked to the former Abia State governor, the *Independent* owned by former Delta State governor, James Ibori, and the *Nation* owned by former governor of Lagos State, Ahmed Bola Tinubu. The EFCC official mentioned that they were able to trace some of the money which was taken from various state treasuries and was used to procure materials for the establishment of some of these newspapers.

One important thing to note is that even here the differences in various regions among the governors who tried to establish these newspapers was clear. All the newspapers owned by governors are associated with southern governors, and this may suggest that the edge in terms of understanding the role the media plays whether for promoting societal or personal interest is higher in the south than in Northern Nigeria.

It also shows a stronger link in terms of media clientelism among southern politicians than northern politicians. This does not mean that politicians from Northern Nigeria do not attempt to have this clientelist relationship with the media. A female respondent from the *Daily Trust* newspaper mentioned that they have been under pressure several times from politicians, urging the newspaper to withdraw stories because the person involved is a northerner. What is different, however, is that some politicians from the south invest directly in the media, making the clientelist relationship more direct, while politicians from the north make it indirect through contact with journalists.

The respondents gave examples on how politicians use the media in promoting or protecting their interest. According to this journalist who is a political editor with a Lagos based newspaper:

> *Whether those we report, whether those of us doing the reporting, do you think Atiku got the amount of exposure he got in the media because they love Atiku; it is not that of love. He was financing it. That is still some other truth.*

The above respondent did not absolve any one from blame. According to him, both journalists and politicians are blameworthy. The examples he cited above with Atiku Abubakar, the former vice president, and a strong politician from Northern Nigeria is a classic example. The vice president found himself in a battle of survival with former president Olusegun Obasanjo. Both sides started exchanging accusations against each other. The senate established a committee to find the truth about those allegations. Both the president and the vice president were indicted by the committee for diverting resources from the Petroleum Technology Development Fund (PTDF) (see Chap. 6).

But the point the respondent was trying to make was that despite the allegations of corruption against Atiku Abubakar, he continued to get a favourable coverage in the press when he launched his presidential campaign. There are at least two reasons within Nigerian context on why the media should be critical in the coverage of Atiku's campaign. The first is the allegation of corruption, and the media, which should serve as watchdog, should be able to analyse and bring out the issues affecting Atiku Abubakar. The second is that being a politician from Northern Nigeria, and the media being regionally biased, this should provide coverage that uses the regional angle to demonise his campaign, yet from the perspective of the above respondent, that did not happen. So what is the reason? According to this perspective as suggested by the respondent, it is because "he [Atiku] was financing it". This perspective suggests there is corruption within the media itself, which we shall discuss later in this chapter.

From the description given by the respondents, clientelism can take different forms. It can be internal, in the sense that when a story touches on the interest of the newspaper, either its publisher or some other interests, the newspaper might give a mild treatment to the story, and that is the point made by the journalist below:

> *The* Sun *newspaper was very cautious in its coverage of the scandalous allegations against Governor Orji Uzor Kalu reportedly the publisher and the newspaper owner. So, you can say there are some inclinations or factors or underlined interest that shapes the general ideology of this coverage by the newspapers. Of recent, there was a banner headline in the* Daily Trust *newspaper which says "Governor Sule Lamido was responsible for scuttling ex-governor Saminu Turaki's bail." It was only governor Saminu Turaki who has not gotten a surety... But I will say that it is generally out of sympathy that the newspaper even went to press with the story.*

The above example suggests some of the views held by some journalists concerning corruption within the media. The example shows that this interest can be found in any of the regions, with the *Sun* being a southern newspaper and *Daily Trust* published in the north. Another point made by the journalists is that the journalist can do his homework and write the story. But when it reaches the editor's desk, it might not be published, as confirmed by the example below, which goes on to suggest how strong the clientelist relationship is between journalists and politicians taking into consideration the experience of the respondent:

> *Once in a while, there is always a slant to a story depending really on who is involved and that I think is general. For example, if the case of corruption is established against somebody that is close to my publisher, for example it's not as if the journalist will not write the story the way it should be written but you can be rest assured that when it gets to the headquarters they will change certain things. Basically, due to the relationship of the person involved.*

The respondents were very clear about the relationship between publishers and politicians, and how they work hard to protect their interest. According to this journalist:

> *To be candid the politicians have infiltrated the newspaper industry. They own the papers, pay the salaries.*

This is a clear case of political clientelism; the journalists know this fact, but they can't do anything because they need their jobs to survive. The editors who determine which stories are published might also be powerless, and so the interest of the publisher will triumph. Equally important is the fact that the newspapers may have certain political interests. In the west, for instance you might have different political and ideological leanings, some papers being right wing or conservative, others being liberal, leftist or centre ground. In Nigeria that may not be the case. Two things might determine the political interest of the paper. First, its location, and second, the interest of the publisher. According to this journalist:

> *I can hardly point to a newspaper that has no political interest. And the political interest is not basically informed by goodwill. It is informed by the man that has the cash.*

Clientelism from the views expressed by the respondents could be influenced by historical factors. That is the historical advantage of pioneering the publishing of newspapers, which make those in that region to master the art of newspaper publishing, and then use it to their advantage if the need be. This was explained by a journalist from *Thisday* newspaper, specifically referring to the advantage the south has over the north:

> *More importantly as a tool of agenda setting, do not also forget the fact that they were in the thick of the struggle for independence and so overtime they have hone their skills on how to effectively use the media. These are historical facts we can't run away from them. I am saying this for you to understand so that it may not appear from the word go some people were destined to own the newspapers, these were the realities. And so, you find an interesting scenario were the bulk of the newspapers are cited in the Lagos-Ibadan axis owned by people from the south-south and to some extent the people from the southwest determines what goes into those newspapers.*

The conclusion from the description given by the journalists above also reveals the complexity involved the newspaper industry in Nigeria. It shows that the south does not refer to a monotonous entity (see Chap. 8 for more on this). It has complexities as confirmed by the journalist above. The southern part of Nigeria comprises of three geopolitical zones. The south-west, which is predominantly Yoruba; the south-east, which is predominantly Ibo; and the south-south, which is a mishmash of different ethnic groups; what is however distinct about the south-south geopolitical zone is that it is the oil producing area of the country, and the point the journalist from *Thisday* was trying to make is that majority of the media owners are from the south-south, while the south-west maintains its advantage of location and management. These factors combined contribute the content of political news. The same journalist elaborated on this point:

The media has never been immune to the political realities depending on trends in Nigeria. When it has mattered they have taken sides, at other times they have tried to hide.

The above point might be one of the reasons why it will be difficult to give a straight explanation about the Nigerian media, because sometimes national issues are given preference over regional issues, and at other times, regional issues are given advantage. Beyond regionalism, other respondents look at the interest of proprietors, those who own the newspapers. According to one columnist and a former editor in Northern Nigeria, the newspapers ignore stories that affect their owners:

If you take for instance the Independent which speculations say is owned by Ibori, and you find that cases that involving him hardly get highlighted in the newspaper. You can see it clearly in the obvious case of Orji Kalu in the Sun; *clearly as far as the* Sun *is concerned Orji Kalu has done nothing wrong.*

Certainly the experiences of the journalists might suggest different forms of clientelism, in the interplay of power between different sections and interests in Nigeria, among the regions and the newspaper proprietors with the press as the tool used in the political interplay.

Adequacy and Prominence

One of the perceptions of Nigerian journalists as expressed by the respondents is the adequacy of reports about corruption scandals, and the prominence given to the stories on the pages of Nigerian newspapers. This is significant because stories about corruption scandals were featuring regularly despite the factors mentioned earlier about clientelism and corruption within the media. A description of how the newspapers take stories about corruption was given by a journalist who reported from the national assembly for the *Daily Trust* newspaper:

So the coverage is very adequate in the sense that an average Nigerian on the street knows that so and so governor is corrupt. I could remember when I was covering the national assembly, the Senate, when the EFCC boss Malam Nuhu Ribadu was in the dock, he was in the Senate chamber addressing them on the list of corrupt governors. He was reading out names and it was beamed on national television and the next morning most of the newspapers were awash with the name of these governors.

This statement brings about two issues, first how the activities of Economic and Financial Crimes Commission (EFCC) made stories about corruption become common knowledge in Nigeria, and secondly, the interest of the newspapers in carrying these stories. With regards to the first, it appears that the EFCC chairman, Nuhu Ribadu was able to articulate his points that the media in Nigeria found in him a person who supplies the news uninterruptedly. The second is how news about corruption can be used in promoting the newspapers themselves. Many of the respondents confirmed that the amount of coverage given to stories about corruption was adequate. According to this journalist from the *Sun* newspaper:

> *It is there, yes, it is very adequate. If you check, if you have been here in the last one week you will discover that oil scam, NNPC is there. So it is adequate if you ask me. I will give it seventy percent out of hundred.*

But not all the journalists agree with the same view, according to another journalist from the nation newspaper:

> *Adequate, no. but condoned within the limit of powers available to them yes. But has never been adequate because there are limitations.*

In the case of the first view that sees the report as adequate, the journalist was looking at it from quantitative point of view. Therefore, if a governor or minister is arrested, and all the papers carry it, and continue to follow the story for one to three days, or even a week, that can be considered adequate. As for the second view, the journalist was looking beyond the quantity; he was looking at it in terms of quality, in terms of independence of the media, and other challenges and limitations that surround news production. What is, however, agreeable is that the newspapers pay attention to news about corruption scandals, but whether that contributes in reducing corruption is a subject of debate.

Different administrations in Nigeria have tried to address the issue of corruption, in particular during the military era. When the country returned to civilian rule in 1999, two bodies were established by President Olusegun Obasanjo. The Independent Corrupt Practices Commission (ICPC) and the Economic and Financial Crimes Commission (EFCC). Though the activities of the EFCC seems to draw more attention than ICPC, many of the journalists interviewed suggest that the establishment of these two agencies contributed in giving prominence to news about corruption as confirmed by this journalist:

> *But from 1999 up to now the issues of corruption are featured more prominently in the media because the government established the[se] agencies, ICPC and EFCC, especially from the EFCC side…in a nutshell I think corruption has been receiving more attention in the media more than any other time, because due to the primary activities of these two Anti-corruption agencies.*
>
> *Almost every day you open the newspapers in Nigeria there are reports about the cases of corruption, either those who have reached the courts or the ones that are being investigated by the police and the anti-corruption agencies.*

The two agencies mentioned above attract the attention of the media, which, as stated by the respondents, gave additional prominence to news about corruption. Another journalist from the *Punch* newspaper believes that apart from the activities of these two agencies, news about corruption attracts attention:

> *Because a corruption story is a very interesting story all the time, I mean people are always interested to hear stories about official corruption and these newspapers are aware of this. The southern newspapers and the northern newspapers are aware of it. But you cannot run away from the fact that in Nigeria the tendency is to dedicate a lot of coverage to political corruption even with some ethnic undertones in it.*

So in terms of the adequacy of the reports and the prominence given to stories about corruption, we can identify at least three different experiences. Those who agree with the amount of coverage and prominence given to the news, those who are more critical of the amount of coverage by looking at the wider picture in terms of challenges and limitations, and those who agree that the reports are adequate, but they may come with regional or ethnic undertones. What this suggests is that there is diversity of views, as adequacy of reporting means different things to different journalists. The category who are satisfied that the amount of time and space given to the coverage of corruption scandals is sufficient, and they are satisfied with what the newspapers were able to cover. The second category, who acknowledge the effort of the newspapers but feel that what is done is not enough and the press needs to do more. And finally, those who may be happy with the amount of coverage, but do not see any departure from the traditional assumption about the newspapers being regionally and ethnically biased.

Unevenness in Newspaper Ownership

While the journalists give different perspectives on the nature of journalism practice in different parts of Nigeria, with reference to stories about corruption, they were mindful to acknowledge the unevenness in the ownership of newspapers between the north and the south. Unevenness in newspaper ownership is one of the common features of journalism in Nigeria, because the newspaper industry is dominated by one section of the country, and reflects the views, politics and lifestyle of the region (Agbaje 1990; Adebanwi 2004; Oyovbaire 2001). To date there are at least twelve to fifteen national dailies published in Lagos, Southern Nigeria, while there are only four major national dailies from Northern Nigeria, and these four cannot compete with the economic strength of the ones published in Lagos. According to this journalist:

> *The way I look at it is that the northern newspapers are not even much, the* Daily trust, *leadership; So corruption is corruption and I don't think there is any particular way because corruption is a big news anywhere whether you are northern or southern newspaper, it is still corruption and it wouldn't make any difference whether somebody was caught in Lagos or your newspaper was based in Lagos or in Abuja corruption is universal.*[7]

As of May 2018, Daily Trust, Leadership, People's Daily and *Blueprint* are the main newspapers published Northern Nigeria. The journalist tried to argue that corruption is corruption, and so irrespective of the location of the newspaper, the story will make the headlines. But that is a simple view, when compared to the views expressed by the journalists in the regionalism sections. However, these views can be seen in the light of the effort of the newspapers to report cases of corruption in spite of who is involved. It can also be seen in the light of the fact that the allegations of corruption under president Olusegun Obasanjo, who comes from the south has created an understanding among Nigerians that corruption is corruption and has no ethnic or regional colouration, a view that hitherto

[7] This point is not a denial of the existence of the unevenness and regional leaning of the newspapers, but the point he seems to be illustrating is that news about corruption sells, and irrespective of who is involved, the newspapers have to report it. One of the interviewees made this point more clearly by saying that the subjective orientation of the papers is more in the opinion and editorial sections rather than in the news stories.

became prominent especially during military rule, majority of whom were from the north. Equally, the view may suggest that the newspapers may have a regional leaning, but that may not be the personal views of the journalists working in those newspapers.

Although the unevenness in the ownership of newspapers between northern and Southern Nigeria is a reality, some of the journalists tried to explain this within a historical context, a point that was highlighted earlier. According to this journalist from *Thisday:*

> *But also, the elite, those who have come in contact with the colonial masters predominate in this particular area. And so it was only natural that it will also be the place that will harbour the newspapers. So, the Nigerian newspapers were born into a struggle. That struggle was in Lagos and all the time Lagos has assumed the status of a fleet street of Nigeria so to say. And you find that a lot of the papers are situated there.*

From the perspective of this journalist, rather than look at it from regional advantage, it should be looked at from historical perspective, which has not been reversed from the inception of newspapers in Nigeria.[8]

There were attempts in the past that tried to address the imbalance, but those attempts were not always successful. According to the same journalist:

> *Then in the north we have had attempts that had failed until* Daily Trust… *came [and] from all indications it is here to stay. Then* Leadership *is also trying to make attempt and a lot of others down. That is why I said I didn't want to make a comparison because how do you compare a thousand to two? Ninety-nine percent of the media are located around Lagos-Ibadan axis.* (see Chap. 8 for a detailed analysis on the influence of location in Nigerian journalism)

The last point made by the journalist is one of the complexities explored in this research, the difficulty in comparing two things that are unequal. While the journalist above works with a southern newspaper, another journalist who made an attempt to publish in the north, but could not succeed, and two senior journalists from *Daily Trust* and *Sunday Trust,* published in the north made similar points:

[8] For details about the history of Nigerian newspapers see Chap. 3 "Historical Landscape of Nigerian Newspapers".

> *I think part of the problem in trying to make comparison is the imbalance in the media themselves. Because invariably if we are talking of newspapers that is the print media; the north has effectively two newspapers [at the time of this interview], the* Trust *and the* Leadership.[9]

> *I am sure you are aware that there are more newspapers in the south than we have in the north.*

> *You see the first problem is that most of the newspapers in Nigeria are southern newspapers, so that is the first problem. So it's difficult to do a direct comparison. Let's say for example in Lagos, we have 12–15 Dailies, that in Abuja you have two, in Kaduna you have 1, and then you have other weak ones. The overwhelming number of the newspapers is southern.*

A look at the imbalance in newspaper ownership in Nigeria is not restricted to the media only, it is a historical issue that is linked to the evolution of Nigeria, almost in every sector of the economy this imbalance can be found.

Does that imbalance always affect the way stories are reported? Not all the journalists share the view that stories are killed depending on the region the person affected comes from. According to this journalist from the south:

> *There is no distinction there, basically we write the same stories. Probably we even have the same sources. But once in a while there is always a slant to a story depending on who is involved, but that one I think is general too.*

From this perspective therefore, publishers establish friendships with a number of people and these people could be business associates, politicians or everyday friends; once the story affects this category of people, irrespective of whether they are from the north or from the south, the story might be censored.

Another perspective brought by the journalists during the interviews was that the imbalance in reporting the cases of corruption may not necessarily come from the newspapers, but could be as a result of government action that takes more punitive measures against certain government officials from a particular section of the country, and soft on somebody from another region. Now the prominence given by the government might be

[9] This part of the interview was conducted before the establishment of *Peoples Daily* and *Blueprint*.

reflected in the way the story is reported. This is the opinion of this journalist who has been an editor, and later worked in some government institutions in the previous administration (1999–2007):

> *This is an issue that even led to a presidential broadcast like at that time they said fifty million but now we are hearing that governors steal billions, you find the Igbo's complaint there, is it because of fifty million naira, there was a Presidential broadcast, the President broadcast to the nation to expose the matter. But later when he came to the issue of Tafa Balogun, a public officer, the Inspector General of Police, a Yoruba man, there was no presidential broadcast and we are talking of billions, I think Tafa Balogun was thirteen billion so you find this one because of fifty million it involves a presidential broadcast, so I will expect the Lagos papers to really celebrate that.*

This journalist was referring to two cases of corruption against two former high-ranking individuals, Adolphus Wabara, the former president of the Senate, and Tafa Balogun, the then Inspector General of Police. Adolphus Wabara was accused of taking a 50 million naira bribe to inflate the budget of certain government ministries. While Tafa Balogun was accused of diverting 13 billion naira. In the case of Wabara, the then president of Nigeria, Olusegun Obasanjo made a presidential broadcast to the nation condemning the act, this led to his resignation as senate president, but in the case of Tafa Balogun there was no presidential broadcast, even though the amount he was accused of diverting was higher than Wabara's. But he was also removed from his position and arrested by the Economic and Financial Crimes Commission.

Second Theme: Journalism and Culture

As discussed in Chap. 1, political culture is seen as the situation where political behaviour is seen in cultural context. Hallin Mancini (2004) emphasised the role of culture in journalism, because according to them, journalism cannot be practised outside the culture of the people. This book is also interested in finding out the role of culture in journalism practice. The respondents have different views on how culture plays a role in the practice of journalism. Two issues came up during the interviews about the differences in culture between the north, and south, and according to some of the journalists, those behaviours are imported into the news room. The first is that a northerner is somebody who does not disagree with those in authority, does not speak badly about his brother, and is careful not to offend. Secondly, a southerner is seen as somebody who can challenge authority, and can argue with anyone. These behaviours according to the journalists play a role in the making of news; here is an example by a woman editor from one of the newspapers published in the north:

> *I don't know whether to say it is the cultural background. I think it is always that because there are times when we report... in the north we are heavily influenced by our Islamic culture for sometimes to downplay your brother's sins. Because it is not recommended in Islam to go in town and say these are all the faults of so and so. And some people that also extend to our public office holders. So many a times our paper will lead with a story that is against a prominent northerner and before the day is over our editor or editor-in-chief will be bombarded with phone calls; he is a brother, he is this and that, how can you do this to such a person. So, we try to enlighten them o.k. we are not exactly after the person... there is nothing personal against him.*

The point made by this editor was that the concept of brotherhood in Islam, which commands people to be kind and not to cause harm to a fellow Muslim, is erroneously constructed to mean condoning evil and covering up for people whose transgression may have an impact on the society. So, people use that as a way of censoring the news indirectly. From the experiences of this editor, people from Northern Nigeria call the editor-in-chief and ask him not to publish stories, because the person is an elder who should be respected.[10] One of the respondents from the *Guardian* newspaper indicated that this attitude is the reason why newspapers could not survive in Northern Nigeria, until the coming of *Daily Trust*, which tries to move away from that tradition.

According to the same journalist, the distinction between journalists from the north and those from the south is that you don't' find this kind of behaviour in the south; they may decide not to publish the story possibly for fear of libel. According to her:

> *I think they don't really pay heed to that, may be sometimes they keep away from certain scandalous things because of the possibility of libel. But not necessarily because it is something that they feel culturally is offensive.*

[10] For a detailed account of what an elder means in the Muslim community in Northern Nigeria, see Last, Murray (2003): *Towards a political history of Muslim youth in northern Nigeria: 1750–2000* available at http://www.ascleiden.nl/Pdf/conference24042003-last.pdf downloaded 24/11/2008.

Some of the respondents have the view that, though the culture plays an important role which may sometimes have an impact on the news production, one thing that journalists find difficult to be impartial about, whether from the north, or from the south, Muslims or Christians, is if the issue of religion is involved. Some of the respondents even believe it is religion that is important and not the culture. According to this journalist who works with a southern newspaper:

> *Take religion for example, when there is religious riot rarely do you find any newspaper that has its head above water. Look at it from your own perspective, oh! They are killing our brothers the Christians, no! They have slaughtered Muslims in Agege in Lagos lets fight back and when you read some of the things that your own colleagues write, is pathetic. But if you find yourself in their shoes what will you do. So these things are still affecting us, we can't run away from it, we have to mature up to the level where we can report objectively on such issues and I don't think there is anything, if you try to publish anything that is against the established national interest in the United States they will stop you, if it means killing you, remember the Aljazeera thing, did it occur to you if when that thing was exposed that US government and the British government were planning to bomb the Aljazeera office.*

Another journalist from Northern Nigeria has expressed similar views about the role of religion as the main issue that influences the culture:

> *Well, yes, but this is probably more of a religion thing than a culture in the sense that the newspapers that come from this part of the country, although you will say that it is* Trust *of all the newspapers that are here that you will say is predominantly Muslim owned. Islam because it abhors 'kwakwa'* [11] *you will find that they are reluctant, not that they don't investigate but even the language they use they tend to be more deferral to the authorities than newspapers from the south. Even when they criticize you find their language more deferential, they don't use strong languages and to that extent yes. So it is more of a religious thing than a culture thing. But except that Islam is the predominant religion in this part of the country so it also affects the culture.*

Some of the respondents clearly stated that everybody is influenced by his cultural background. As such, what might be seen as a story worth making big headlines might not be seen in the same way in other cultures. He gave an example:

[11] Excessive curiosity or going beyond limit.

Everybody is influenced by his cultural background. You know there are some things that are seen as corruption in other lands which here due to our own cultural circumstances we don't see it as corruption or as scandals. For example, the Western media could make a big hive out of a politician having a mistress somewhere. Here in Nigeria this is not regarded as a corruption if a minister has a mistress somewhere. If his wife finds out she talks to him, it's not the kind of thing you publish and say so-so minister did something. Even the definition of corruption somehow culturally determines some things which people do here which society does not regard it here as news. So, there is no doubt we are influenced by our own cultural conditions.

The position of these journalists corresponds with the position of Bayley (1966), whose work has been discussed in Chap. 1. His position is that corruption is culturally conditioned, and what is seen as corruption in one society might be normal in another.

But another journalist has a contrary view. For him, the cultural background of journalists as northerners or southerners is melting. Because these journalists interact together, and so they develop the same culture of practice. They have common values, they sometimes do things right and sometimes do things wrongly:

So the cultural background I was talking about earlier is beginning to melt and you find that all these journalists now have common values that drive them all over the place. They take bribe, those that have integrity have integrity, those that take bribe take bribe and they mix freely.

However, some of the examples given by the journalist reveal the differences in culture which might perhaps show the differences in attitude, between people from the north and those from the south. According to this journalist from the south, such differences are beginning to manifest with the change of political power from the south to the north:

I was talking to somebody yesterday who is a journalist and he said the villa [official residence of Nigerian president] is getting better because at least we will be getting more money unlike Obasanjo who was stingy. You see it is just the impression we have that northerners are free with money than the southerners; whether it is true or not I don't know. But it is easier for you to get money from a northerner than from a southerner and that is the culture.

So, by implication, this journalist is saying that the attitude of people from the north and people from the south is so obvious that a southern president is seen as stingy and northern one as generous.[12] True to his words, people from the south see northerners as people who are stupidly generous, and you can easily make money out of them. On the other hand, people from the north also have an impression that southerners are less respectful and can be dubious. One respondent, who is a Christian from Northern Nigeria, but worked with a southern newspaper until he left to work for the BBC, made this long comparison about the cultural differences between people from the north and those from the south, and according to him, these attitudes are also imported into the newsroom.

> *You find in the northern culture even the way you interact with an elder, if you look at them straight in the eye it's considered rude in most cultures. If your elder is speaking to you, you lower your head out of respect for him. In the south it's not uncommon, it is not strange to hear a Yoruba boy for instance, his father telling a story about what he did in the office or in the army during the war and [the] kid will just say 'iro ni baba' meaning you are lying father, that is unthinkable in northern culture. You don't even think of it let alone do it but in the southern culture this thing is ok, this boy is telling his father you are lying baba. So that is the sort of thinking we grew up with and that sort of thinking we take to our newsrooms. So you find the southern newspaper reporter bringing his 'iro ni baba' into the newsroom and report it. And the northern reporter is bringing the way he puts his eyes down when he is listening to an elder that also finds its way into the newsroom inevitably because that is his makeup, that is his orientation that is his mental makeup, that is the way he approaches the world that is his world view. So that is why I talk about restraint on the part of the northern newspapers not because they condone corruption, no. But because of the culture.*

What comes out of this section is that the respondents do acknowledge the role of culture in news production, and how that makes an impact in deciding or censoring what comes out as news? It is difficult to draw a conclusion about the extent to which the views expressed by the respondents play a role in shaping news values. But the points raised by the journalists suggest that journalists are products of their own culture, and their cultural orientation may contribute in shaping their journalistic attitude.

[12] See the earlier discussion the qualities of *mutumin kirki* by Kirk-Greene.

Third Theme: Fourth Estate Role of the Media

The fourth estate role of the media has been discussed by scholars from a historical context to its application and limitations (see Albuquerque 2005; Schultz 1988); the respondents in this research have expressed different views about the fourth estate role of the press in Nigeria. According to this journalist from *Thisday* newspaper:

> *I think the Nigerian press has performed creditably. But then a whole lot of things have to be done to ensure that the watchdog role is strengthened. And that is why there has been this clamour for more access to information. The FOI bill was supposed to provide that platform for us to get access to information. But then what happened to the bill, the former president didn't sign it into law. If it had been signed into law the Nigerian journalists will have had a legal platform to be able to demand federal access to certain information. Because if you are able to establish the trail; nothing stops you from going all the way to get to the root of the matter.*

This journalist has within the context of Nigeria given a pass mark to the fourth estate and watchdog role of the Nigerian press, but with reservations. In particular he has brought out the issue of the freedom of information bill, which has become a subject of controversy in the national assembly, though former president Goodluck Jonathan has signed the FOI bill in 2011. What, however, was not made clear by the journalist is what he understood by the fourth estate role of the media and if there is consensus on the fourth estate role as he understands it (see Schultz 1988; Albuquerque 2005). The executives including the legislators do not seem to be comfortable with the FOI bill. The House of Representatives even threw the bill out during one of its deliberations.[13] Many of the journalists expressed concern that without the bill, it will be difficult for the media to play its role as the fourth estate of the realm. Some of the respondents indicated that having the freedom of information bill passed will contribute in reducing corruption in Nigeria. Though the idea of the FOI bill reducing corruption is highly debatable looking at the myriad of corruption allegations during the jonathan administration that signed the bill. Despite the constraints, the journalist feels that the press in Nigeria is trying its best. He gave the following account:

[13] For reports on throwing out the bill, see http://allafrica.com/stories/200806040567.html

I think somehow it reduces corruption. If I have facts now, I have documents I don't care, I will write about whoever I will want to write about. But if you don't have access to information it is always difficult. My next piece for tomorrow I wrote on Jonathan because I find it to be insulting really that a Vice President will make public his assets form and he will tell me that the only car in his garage is 15.8 million Naira car given to him by somebody. I asked the question 'does it mean that this man has never used his money to buy a car before'. He is a PhD holder and a lecturer and the only car you are declaring is a BMW worth 15.8 million naira given to you. And I said he must be hiding something.

The example he cited above refers to the then vice president, Goodluck Jonathan (later president of Nigeria from 2011 to 2015). It was one of the stories attracting attention during the week of this interview. And the respondent angrily stated that he will write an article in his column to condemn the attitude of the vice president, first for not declaring his assets willingly until he found himself under pressure, and secondly, for trying to play with the intelligence of the people. The point made by this journalist shows the kind of freedom the media enjoys, especially when you compare it with other countries in Africa. And that is the position of majority of the interviewees, though they feel the media could still do better in Nigeria.

To illustrate the watchdog role played by the media, some of the respondents believe the media proved to be better than the national assembly in the watchdog role. According to this senior journalist from *Daily Trust*:

You see, the way it is in Nigeria now, if any executive officer is going to abuse his office, he will be more afraid of that information falling into the hands of the media than falling into the hands of the National Assembly. It is as simple as that. If the President or a minister wants to do anything, he will be more afraid of media exposure than being called before a committee of the National Assembly and sanctioned. So also if the media blow open a case of corruption it becomes very difficult to cover up.

If you ask me, the watchdog role of the newspapers right now is more effective than the watchdog role of the national and state house of assemblies. I mean in terms of checking corruption and govt excesses.

But some of the respondents disagree. According to the journalist below, the media continued to dance to regional sentiments after the return of the country to civilian rule in 1999 for at least four years, until the allegations of corruption under Obasanjo became an issue of public discourse:

The newspapers especially the predominantly southern papers turned a blind eye to corruption and to all the bad things that Obasanjo was doing. In fact, they were focusing at that time on the National Assembly especially the National Assembly leadership which they say it was corrupt even when they came out with clear evidence.

Another senior journalist also disagrees, but from a different perspective. He feels that there are certain factors that militate against the attainment of the fourth estate role of the Nigerian press:

No, I am not satisfied at all. I am not satisfied because of these critical factors that I talked about. There are so many issues that are not covered. One is that we cover too much politics and we leave other areas of national interest. For instance, even the business and economy, you do not find people following the cash, following the money train especially the business and economy desk. We cover too much of politics in business rather than the real business. We also do not have enough correspondents these days to cover science and technology issues. And you find that editors are not actually asking correspondents to pursue those issues. They pursue issues in the National Assembly, the federal executive council.

One interesting point mentioned by the respondent above, is too much coverage of politics. This is a subject for another research. Why should the media concentrate on politics? Is it because politics is so attractive that journalists want to be part of it, or is it simply responding to the needs of the audiences who may also be interested in political news?

Fourth Theme: Investigative Journalism

Investigative journalism is a segment of the fourth estate role of the media. (See Chap. 1 for further details on investigative journalism.) The view expressed by the journalist below reveals the picture on investigative journalism in the Nigerian press.

One of the things I have not been able to get right in the Nigerian media is investigative stuff. We have not gotten that right, perhaps because of the fact that investigative journalism is a very expensive enterprise. You need to put people permanently; you need to mobilize resources in that particular area and all of that. We are in a society where people are looking for shortcuts and that also includes the media. Nobody wants to put his money in a long-term investment and investigation as far as the media is concerned is a long-term investment. And so, people will start looking for the breaking story and by so

> *doing the media has deprived the sale of perhaps the most important aspect of its responsibility which is as a check. Because if a government made a budget today and say in the next one year this is what we are going to spend, as media people we should look down the line and look at the budget and the reality on the ground. Is there a match or mismatch between what was budgeted and what is on the ground?*

In this section, the respondents described a lot of issues related to investigative journalism. These include clientelism, the understanding of the concept, its application, corruption within the media and the challenges faced by the journalist.

Clientelism and Investigative Journalism

Clientelism is a form of "social organisation in which access to social resources is controlled by patrons and delivered to clients in exchange for deference and various kinds of support" (Hallin and Papathanassopoulos 2002: 182–183). Clientelism is seen as a feature of societies where little distinction is made between public good and personal interest. It is a system whereby rules and procedures are less important than personal connection (Roudakova 2008: 42), and media organisations will only succeed if clientelism is weakened and discouraged (Lee et al. 2007: 39).

While the aim of investigative journalism is to be impartial and report facts as they are for the good of the public, exposure to clientelism could be an obstacle in achieving that aim. Accounts from the respondents interviewed have shown that clientelism is one of the features of journalism practice in Nigeria. According to this journalist:

> Daily Trust *was punished several times by Nasiru El- Rufa'i. He was giving advert but not to* Daily Trust *because he believes he was fighting* Daily Trust, *he believes* Daily Trust *was fighting him…Nasiru El-Rufa'i for example felt as a Northerner, the* Daily Trust *has an obligation to support him.*

Nasiru El-Rufa' was the minister of the federal capital territory, Abuja, and the governor of Kaduna state since 2015; the issue under discussion took place when he was a minister, and from the perspective of this journalist the relationship between El-Rufa'i and the *Daily Trust* newspaper should be determined by regional loyalty rather than professionalism. If *Daily Trust* had bowed to the pressure, many stories emanating from the federal capital territory might be compromised. Even with that, the paper was punished for refusing an advertisement. That is why many journalists that develop close relationships with politicians and media organisations "end up serving intra-elite communication needs rather than looking for the public interest or the common good" (Roudakova 2008: 43).

One of the ways in which clientelism undermines investigative reporting is that politicians and public office holders have rivalry among themselves, and they can use the personal relationship they have with journalists in order to bring down their opponents, something that can easily be camouflaged as investigative journalism. Such behaviour was confirmed by this senior journalist from the *Guardian* newspaper:

> *That is because always there are adversarial sources of information, you have your enemies all out there, and they will release all that concerns you to me if they lay their hands on it.*

As discussed earlier by (Roudakova 2008), concerning the rapport established by politicians with journalists, one of the respondents working with *Thisday* newspaper confirmed that some politicians think that when they fall into trouble their journalist friends will help them to get out of it:

> *As long as they can perpetrate corruption and they are not exposed, they are happy. That is why some of them go out of their way to befriend journalists. Once they get their way to befriend the journalists, their belief is that when they run into trouble they will get protection from the journalists. That is the base for the friendship between politicians and journalists.*

Understanding of Investigative Journalism

From the responses gathered, Nigerian journalists have different understandings of investigative journalism. Some of the journalists see it as a way of digging out the truth as pointed out by this journalist:

> *Investigative journalism by my understanding is where the media focuses on exposing corruption in public places. Not just exposing corruption but trying to dig out the truth.*

Other journalists have a wider conception of investigative journalism, looking at it from the way the data is compiled about the subject of investigation and producing an accurate description of the situation as explained by this journalist from the *Nation* newspaper.

> *Investigative journalism is dependent on different things. People will say when you do a thorough job; you get your documents, get your sources right from the appropriate quarters before you go ahead and publish it…If you want to do it you must have funding.*

The above description shows that the journalist does understand that investigative journalism is beyond routine journalism where the journalist relies on news releases or press conferences, but it means going an extra mile to solicit for information and compare the facts. According to these two editors:

> *Usually that means going after exclusive stories, exposing something that somebody is trying to hide.*

> *Well I guess it is when you come across a topic which is of public interest and you pursue it to the very end whatever the troubles ahead.*

From the conception of these two editors, the watchdog role of the media is at play. Investigative journalism is involved where public office holders try to hide something from the public, whether it is the declaration of their asset, inflating contracts or using their office for self-enrichment. It also means going after any story that might be of interest to the public. Other journalists see it from a more journalistic perspective, that is making a thorough investigation on stories that are already making headlines, so that the public will be more informed as described by this young journalist.

> *It is just a way of going an extra mile into finding more facts, figures or even more information about an event or an issue that is making the news.*

From the various responses derived from the respondents, investigative journalism can be defined as the compilation of information from the effort of the journalist to find stories that may otherwise remain hidden and provide an accurate and sound description of the issues in order to educate the members of the public.

Application of Investigative Journalism

But the question to be asked is do Nigerian journalists believe that they practise investigative journalism? The responses vary. According to this journalist from the *Guardian* newspaper:

> *Well investigative report is not something that you will do within a week or within 1 or 2 or 3 days. You spend a lot of money, a lot of time; you need a lot of documents a lot of interviews of all the characters that are involved. But we don't have time to do that now – because we don't have the resources to do so.*

From this perspective, it can be understood that investigative journalism takes time and resources, both of which are difficult to manage. Even those who claim to practise investigative journalism are careful in their assertions as exemplified by this journalist from *Sunday Trust*:

> *I will say that since we started our* Sunday Trust *paper we have done quite a bit of investigative stories which have gotten a lot of response in the government circle. Since it is because of the public interest we go out of our way to investigate things that have to do with the government and its policies.*

One of the consequences of investigative journalism is that sometimes it results in resignation from office (as in the Watergate scandal), litigation or a punitive measure taken against the erring individual. According to this journalist:

> *You know Nigerians don't resign anyway, even full plane crashes under one minister and nobody told him to go and he was not willing to go.*

The statement above will bring forward different questions that require some explanation. Is it because investigative journalism in its ideal form has not yet taken root in Nigeria? Is it because of the media elite integration, whereby the journalists are compromised into a relationship that is simply defined by clientelism? Or is it because those involved have little concern over public interest? The answer may not be a categorical yes or no, but as identified by many of the respondents it could be as a result of a combination of these factors and the nature of Nigerian society itself, where it is easy for the mighty and the powerful to get away with apparent wrongdoings.

But other journalists see investigative journalism not just from the perspective of public office holders, but through undercover reporting that exposes maltreatment of workers as suggested by this respondent:

> *But in the Sun we do. That is one of our greatest strength because we have in the* Saturday *Sun investigative series. Our reporter Emmanuel has won three consecutive times investigative reporter of the year. Wole Soyinka prize of investigative reporter. He was once posed as a worker in a factory were Indians were using Nigerians, I mean maltreating Nigerians.*

From the responses above, Nigerian journalists do understand that investigative journalism is different from day-to-day reporting of events and they do understand that investigative journalism can only be practised when there is support for it, both from the media organisation and the society at large. It is important to point out that although the journalists do understand investigative journalism, it is not a shared understanding; there are differences in their conception. One of the respondents confirmed that investigative journalism is not something we do here. Others suggest that it is done but the effort is limited. What this suggests is that although the journalists may theoretically understand what investigative journalism means, and some of the journalists may want to pursue that line in their career, the political, economic and environmental factors needed to make it thrive may not be there. The frequent reference by the journalists on the lack of passage of the freedom of information bill is a pointer to that. Beyond the passage of the freedom of information bill, the fact that those in authority hardly take responsibility for their actions unless in certain isolated cases, can undermine the effort of the journalists to practise investigative journalism.

Obstacles

No doubt there are challenges; these challenges could be physical in which the individual journalist is harmed as exemplified by this respondent:

> *Do you know what happened to my face, I believe so much in investigative journalism and somebody thought I was being too irresponsible and wanted to stop me – That was about fifteen years ago. I still carry the scars today, Remember Dele Giwa, his own case he died, mine I am alive to show all my colleagues, if you go too far your handsome face will turn this way.*

The above respondent was a senior journalist, and half of his face was burnt, because he tried to investigate the wrongdoing of a senior government official from his state. He was working for a private newspaper, yet an attempt was made to destroy his life.

For the government-owned media, it is even more difficult, because journalists cannot even publish stories against the government, otherwise they will either be suspended, frustrated or be forced to resign. According to this editor who was suspended for publishing a story against the federal government while working for a government-owned newspaper:

> *As a general rule the* New Nigerian *does not dig up stories by fact of government ownership just like NTA does not do in exposing of anything.*

The *New Nigerian* was one of the newspapers owned by the federal government, while NTA, the *Nigeria Television Authority* is the main television station owned by the federal government. It is common knowledge that these two media organisations have been reduced to government mouthpieces without room for sound and critical journalism, even though they are meant to serve the interest of the public.

Another challenge identified by the respondents is "poor capitalisation". Lack of strong capital base according to the respondents, poor capitalisation seriously undermines the effectiveness of journalism in Nigeria. See Yusha'u (2018) for detailed study on poor capitalisation of the media in Nigeria. According to this journalist, who is a bureau chief of one of the leading newspapers in Nigeria:

> *So we do not have too many journals in Nigeria and organs of mass communication and even electronic media that can begin an investigation that cannot be interfered with by big business bureaux. It is because of this poor capitalisation.*

This, according to the respondents, provides senior politicians and business owners to invest in the media organisations, but the consequence is that what goes against their interest will not be reported. In fact, during the interviews there was a statement mentioned by almost all the respondents, "He who pays the piper, dictates the tune"; the journalists were unanimous on this.

Corruption within the media itself is another challenge. Journalists are seen as beggars because they either use their positions to make money, or even extort public figures as testified by this political correspondent:

A whole lot of good stories would have been investigated and Nigerians would have been better for it... At the end of the day they do not get investigated because people that are involved succeeded in getting the journalists to get off the investigation.

According to some respondents, the media organisations themselves are not interested in investigative reporting due financial constraints and other factors as confirmed by this reporter:

Not enough because of constrains like financial constraints. Most newspapers don't finance it anymore.

Corruption Within the Media

Many of the respondents agreed that reports about corruption are receiving more attention now than before. But they also blame the media for being part of the problem, because of the corruption within the media itself. As indicated by this journalist:

The media is corrupt not could be corrupt. Why has nobody said anything about Odili?[14] *Come on, let us ask ourselves questions, the governors we have are not the most corrupt the ones that have been tried are not the most corrupt. Somebody is paying so that these things do not come out in the open.*

So beyond regional and ethnic divisions in Nigeria, people can also plant stories or bribe the journalists to ignore certain stories. This will make the reporting of corruption much more complex by allowing the media to be a platform for political opponents to settle scores and increasing corruption by making political office holders to take money from the treasury in order to satisfy journalists who use the privilege of their position to either promote or blackmail people. This journalist from a leading newspaper in the south added this point:

Bitter truth. We are all corrupt, whether those we report, whether those of us doing the reporting. You think Atiku got the amount of exposure he got in the media because they love Atiku; it is not that of love.[15] *He was financing it.*

[14] Peter Odili is the former governor of Rivers State, one of the oil-rich states in Nigeria.

[15] Atiku Abubakar was former vice president (1999–2007); he was together with President Olusegun Obasanjo accused of diverting money from the Petroleum Technology Development Fund (PTDF) by a senate committee.

The two examples given on Odili and Atiku could mean that the section of the media that is corrupt as alleged from the statements above do not care where a person comes from as long as he can finance his stories or bribe the journalist to remain calm in his or her activities. Atiku is from the north, and Odili from the south-south part of Nigeria; none of them is from the south-west which is the media capital of Nigeria.

However, according to another journalist, there is a reason that forces some journalists and media organisations to collaborate with politicians in blackmailing or hiding the wrongdoing of others:

> *Poor capitalisation does not allow editorial independence. Most of the organs either in the south or in the north are owned by either business men who have interest in politics, or are owned by political leaders, or some political leaders have invested because of poor capitalisation, some of these organs depend on daily basis on handouts from political leaders who are using public funds, that is why so many newspaper stories are sponsored, columns, articles, some of them are full of impurities.*

The factor mentioned by the journalist above shows some of the difficulties faced by journalists who are genuinely interested in promoting the profession. And the result of that will be the example given by this journalist:

> *If you don't have money to pay your staff, you don't have money to buy the latest software, you don't have money to buy newsprint, it means that you will depend on people who are either in business or in politics to run operations, so how independent can you be? That's part of the problem, corruption in the mass media make journalists to lose credibility in the eyes of members of the public. Some of the newspapers are owned by former governors, how independent can you be when some of those governors are being haunted by EFCC.*

The elite have seen the potential of the media in protecting their interest. That, therefore, might explain the reason why they invest in the media. But the implication of that is more politicisation of journalism and forcing journalists to be tools that can be manipulated by those who have the capital to establish the media organisations. However, this journalist suggests that such newspapers established with money from suspicious sources have no basis to be in the market:

I just find it interesting that the media never beams the searchlight on itself. Very rare do they beam the search light on themselves. A governor is being tried in Nigeria today for money laundering, thieving and stealing. The former governor of Abia state, Orji Kalu and this man owns a newspaper, a tabloid, its account were recently frozen by the EFCC and so they were having difficulties running and so they began to link that to the political difficulties of their owner. But for me I saw it a little bit beyond that, if a newspaper is running on the basis of funds acquired fraudulently, what basis does it have to be a newspaper.

Poor Capitalisation

One of the issues of concern to many of the respondents is poor capitalisation, which they see as one of the problems encountered by the press. Poor capitalisation here refers to the absence of a strong capital base that would allow the newspaper to be financially independent. The journalists see poor capitalisation as one of the issues affecting the credibility of the profession, because without strong capital, there will be challenges which the media will find difficult to overcome. One of the reasons for the poor capitalisation is in the nature of ownership, in which politicians and businessmen invest in the newspaper industry without much concern for the welfare and credibility of journalism. According to this journalist from the *Guardian* newspaper:

The building block of credibility in the media is trust. If people no longer trust what you put there because they believed that some political leaders in one opposition party or another are sponsoring what you are broadcasting, it is a problem.

The problem of poor capitalisation has made it difficult to carry out such tasks as investigative and in-depth reporting, which is required in order to keep the public fully informed on the affairs happening around them. This senior journalist elaborates on how poor capitalisation affects journalism practice:

We are constrained because of poor capitalization. Investigation either in the media or in security services consumes a lot of money. But the publishers and the editors do not pay attention to special desks that can do investigation. If you don't have the money if you want to investigate corruption or corrupt practices, if you yourself cannot pay your way to where you are going to investigate; it means that the people you are going to investigate can influence you, they can pay you. They said you haven't paid your house rent of 200,000 Naira and they give you 1 million naira. So poor capitalization is the trouble with the Nigerian mass media.

The journalist above is citing an example of how the absence of strong capital base affects even the payment of salaries. In this case if the rent of the journalist is 2,000,000 Naira[16] per annum in Abuja, the capital, for instance, and his annual income is just a little above his rent, or even much lower than that in many cases, how will he avoid the influence of the people who would like to take advantage of his situation to influence the stories he writes? This could perhaps suggest the reason why so much attention is given to the coverage of politics, because of the favours that might come with it as suggested by the journalist below:

There are so many issues that are not covered. One is that we cover too much of politics and we leave other areas of national interest. For instance even the business and economy, you do not find people following the cash, following the money train especially the business and economy desk. We cover too much of politics in business rather than the real business.

As identified by the journalist above, there is much to cover, yet the coverage of politics is receiving more attention. It is not bad to cover politics; what may be bad is using the coverage of politics for personal gain. From the accounts of the respondents, if the condition of the journalist is not improved, political sources, especially those in position of authority will look down on the journalist. According to the journalist below, a media organisation should be strong enough to invite a politician or any other person no matter how highly placed. But when the journalist looks hungry and in shambles he will hardly get the respect he deserves, let alone make a serious impression on his source:

By the time I pay my way to talk to a minister or a public office he may know that it is a very serious matter and he cannot influence me... And he cannot even think about it because he knows I am independent. The way I dress, the way I talk and even the quality of my hotel room, where I stay will dictate to him that this one is a serious matter. But when they know where you are coming

[16]This figure has more than doubled after the interview and also due to the economic recession following the 2015 election.

> *from, they look at the quality of your tie and shoes they know that you need better tie and shoes and they begin to talk about that and that is the end of the story.*

Therefore, poor capitalisation can retard the input a newspaper can make in the political communication process of a country, especially a developing one like Nigeria, which requires a vibrant press that can assess the political situation and provide honest and impartial account of issues.

Bad Working Conditions and Inadequate Professional Training

Among the issues identified by the respondents, which are related to the points raised earlier, is the nature of the working conditions of the journalists. The respondents suggested what they think can be done to improve the quality of journalism in Nigeria; the journalist below provides an example.

> *Better education, better equipments, faster communication and greater ethical reorientation. But the single most important thing that will improve Nigerian journalism as far as I can see is having the FOI act more than anything. Because having the FOI will automatically eliminate rumour mongering and inaccurate reporting.*

From the account above, five important points have been raised. These are; better education, better equipments, faster communication, ethical reorientation and the FOI (freedom of information) bill. Education is important; it provides the basic background and shapes the thinking of the journalist. Equipment makes the work easy, faster communication will increase efficiency, ethical reorientation will teach the journalist the values of the profession and the trust he should seek to establish and defend. But if the working conditions are not good, those with the relevant education will move to other sectors of the economy, and those who agree to join the profession may do so as a gateway for other opportunities, and this can create a serious problem in terms of reporting and the credibility of the newspaper and the journalist himself. But the FOI bill may not necessarily solve the problem of inaccurate reporting, and with the emergence of fake news, which is being strengthened by social media, more training is required to ensure accurate reporting. A senior editor from the *Daily Trust* believes that is it is poor pay that creates corruption among journalists:

> *Corruption in the media is due to poor pay and also in some cases irregular pay and in fact in some newspaper houses no pay at all. There are some small newspapers that don't have a pay roll and they say that the reporter's ID card is his pay roll meaning they are encouraging him to go out and seek brown envelope.*

Though some journalists might engage in corruption because of poor pay, some may do so simply because of greed, as explained further by the same journalist:

> *But of course, as a human being I know that is not enough because there is the greed factor and you know when somebody is greedy if you give him a million he may want two million, if you give 2 million I want 3 million. So that one I don't know as long as there is overall corruption in the community the newspapers are bound to suffer somehow.*

Another factor that can create problem in terms of what gets reported is the interest of the publisher. Many of the respondents confirmed that politicians and businessmen establish newspapers in order to get access to the government. Therefore, these publishers will make sure that what gets reported does not go against their interest. That is the point made by a journalist from *Thisday* newspaper.

> *The man who owns the business like I was taught in the communication school is the man who decides. Your interest cannot be higher than that of the man who owns it…you know the world over, that the man who owns the newspaper would determine his editorial direction. He can give you a free direction, not even that. Advertising and advertisers would naturally influence it. They are the ones who sustain your paper. That is one powerful force stronger than the owner of the paper.*

The comment above raises some questions regarding the independence of the press, because the journalist as a gatekeeper may be constrained by other factors like the interest of the publisher and the power of advertisers, who may even be more powerful the publisher himself. (For details on the power of advertising in influencing the news, see Herman and Chomsky 2002).

One of the respondents asked rhetorically, how do journalists survive despite the above challenges? Some of them are living a lifestyle which is beyond their earning. According to this journalist, somebody might be paying for it.

The question to now ask yourself is how do the journalists survive? How do they manage to drive the cars they are driving? That is the question. Somebody is putting the bills somewhere. A publisher once told his staff, what do you think I gave you that identity card for?

The reference to the identity card is about one of the publishers who, according to the respondents, does not pay salaries on time; he simply tells the journalists that their identity card is enough to make them earn a living.

However, one of the respondents, a former managing director of a newspaper publishing company, and at the moment a leading columnist in the country offered some suggestions which he thinks can help in addressing some problems affecting the newspaper industry.

The solution invariably we must be up and doing, we must eschew tribalism and ethnicity. We must eschew religious bias. Of course, we all have our biases but the most important thing is when you come to do your reporting, try as much as possible to put it aside. It is not easy, but you must try. Trying is not too difficult, achieving the end of it, balance; objective, fair reporting is difficult. But at least making the attempt is not that difficult. All it involves is when any issue comes up, try and get all the parties involved.

The points raised by the above respondents showed the need for training apart from other considerations that must be made available if journalists are to practice in an ideal environment, where they will uphold the principles of honesty and impartiality.

Solution

The respondents have offered different views on what they think might serve as a solution to the challenges faced by the Nigerian media. According to this journalist from the *Nation* newspaper:

This solution is to have more resources, better training for our staff and the lowering of some of the obstacles in the official, private and cultural circles. You know we have to bring these things down so that we can do our job easily. We need a little more courage from journalists and reporters too; and a little belief in the sense of justice.

This view further suggests some of the issues discussed earlier in the section on obstacles and poor capitalisation. Resources are very important if the media is to become independent in Nigeria. Another journalist looks at the solution from the challenges of information technology and support from other institutions that will complete media effort. According to him:

> *They can be improved. I hope with the Nigeria's recent opening to international system and which means the standard will be raised higher because you have challenges coming in as these borders open up and so you are challenged by a new level of practice to want to step up your game. So, there is also the internet which has brought this big boom and people watch what others are doing and so they are challenged to try to improve the system so that is helping. But we can also help with law, the legislation, and the freedom of information bill; if it ever gets to be passed in this country it will improve journalism practice in Nigeria in no small measure.*

Another important issue raised by the respondents which they suggest will help in improving journalism practice is training. During the interviews, the respondents stated that some journalists simply join the profession as a means of earning a livelihood, and some proprietors do not care to provide them which sufficient training before going into the field. So according to this senior journalist from the *Sun* newspaper, the starting point is:

> *Pay well, give them good training and then motivate them because they are performing a role that is constitutionally recognized. It is very tough; it is like an anti-corruption crusader who has no money. He will be tempted.*

Good salaries and training will help journalists to practice professionally, but also to be equipped intellectually. The same journalist elaborated on the consequences of lack of payment and training:

> *I am sure you could ask some of them how many books they have read in the last one month, you can't perform your educating role when you yourself you are not equipped. There are no trainings; people don't go for refresher courses. It is not about poor pay alone, if you do not read how then do you write, how do you inform others?*

Apart from training, other journalists emphasised the need for investment. This may not be unconnected with the way some proprietors make money from newspaper publishing but channel the resources elsewhere rather than investing more in the newspaper industry. This point was emphasised by an editor from *Thisday* newspaper:

> *Some of us have been privileged to attend some BBC programs and fellowship. But a whole lot of people have not got that benefit. More investment in the media so that we look at a long time gestation, investigative stuff so that we better hold our leaders accountable.*

But training and investment may not be the only solution to the challenges faced by Nigerian journalists. There are other issues related to the culture, regional and political interests, and the journalist below who runs a column with *Daily Trust* emphasises that angle:

The solution invariably we must be up and doing, we must eschew tribalism and ethnicity. We must eschew religious bias. Of course, we all have our biases but the most important thing is when you come to do your reporting, try as much as possible to put it aside. It is not easy, but you must try. Trying is not too difficult, achieving the end of it, balance; objective, fair reporting is difficult. But at least making the attempt is not that difficult. All it involves is when any issue comes up, try and get all the parties involved.

Ensuring objectivity, fairness and balancing may be important, but the policies from government that will allow journalism to prosper are equally important in ensuring that journalists do practise in the best way they can. According to a senior journalist with the *Guardian* newspaper:

> *Definitely public policies that will favour this media practice. Beginning from these consumables, regulatory authorities to be in place. May be consolidation, because I don't mind to tolerate a situation, as a journalist I am ashamed of my colleagues are not paid for one year or six months. And I don't think that they will be proper journalists.*

The same journalist also recommends that journalists should practise with passion and work hard to ensure that they restore the dignity of the profession as he explained in the following words:

> *My own recommendation is that we should begin to restore value to the practice of journalism. We should reinvent it because I still believe like people including this [former] CNN man who has this interview every day, Larry King, he said that journalism is the best profession in the world and I still believe in it.*

Conclusion

This chapter has analysed the interviews conducted with Nigerian journalists. The discussions were framed under four different themes. Corruption/ scandal, journalism and culture, fourth estate role of the media and investigative journalism. In each theme, different forms of understanding were identified, and relevant quotations from the interviews were used as examples to explain the understanding of the journalists. The analysis has shown the complexity of the media in Nigeria. The respondents provided different views that sometimes converge, and sometimes disagree with each other. But what is clear is that the press in Nigeria is alive and journalists have realised this, but there are challenges that must be addressed in order to strengthen the media and the journalists in their political communication role.

It is noteworthy that the conceptions of the journalists under the first theme of the interviews in which some of the journalists have a consensus that there is no difference in the coverage of corruption between north and south, but counteracted by the journalists who expressed the biases of the Nigerian press in terms of regionalism only strengthens the need for an intranational comparative research which this research has pursued. Some of the issues raised by the respondents in terms of the unevenness in newspaper ownership, and the cultural differences between journalists from different parts of Nigeria suggest the diversity of the country and the need for a research that will investigate the nature of Nigerian media system.

As the data revealed, the journalists truly see their work as that of the fourth estate role of the media, but they acknowledge the constraints that militate against such an objective. Some of these factors could be internal like poor training, corruption within the media and others are external like political clientelism and lack of support from other institutions that can help in strengthening the fourth estate role, like the judiciary and the legislator.

As discussed already in Chap. 1, among the ways of uncovering corruption scandals is through investigative journalism. The issues raised by the journalists suggest that investigative journalism is not practised in Nigeria as it is understood theoretically. This is due to factors that equally challenged the fourth estate role of the media. The relevance of this is that the findings of this book are suggesting that the prominence given to news about corruption scandals is not because of the efforts of the journalists, but it is a reflection of the tide of activities related to the works of the Economic and Financial Crimes Commission and the Independent and Corrupt Practices Commission that provided news that was attractive and helped sell the newspapers. But the interest shown by the press in reporting these cases suggests the kind of freedom enjoyed by the press in Nigeria despite the challenges it faces and is consistent with the nature of the Nigerian press before and after independence when it comes to issues of national importance, as discussed already in Chap. 3, on the Nigerian newspaper landscape. The interviews have also identified some of the challenges faced by the Nigerian press, which includes corruption within the media, poor capitalisation, bad working conditions, poor remunerations and clientelism.

The views expressed in this chapter by the journalists on the nature of journalism practice in Nigeria further suggests that it is difficult to have a single model of journalism that can be applied in every society. As such, the works of Hallin and Mancini on *Comparing Media Systems* (2004), where the framework of this book was adopted and modified to suit the Nigerian newspaper landscape, remains an important contribution.

However, as with other works that seek to explore the nature of journalism practice, their work, although useful in suggesting a framework for comparative research, remains inadequate in creating a picture of journalism practice that can be applied globally. To do that, the work of Hallin and Mancini needs to be expanded to other continents beyond Europe and North America, which they have attempted in their book *Comparing Media Systems: Beyond the Western World* (2012). Even that is not enough, especially from African perspective, where South Africa was the only country that featured from Sub-Saharan Africa. In Chap. 8, this book will focus on strengthening the issues raised by the respondents in this chapter. Regional Parallelism as opposed to political parallelism as a framework for comparative research in Africa will be discussed in detail.

References

Adamu, A. U. (2007). *Transglobal Media Flows and African Popular Culture: Revolution and Reaction in Muslim Hausa Popular Culture*. Kano: Gidan Dabino Publishers.

Adebanwi, W. (2004). Hegemony and Spatial Politics: The Press and the Struggle for Lagos in Colonial Nigeria. *Africa Development, XXIX*(4), 75–91.

Agbaje, A. (1990). Freedom of the Press and Party Politics in Nigeria: Precepts, Retrospect and Prospects. *African Affairs, 89*(355), 205–226.

Bayley, D. H. (1966). The Effects of Corruption in a Developing Nation. *The Western Political Quarterly, 19*(4), 719–732.

BBC News. (2007). *Nigerian Ex-governors on the Run*. Available at http://news.bbc.co.uk/1/hi/world/africa/6702443.stm. Downloaded 19 June 2008.

de Albuquerque, A. (2005). Another 'Fourth Branch': Press and Political Culture in Brazil. *Journalism, 6*(4), 486–504.

Hallin, D. C., & Mancini, P. (2004). *Comparing Media Systems: Three Models of Media and Politics*. Cambridge: Cambridge University Press.

Hallin, D., & Papathanassopoulos, S. (2002). Political Clientelism and Media: Southern Europe and Latin America in Comparative Perspective. *Media, Culture & Society, 24*, 175–195.

Haruna, M. (2008). *June 12, Me and Dare's Diatribe (II)*. Available at http://www.dailytrust.com/index.php?option=com_content&task=view&id=14975&Itemid=71. Downloaded 23 July 2008.

Herman, E. S., & Chomsky, N. (2002). *Manufacturing Consent. The Political Economy of the Mass Media*. New York: Pantheon.

Last, M. (2003). Towards a Political History of Muslin Youth in Northern Nigeria: 1750–2000. Available at http://www.ascleiden.nl/Pdf/conference24042003-last.pdf. Downloaded 24 Nov 2008.

Lee, C.-C., et al. (2007). Party-Market Corporatism, Clientelism and Media in Shanghai. *Press/Politics, 13*(3), 21–42.

Okome, O. (2007). Nollywood: Audience, Spectatorship and the Sites of Consumption. *Postcolonial Text, 3*(2), 1–21.

Olayinka, A. (2008). *EFCC: Before We All Fall Victim*. Available at http://www.tribune.com.ng/22102008/opinion.html. Downloaded 17 Nov 2008.

Oyovbaire, S. (2001). The Media and Democratic Process in Nigeria (1) available at http://www.waado.org/nigerdelta/Essays/Oyovbaire.html downloaded 15/08/06

Roudakova, N. (2008). Media Political Clientelism: Lessons from Anthropology. *Media, Culture & Society, 30*, 41–59.

Schultz, J. (1988). *Reviving the Fourth Estate: Democracy, Accountability & the Media*. Cambridge/New York: Cambridge University Press.

Yusha'u, M. J. (2018). Poor Capitalization and Corruption Within the Nigerian Press. In H. Mabweazara (Ed.), *Newsmaking Cultures in Africa* (pp. 185–205). London: Palgrave Macmillan.

CHAPTER 8

Regional Parallelism

Introduction

In Chap. 7, we have seen the diversity of opinion expressed by Nigerian journalists on a range of issues related to journalism practice. Key takeaways from the chapter suggest that there is deep regional divide in the perception of journalists on how journalism is practiced in the country. We have seen how newspapers like the *Punch* and *Daily Trust* (Chap. 6) use different approaches in their selection of language when reporting corruption scandals, with the region of the alleged culprit directly influencing the selection of language. The chapter also highlighted how the media itself is not the saint it might pretend to be, because it is also awash with allegations of corruption through brown envelope journalism.

The outcome of the interviews provides credence to the proposition in Chap. 1 on the need to modify the political parallelism framework suggested by Hallin and Mancini (2004) as discussed in Chap. 1. It also highlights the need for serious research on journalism cultures beyond European and North American borders.

In this chapter, an analysis of the issues raised by the respondents are presented in order to identify various meanings that could be ascribed to the issues raised by the respondents. Following the introduction, the chapter analyses the themes that emerged from the journalists' conceptions as categorised in the previous chapter. This includes regionalism, in which different classifications were provided to explain some of the factors that influence the regional biases of the media or what this research refers

M. J. Yusha'u, *Regional Parallelism and Corruption Scandals in Nigeria*, https://doi.org/10.1007/978-3-319-96220-7_8

to as regional parallelism. The chapter will also discuss such issues as journalism culture, in which the differences in culture between northern and southern journalists, affects their work. Other conceptions that emerged during the interviews such as clientelism, lack of professionalism and bad working conditions are elaborated upon. Additional analyses of the solutions suggested by the respondents are also discussed. This chapter contributes towards understanding the complexities involved in the practice of journalism, such that the reporting of corruption scandals can be seen within a context that is shaped by the specificities of Nigerian media landscape.

Regional Parallelism

Following the work of Hallin and Mancini (2004) who suggested "political parallelism" as a framework that can be used in understanding the media systems of different countries, and the modification of that framework into regional parallelism as suggested in Chap. 1. The findings suggest that what obtains in Nigeria could be termed "regional parallelism".

Here it will be pertinent to elaborate on the meaning of regional parallelism. Regional parallelism within the context of this book refers to the influence of regional and ethnic considerations in the practice of journalism. It is rooted in the historical realities of a given country. It is important to note that regional parallelism can be linked to the concept of clientelism discussed by Hallin and Papathanassopoulos (2002) and Hallin and Mancini (2004) whereby personal connection and respect for procedure are less important compared to personal loyalty and connection.

Regional parallelism is evident because the views of the respondents have shown both elements of political parallelism and clientelism, but also because Nigeria's historical and political development was regionally developed since the amalgamation of the country in 1914 by the British colonialists. As such, it would be difficult to divorce the regional element from the historical realities of the country, despite the transformations that took place in later years. Even the power sharing arrangement in the country at the moment reflects the regional divide. The selection of candidates for public office especially at the federal level reflects this regional divide otherwise the media itself would start crying for marginalisation of the section of the country that is perceived to be the looser in the power sharing arrangement. If the president is from north, the vice president would come from the south. At present, Muhammad Buhari, the president of

Nigeria, is a Muslim from Northern Nigeria. His deputy, Yemi Osinbanjo, is a Christian from south. From 1999 to 2007, Olusegun Obasanjo, a Yoruba Christian from the south was the president of Nigeria, his deputy Atiku Abubakar was a Muslim from the north. The distribution of other political offices such as the president of the Senate, speaker of the House of Representatives, the chief justice of the Federation, even the appointment of military service chief reflects this regional divide. Any section of the country that feels under-represented would claim to be marginalised. These claims of marginalisation find a natural space on the pages of Nigerian newspapers. The views expressed by the journalists in the previous chapter is a pointer to this fact.

From the data collected in this research, the following characteristics can be associated with regional parallelism: (1) it is determined by location, (2) it is supported by the elites, (3) it is promoted by political and business interests, (4) it is made obvious by the economic imbalance in media ownership, (5) it is surrounded by the complexities that characterised the society, and (6) it is flexible. Each of these factors can be identified from the views expressed by the respondents during the interviews.

Location

Starting with location as a factor in Nigerian journalism, this became a factor because of the advantages of history, Western education, political and economic power and the emergence of middle class. In terms of history, the south-western part of Nigeria, and Lagos in particular, was the gateway to Nigeria; that was how the missionaries who established the first newspaper in Abeokuta in 1859 gained access to the country. The region, therefore, had the advantage of having the first newspaper, the first trained editors and the first audience to read the newspapers. Although the northern part of the country had the earlier advantage of literacy because of Arabic and Islamic education, but the region was left behind in terms of Western education that later became the legacy of British colonialism and the leading means of communication in the Nigerian media to date.

The first major institutions of learning in contemporary Nigeria were also established in the south-western part of the country, including the first university in Nigeria that helped in producing the early set of intellectuals whose moral and professional support is needed for the survival of newspapers. The region was also the economic and political power-house of Nigeria; the federal government was also located in Lagos. Following a series of reforms after 1999, if the GDP of Lagos alone is taken in isolation from the rest of Nigeria, it would be the seventh largest economy in Africa after Nigeria, South Africa, Egypt, Algeria, Angola and Morocco. The economy of Lagos is even bigger than those of Kenya and Côte d'Ivoire, both of them major regional economies in East Africa and West Africa respectively (Quarts Africa 2016).

Apart from the influence of literacy, Western education and commercial activities in Southwestern Nigeria, another part of Southern Nigeria, Calabar, had played a prominent role in establishing the early Western schools in Nigeria and printing press in Africa. This has been documented in the work of Behrendt, Latham and Northrup (2010) in their work on the Diary of Antera Duke. Historical evidence has shown that by 1872 there were at least three running schools in Calabar (Latham 1973: 108–110).

Hope Waddell Institution has a printing press as far back as 1903. Hope Waddell has also produced some of the early journalists in the history of Nigeria, such as Dr. Nnamdi Azikwe and Dr. Patrick Okon. In a 2014 interview with *Daily Trust* newspaper, the principal of Hope Waddell recounted how the school printing press aided the publishing of several newspapers in Nigeria. What is even more interesting was that the school in those early years of colonial rule had its own magazine, the *Gateway Magazine*, which is still being published by Pressby Press, the current name of the printing press (Ujorha 2014).

There are lots of lessons to be learned from the role of Hope Waddell School, because some of its alumni, like Dr. Nnamdi Azikwe, became leading newspaper editors and used it to fight for Nigerian independence. To date, the influence of location remains a major factor in Nigerian journalism, because as it was in the 1900s, newspaper ownership and editorial control is largely managed by proprietors from south-western and south-south or the Niger Delta part of Nigeria. The most influential newspapers to date, such as the Nigerian *Guardian*, the *Punch*, *Tribune*, *Thisday*, *Vanguard* and the *Nation*, are either owned or controlled by people from the south-west or Niger-Delta regions.

The northern part of Nigeria was left behind for several reasons. Western education, which is the main medium for publishing newspapers, came to the region much later. The colonial policy of indirect rule also discouraged the promotion of Western education in Northern Nigeria because of the fear of the colonial government that combining Western and Islamic education among the population could make governance difficult for the British. A third factor was the resistance of the people to embrace Western education because of its connection with missionaries (Sanusi II 2017).

These factors contributed greatly in establishing a middle class whose support is needed in sustaining newspaper publications, through readership, contribution of comments and analysis and other forms of support. While the factors mentioned above remained true in the country, it will be interesting to see the changes that will occur over time because of the relocation of the federal capital to Abuja. Still, Lagos remains the commercial capital of Nigeria. But the economy is still largely under government control. Some newspapers, like *Daily Trust, People's Daily* and *Leadership*,[1] have established their headquarters in Abuja, the new capital, while other newspapers either have large offices or bureaus, like *Thisday* newspaper, or have opened regional offices. At the moment there is a dichotomy in terms of economic activities, while private companies and other private commercial opportunities remain in Lagos, government business has shifted to Abuja. Though this is beyond the scope of this book, it will be interesting to see how Abuja as a centre of government business influences the locational domination of Lagos in the newspaper industry.

The Elites

The second feature of regional parallelism as drawn from the interviews is the support of the elites in sustaining these newspapers. The elite in Nigeria have understood the complex nature of Nigerian society, with different ethnic groups and religious affiliations, both of which struggle for relevance and self-assertion investing or providing moral support to the media. To achieve this, there is the need for a strong media that will articulate the position of each group. With the advantage of location or ownership of a newspaper, the elite effectively utilise the media either to promote their interest, their region and their personal interest or even manipulate public opinion to their advantage. That is one of the points explained by some of the respondents on how the newspapers complement the interest of the elites who use regionalism to maintain their political relevance. According to Haruna, one of the leading columnists in Nigeria:

[1] Both *Daily Trust* and *Leadership* are seen as northern newspapers.

> The sad thing about Nigerian journalism is that it seems so blinded by ethnic and sectarian considerations that it does not admit even a minimum standard of objectivity. For most Nigerian journalists, it seems to be the case of my kith and kin first, right or wrong. Not surprisingly, politicians always try to exploit this weakness of journalism practice to put an ethnic or religious spin on the slightest trouble they manage to get themselves into—there are many other issues of journalism ethics that should worry anyone with a care for the integrity of Nigerian journalism. Of all these other issues, probably the most important is the ethnic and sectarian divisions of the mass media.[2]

Political Interests

The third feature of regional parallelism is the promotion of business and political interests. Many of the respondents interviewed agreed that one of the problems of journalism in Nigeria is that the political and economic class invest in the media to promote their business interests, get easy access to senior government officials or promote their political agenda. Many of the respondents cited an example with one of the leading newspapers in the country whose proprietor distributes identity cards to his staff and leave them to survive on the courtesy of their sources.

This political interest is increasing by the day with serving politicians establishing newspapers and using the media to promote their political interest. Though as suggested by Hallin and Mancini (2004) that no right-thinking analyst will argue that the media is value neutral, what is at stake here is the use of the media to create further division and tension among the people by the members of the elite. An editorial by the *Daily Triumph* newspaper will be useful here for further analysis:

> One of the communiqué's nine-point observations stated inter-alia "the media have through sensationalism, inaccurate reporting and fraudulent manipulation of facts fuelled religious and community crises." It further noted that the elite are the culprits often involved in inciting people and fomenting social unrest to promote political or personal agenda.[3]

[2] See *The Problem with Nigerian Journalism* by Mohammed Haruna available at http://www.gamji.com/haruna/haruna.htm downloaded 25/11/2008.

[3] See Media, Elite and Religious Crises, which is an editorial by the *Daily Triumph* of 27/11/2008 published in Kano, available at: http://www.triumphnewspapers.com/med27112008.html downloaded 28/11/2008.

The editorial was a reaction to the communiqué issued by the Nigeria Inter-Religious Council (NIREC) co-chaired by the president of the Supreme Council for Islamic Affairs[4] in Nigeria and the chairman of the Christian Association of Nigeria.[5] They issued the communiqué during a meeting in Kano on November 27, 2008. What this highlights is that the views expressed by the journalists have been confirmed by members of the elite themselves, that the media is monopolised to satisfy sectional and political interest of some individuals. But, as acknowledged in the later part of the editorial, it is not simply because the elite utilise the media to their advantage, but the government has consistently failed in punishing those who use their position or the media to create tension in the country.

Economic Imbalance

Economic imbalance in media ownership is the fourth feature of regional parallelism. One of the factors that promote the differences between the regions is the imbalance in newspaper ownership. Many of the respondents interviewed pointed out that it is even difficult to make comparison between newspapers as most of the newspapers are located in one region, while other parts of the country struggle with few strong newspapers and few weak ones. This economic imbalance as a factor in promoting regionalism was mentioned by one of the respondents from a newspaper in the north who wants to extend their business to the southern part of Nigeria because the paper is stronger in the north, and they decided to launch their operation in Lagos. During the launching one of the speakers asked them why they bothered to be a national newspaper when they can still maintain their regional identity and have their paper circulated nationally. Another issue that came during the interviews is the nature of recruitment. In almost all the national dailies, from each of the regions in Nigeria, the majority of the staff of the newspapers came from the region the newspaper is identified with (see Chap. 5 for a similar trend in Kenya). The influence of recruitment in news judgement was discussed by Hallin and Mancini (2004) when discussing "political parallelism" by explaining that "news incorporates political values, which arise from a range of influences,

[4] The current chairman of the Supreme Council for Islamic Affairs is the Sultan of Sokoto, Alhaji Muhammad Sa'ad Abubakar.

[5] The former chairman of the Christian Association of Nigeria is the Archbishop of Abuja, John Onaiyekan.

from a routine information gathering to recruitment patterns of journalists and shared ideological assumptions of the wider society" (p. 26). Hallin and Mancini stated that journalists might be committed to the idea of objectivity in journalism, but some of the influences mentioned could constrain them from being neutral.

Complexity

The fifth feature of regional parallelism is its complexity. The character of Nigerian journalism is not plain north/south dichotomy. It reflects other complexities of Nigerian society. This complexity can be interregional between north and south, intra-regional, interethnic or inter-religious. As discussed by some of the respondents during the interviews, the majority of newspaper owners in Nigeria are not from the south-west or Lagos in particular, they are from the south-south region, the oil producing area of Nigeria. But because Lagos is the economic and business capital of Nigeria, for these newspapers to survive they have to be located in Lagos. Beyond that, for the newspaper to succeed, these proprietors employ people from the south-west, the Yoruba in particular to serve as editors because they are more familiar with the intricacies involved in terms of securing advertising and even the nature of the readership. This is because of the historical and economic advantage the region has. Another complexity involved is the issue of corruption within the media itself, which was pointed out almost by all the respondents. Corruption within the media goes beyond regional considerations; it is for those who are willing to pay. In the words of one of the respondents, a lot of the news, articles and columns are "full of impurities". Part of the complexity as identified by some of the respondents is that the bias of the newspapers does not necessarily come in news stories; it is mostly in the commentary and editorial sections of the newspapers.

Flexibility

The final feature of regional parallelism is that it is flexible. It is flexible in the sense that the newspapers do not side with their region because of a deliberate conspiracy or consensus between them. A number of the respondents, even though they pointed at the apparent nature of regionalism in journalism practice, they indicated that many of the newspapers from any part of the country can be balanced in their reporting, as confirmed by these two examples, the first from a senior journalist in a southern newspaper, and the second from a senior journalist in a northern newspaper.

> *Now the northern papers had the tendency to do what you call "namu ne", that for a long time did not help the newspapers that were coming from the north until* Daily Trust *blessed the trail, it is not that it does not exist in* Daily Trust *but they try as much as possible not to show it.*[6]
>
> *I think it will be risky for one to make a generalised statement because so many of them have been fairly balanced, depending on whom the proprietors are, because there is quite a variety in the south.*

Some of the journalists interviewed also suggested that a new era in Nigerian journalism is on the way because a number of the senior journalists at the moment received their training in journalism and university education after the civil war which took place from 1967 to 1970, but the ones joining the profession at the moment received their education and training under different circumstances. Though it may take time, but the new era may gradually set in.

Nigerian newspapers have a long history of establishing a national consensus when it comes to issues of national survival, from the colonial era when the country was struggling for independence, to the struggle especially in the 1980s and 1990s to purge the country out of military rule, to the criticism against government policies that might have negative consequences on the polity, or an attempt by some politicians to amend the constitution in order to elongate their stay in power.[7] (See Chap. 3.)

Perhaps one of the factors that will contribute in the new era in Nigerian journalism is the war against corruption; despite the criticism on how the anti-corruption agencies conduct their affairs, a number of the newspapers that may be accused on some occasions of siding with their region, or commentators seen as ethnic chauvinists, collectively they condemn the politicians accused of corruption. Many of the respondents interviewed agree that corruption has no ethnic or regional colouration, it is individually based.

Nigerian newspapers dedicate space and give prominence to stories about corruption. It was one area that almost shows the patriotic face

[6] *Namu ne* means he is ours, who belongs to us.

[7] See Chap. 3 for more on the historical landscape of Nigerian newspapers.

Nigerian newspapers. News headlines like "Anti-graft war has come to stay in Nigeria, says Buhari"[8] by the *Vanguard*, a southern newspaper, while the *Daily Trust*, a newspaper from the north, calling for "Rethinking the fight against corruption" under the Buhari administration due to some of the perceived lapses in the anti-corruption war.[9]

However, many of the respondents also pointed out that political office holders are afraid of media publicity, and it is their view that the media was more active in the last eight years of civilian administration than some of the arms of government.

According to Oyovbaire (2001), in his discussion of Nigerian media landscape, the coverage of news in the Nigerian media is drawn from the complex and plural nature of the country. He summarised the entire picture of Nigerian media in the following words:

> We have identified that the south-west of the country is the materialist location of the Nigerian media which coincides with the Yoruba nationality, early evangelisation of Christianity, propagation of western education and establishment of the seat of colonial and post-colonial government together with the large and flourishing market forces and patronage which aided the locational stimuli of the media. The readership audience for marketing its role, mandate and products was the south-west, this historical location continued to provide the arrowhead for opinion formation, legitimisation of media contents, agitation and agenda-setting.

This highlights the difficulty among journalists to shun away from issues of regionalism, because it is part of the make-up of the country. For example, the newspapers always pay attention to appointments by the sitting president, if one section of the country is seen to be favoured over the other, the newspapers from the section of the country that feels marginalised will complain about it. The following examples from The *Guardian* newspaper, published in the south, and *Daily Trust*, published in the north, will be illustrative. Two leading columnists from these newspapers have at one time or another complained about committee compositions by the federal government. First, Mohammed Haruna who runs a column

[8] See https://www.vanguardngr.com/2018/01/anti-graft-war-come-stay-nigeria-says-buhari/ retrieved 17/05/18.

[9] See Rethinking the fight against corruption available at https://www.dailytrust.com.ng/rethinking-the-fight-against-corruption.html retrieved 17/05/18.

in the *Daily Trust* mentioned this about the national political reform conference[10] called by former president Olusegun Obasanjo:

> The controversy surrounding the composition of the leadership and membership of the National Political Reform Conference has once again brought to the fore the importance of the mass media in shaping public opinion and in policy making and implementation. When President Olusegun Obasanjo decided to make virtually the entire leadership of the NPRC Christian and also decided to give them a nearly two thirds majority edge over Muslims in its membership in a country he himself says is 50:50 Muslim/Christian, he knew he could count on the conspiratorial silence, if not the support, of most of the Nigerian mass media in his flagrant breach of the same Nigerian Constitution he has sworn to defend. Clearly the president has not been disappointed. Three weeks into the Conference, there has been a deafening silence from most of the Nigerian mass media over the president's blatant act of injustice.[11]

During the political reform conference there was anger particularly among Muslims and people from Northern Nigeria because as stated by Haruna, majority of the members were Christians including the chairman and the secretary. While the secretary of the committee, Reverend Father Mathew Hassan Kukah, was from the north, which partly conforms to the tradition of regional balancing or federal character in appointments, usually such appointments combine either a Christian from the south and a Muslim from the north and vice versa except in exceptional circumstances.[12] Therefore, Muslims felt underrepresented in the composition of the committee, and that was the point being made

[10] The national political reform conference was called by former president Olusegun Obasanjo to discuss issues of national importance like resource control and allocation, the system of government that best suits the country between presidential and parliamentary or other systems of government. However, there is the view that the main reason for the conference was to suggest the amendment of the constitution so that the former president could have the opportunity to succeed himself.

[11] See *Muslims and the National Conference: the Case of Blaming the Victim* available at http://www.gamji.com/haruna/haruna.htm downloaded November 20, 2008. The Columns written by Mohammed Haruna on Wednesdays in the *Daily Trust* newspaper are also available in his web page *people and politics* hosted by www.gamji.com

[12] The federal government finally appointed Professor Ishaq Oloyede, then deputy vice chancellor (academic) university of Ilorin to serve as co-secretary alongside Rev. Mathew Kukah in order to balance the composition of the leadership of the National Political Reform Conference. See *Islamic Group, Lawyer Hail Oloyede's appointment* available at http://www.thisdayonline.com/nview.php?id=12050 downloaded 20th/11/2008.

by Haruna, that former president Olusegun Obasanjo being a Christian from the south is marginalising the Muslims.

The second example is on the composition of the police reform committee established by the president, Umaru Musa Yar'Adua, a Muslim from Northern Nigeria. Commenting on this in his column, Dr. Reuben Abati, who was chair of the editorial board of the *Guardian* newspaper stated this in one of his columns:

> On Tuesday, President Umaru Yar'Adua inaugurated a 16-man police reform panel led by Alhaji M. D. Yusufu, a retired police man. There have been complaints about the composition of the panel, focussing mainly on its lack of ethnic balancing, and its domination by former police men and women whereas the panel ought to be more representative, to include other stakeholders particularly civil society groups who are directly affected by police functions.[13]

The complaint is about the composition of the committee by having more northerners and Muslims. What the complaint signifies within Nigerian context is that Yar'Adua was favouring Muslims and northerners since he is both Muslim and from the north. This position taken by two leading columnists in the *Guardian* and *Daily Trust* is not new; it has been part of the character of the Nigerian press. While the views expressed by both journalists may be their personal opinion, but it will be difficult also to divorce it from the societal pressure and the interest of readers of both papers. With regards to the police reform committee, *Afenifere* even issued a statement calling on the attention of the president that there is no Yoruba in the committee.[14]

[13] See *Much Ado about police reform* available at http://www.nigerianmuse.com/20080111111038zg/nigeriawatch/abati/Much_ado_about_police_reform by_Reuben_Abati downloaded November 20, 2008. Articles published in the *Guardian* by Dr. Reuben Abati are available in different websites managed by Nigerians.

[14] Afenifere is the leading Yoruba sociocultural and political organisation in the south-west. "In a statement by its National Publicity Secretary, Mr. Yinka Odumakin, the group said the non-inclusion of a Yoruba person in the 16-man panel was unacceptable to the south-west people: "In an ideal situation, we would have expected a broadminded President to ensure that each geo-political zone in the country has at least three members in a 22-man committee. Or is the President saying the Yoruba do not need policing? Or are we no longer part of Nigeria? We will not buy any argument that Yar'Adua is only picking people on competence without geography. Will that explain why the chairmen of his Political Reform Panel and Police Reform Committee are both from Kastina, while the chairman of the Energy Council is from Zaria?", queried the group." See *President on the spot over "Northernization of Nigeria" by* Oluokun Ayorinde

Journalism and Culture

According to Mancini (2007), "There is one main reason why I believe that the idea of journalism culture can be very useful: it allows journalism to be placed in the widest social and political context in which it develops", this is because "Unlike other professions, journalism is not a neutral, aseptic profession that can be separated from the surrounding social and political reality" (p. 1). Thus, journalism practice in Nigeria is not an exception, and the views already expressed by the respondents points to that. This does not mean that the views of the respondents should be seen as sacred facts; rather, they were able to capture a view already held by the scholars. Because it is the culture which produces the national political culture[15] through which individuals understand and interpret issues whether in relation to corruption or otherwise. Therefore, it will be helpful to elaborate on the cultural specificities of the Nigerian society.

Islam is an integral part of life among Muslims in Northern Nigeria, and it is an important yardstick in measuring who is of good behaviour over a deviant, or is responsible or irresponsible, and these moral codes determine the kind of respect you receive from the society. On the other hand, those moral conducts shape how an individual also deals with other members of the society. An important contribution in this area is Kirk-Greene's thesis of *Malam Bahaushe Mutumin kirki* (meaning "a good Hausa man").[16] The thesis suggests that there are ten qualities that define *mutumin kirki;* they are: *gaskiya* [truth], *amana* [trust], *karamci* [generosity], *hakuri* [patience], *hankali* [sense, common sense], *kunya* [shame (bashfulness), modesty], *ladabi* [good manners], *mutunci* [humanity], *hikima* [religious wisdom], *adalci* [religious scruples] (Hunter and Oumarou 1998: 168). These, according to Hunter and Oumarou, "are the qualities that build *hali* [character]" and they define the personality and language

available at: http://www.thephctelegraph.com/stories/June,%202008/2206feat_05.html downloaded November 20, 2008.

[15] See Chap. 1 for additional details on political culture.

[16] Hausa is both a language and an ethnic group found in many parts of west Africa, especially in Nigeria, Niger, Ghana, Cameroon and Chad. The majority of them are Muslims, and they constitute the single largest community in Northern Nigeria. But there are a lot of Muslims in Northern Nigeria who are not Hausas, like Fulani, Kanuri, but many of them also use Hausa as their lingua franca. Intermarriages and cultural proximity is also breaking the cultural differences among them. The term Hausa in certain circumstances means these three ethnic groups, especially the Hausa and Fulani. In fact Hausa-Fulani is now a popular term used to refer to Muslims from Northern Nigeria.

behaviour of the person (Hunter and Oumarou 1998: 169). These moral codes which define the character of the "ideal" Hausa person, "will have direct link to Islam, which is the matrix of life and behaviour for the Muslim Hausa" (Adamu 2000: 8).[17] Over time, these qualities were assimilated into the culture, and they are seen more as cultural rather than religious values.

At least two lessons can be derived from this book in relation to the practice of journalism, especially among the Muslims from Northern Nigeria. First, if we take the example cited by the editor above that they face pressure from people to censor stories because the person is an elder or a brother, then perhaps it is an indication that the elites selectively exploit some of the qualities of ***mutumin kirki*** such as ***kunya*** [shame, modesty] and ***ladabi*** [good manners]; the two qualities as they are applied among the Hausa people suggest a person who remains calm and reserved as a courtesy to someone he respects, even though he may disagree with him or disapproves of his actions. Secondly, what will make the journalists counter the elite may depend on their ability to apply some of the qualities of ***mutumin kirki*** like ***gaskiya*** [truth], and ***amana*** [trust], terms that fit into the values of journalism in its ideal form. Where the journalists failed to uphold these principal values, that is, perhaps, when the issues raised by some of the respondents that northerners are deferential to the authorities may hold water.

The work of Schultz (2007a, b) will be relevant in understanding journalistic culture and how the production of news is influenced by economic, cultural and environmental factors. Although reporters may go ahead and write their reports, the editors decide the angle that the report should take. This according to Schultz might explain why a single report might be reported in different ways. Such differences may explain why specific journalistic cultures shape journalism practice, and this, according to Shultz, is where the contribution of Hallin and Mancini (2004) on *Media Systems* becomes more relevant, because it seeks to contextualise journalistic practice within cultural and historical space. With this in mind, since this research also is rooted in the works of Hallin and Mancini (2004), it is easier to understand how the issues raised by the respondents in terms of the historical, economic and cultural factors shape the orientation of journalism practice in Nigeria.

[17] Adamu has further refined the *Malam Bahaushe Mutumin kirki* theory in the same work by merging it with the works of Habib Alhassan, Usman Ibrahim Musa and Rabi'u Muhammad Zarru to produce eighteen codes of behaviour.

Drawing from the ideas of Bourdieu, Schultz discussed the concept of field which is one of the contributions of Bourdieu in which the field seeks to explain the relationship between journalism as a field, and the economic and other social practices that influences it. What this suggests according to Schultz is that newspapers for example are not autonomous in themselves, but they are autonomous in terms of their political or ideological linkage when they are compared to other newspapers. As such it can be argued that the *Guardian* of London is left-wing or left of centre when it is compared to *Daily Telegraph* which is seen as right of the centre. This argument is significant for this book because in addition to further explaining the relevance of the data used, it suggests that issues of regionalism, north and south, Muslims and Christians become relevant when they are compared to each other. In Bourdieu's perception about the field theory "positions are defined by opposition, such as teacher=student, author=literary agent..." (Hanks 2005: 72). This could further suggest that though journalists are conscious of the regional and ethnic divide in the way journalism is practiced in Nigeria, but overall what is happening is a struggle between the social structure of the society, and the newspapers are serving as the medium where the competition between these social forces is revealing itself. Still drawing from Bourdieu, Shultz suggests that journalism in this respect should be seen as part of the means of cultural production.

Journalism and Clientelism

Journalism as a profession claims to uphold certain principles, these principles include honesty, impartiality, accuracy and so on, but this is the ideal picture; a common feature in many countries, which contradicts those "ideal" principles, is clientelism. Although it exists even in developed societies, it is more visible in countries that are still struggling with the challenges of development. Clientelism "is a particularistic form of social organisation, in which formal rules are less important relative to personal connections" (Hallin and Mancini 2004: 58). According to Hallin and Mancini, the culture of clientelism can be found both in the private and public media. Appointment of chief executives of media organisations are made to fulfil certain political obligations and failure to abide by the unwritten expectations may result in the dismissal of the official. In the case of private media organisations, the proprietors have access to government officials and they use the media outfits to satisfy the needs of their political friends. Government officials also use their positions to punish those who refuse to do their bidding.

In discussing clientelism and corruption in Nigeria, reference has to be made to the scholarly contribution of Richard A Joseph's book on *Democracy and Prebendal Politics in Nigeria* (1988). The work studied Nigerian politics in the second republic and how different ethnic, regional and other interest groups struggle to accumulate the resources of the state for personal or sectional reasons; a situation which ended up promoting excessive corruption and clientelism. According to Diamond (1989):

> Joseph's crucial contribution is his notion of "prebendal" system. Drawing heavily (but not inflexibly) on Max Weber, Joseph uses the term prebendal to define 'patterns of political behaviour which rest on the justifying principle that [state] offices should be competed for and then utilised for the personal benefit of office holders and as well as of their reference or support group'...part of the value of Joseph's approach is his deep and well documented appreciation of the pressures and norms from below which help to propel and legitimate the system. (pp. 284–285)

This is a significant contribution in trying to understand the relationship between clientelism and journalism practice in Nigeria. Nigerian political landscape, politicians and even members of the public have not changed from the depiction of Joseph in his thesis of prebendal politics in Nigeria. The very politicians, whose view of public office is to gather resources for personal use or to serve certain interests, are the very ones who invest in the media. Beyond that it is common for members of the public to view the newspaper or other media of communication as representing their interest or that of their region or ethnic group. The views expressed by the respondents in Chap. 7 on how some ministers tried to punish some newspapers for not supporting them because of regional affiliation, or the killing of stories because of the political position of a politician within a particular ethnic group is simply a reflection of the larger society. As discussed by Bayley (1966), this is one of the reasons why it is important to pay attention to the role of culture in defining corruption.

Clientelism and Professionalism

One of the effects of clientelism is that it compromises professionalism for other political and cultural considerations. According to one of the respondents with the *Guardian* newspaper, one of the reasons why newspapers could not survive in Northern Nigeria, is not necessarily because of lack of advertisement, but because of what in his words described as "namu ne", meaning "he is ours", and he stated that such attitude began to change when "*Daily Trust* Blessed the trail", and that is perhaps why *Daily Trust* refused to succumb to the pressure from the minister. This situation is common in most of the newspapers. According to one of the respondents who worked with the *Punch* newspaper, the major challenge he faced in his job was when he writes and criticises President Olusegun Obasanjo; at the end of the day he was dismissed from his job on the excuse that he purchased an expensive car which he couldn't afford to buy from his salary.

This culture of clientelism has an in effect in the practice of investigative journalism, because of the connection between senior government officials whose wrongdoings might be investigated, and the proprietors who might be interested in government favours. As confirmed by the respondents, it is a common knowledge that some journalists initiate investigation into the profile and private life of high-ranking government officials in order to identify a scandal; once they discover something that might interest the public, they present it to the official and threaten the official to pay for the story or else they will get it published, and many officials succumb to this blackmail. The paradox here is that the investigation has been carried out, the facts have become obvious, but the intention is simply to extort the victim.

Clientelism and Investigative Journalism

So clientelism, which is a feature of many developing countries, interferes with the ability of journalists to investigate corruption scandals. And it is clear from the views expressed by the respondents that both politicians and journalists are interested in this clientelist relationship because it serves the following purposes. First, politicians take advantage of their regional or ethnic affiliation with either the journalist or their proprietors to draw sentiments that will make the politicians have their way. Second, proprietors and editors are interested in the advertising revenue and other patronages they can receive from the officials, hence making them kill or ignore stories affecting their clients. However, this may not always be the case, because the frequency of stories about corruption scandals is increasing by the day, principally due to the activities of the Economic and Financial Crimes Commission (EFCC). The activities of this commission has created a sense of competition among Nigerian newspapers; newspapers will seldom ignore stories about corruption even if it involves their proprietors. Perhaps there could be differences in the use of language. For instance the *Sun* newspaper allegedly owned by former Abia State governor, Orji Uzo Kalu, reported his arrest as "Kalu held", and one of the respondents from that newspaper rhetorically asked what the difference is between "Kalu held" and "Kalu arrested", the latter being the phrase used by some newspapers. But going through the comments in the newspaper, the reports took the perspective that Kalu was simply being victimised by the EFCC because he was a critique of former president Olusegun Obasanjo, and the EFCC was simply hunting the enemies of the former president. Thirdly, clientelism takes the form of blackmail, especially when journalists use the wrongdoing of a politician to extort him.

What this indicates is that, investigative journalism may exist theoretically, but the way it is used in exposing corruption scandals may be surrounded by other factors associated with the internal dynamics of the society such as clientelism, corruption, ethnicity and regionalism, and the understanding of these factors will help a lot in the way questions such as journalistic autonomy and professionalism are addressed.

However, there is a variation in the way the journalists express their understanding of investigative journalism. Some of the respondents look at investigative journalism as giving exposure to stories that will expose the corruption of public office holders. The emphasis is on what Tumber and Waisbord (2004) described as "moral transgressions" in which public office holders fail to live up to the standards expected of them, and once such stories get to the media, they attract public attention.

Some of the respondents pay attention to the digging out of facts; looking beyond the surface evidence. As identified by one young journalist, investigative journalism *"is just a way of going an extra mile into finding more facts, figures or even more information about an event or an issue that is making the news"*.

The journalist above was able to identify at least three key points required in investigative journalism. The first is going "extra mile"; that is, going beyond the routine, or reliance on handouts from news sources, who may perhaps try to control what goes out. This point corresponds with what (Brennen 2000) explains as going beyond the routine by serving as keepers and educators of public conscience. The second point, "finding more facts" and "figures", means that going beyond the routine itself is not enough; all allegations must be supported by facts or figures, and that is what differentiates quality journalism from its opposite. And the third point has to be on "an issue that is making the news". This is the point where the connection between scandal and corruption is established from communication perspective. One of the characteristics of scandal as discussed by Lull and Hinerman (1997) is that it attracts public attention through the news media.

As explained by Goddard (2006), investigative journalism is done to promote public interest. The understanding of investigative journalism by some of the respondents reinforces Goddard's position as confirmed by this woman editor, "*Well I guess it is when you come across a topic which is of public interest and you pursue it to the very end whatever the troubles ahead*". From the perspective of this journalist, two things are important: the notion of public interest, and the trouble that might come with it.

Scholars who defined corruption gave similar emphasis on the notion of public interest. Sandcholtz and Koetzle (2000)[18] in their classification of corruption started by identifying a public interest definition of corruption which focuses on the behaviour of the public official in discharging his responsibility and the extent to which he violates public interest. Looking at the revelations coming from various newspapers about allegation of wrongdoing by politicians, for example the revelation that over $16 billion has been embezzled by the administration of former president Olusegun Obasanjo, or the use of $5 million dollars by the former speaker of the House of Representatives Patricia Etteh and her deputy, Babangida Nguruje, to renovate their houses and purchase new cars even when university teachers constantly go on strike, it is only fair to assume that the notion of public interest will be in the conscience of journalists in practising their profession.[19]

[18] See Chap. 1 for more on various definitions of corruption.

[19] For details about the $16 billion allegation, see the Nigerian Tribune of March 18, 2008 which reports that "The House of Representatives was a focus of attention last week as it began a public hearing on investigations into how the last administration spent $16 billion on the power sector without much to show for it". Also see the story on former speaker Patricia Etteh, see "Nigeria's speaker goes in graft row" reported by the BBC on October 30, 2007.

While there are differences in the way the journalists framed their understanding of investigative journalism, what their views suggest is that investigative journalism has a common purpose, educating the public and standing for truth. But to be successful in investigating stories, there are some factors that should be available. Investigative journalism cannot be practised in isolation; simply because a journalist likes to uncover a scandal, he doesn't just pick his pen and paper and go into the field. He needs resources from the organisation; the judiciary should be strong enough to stand against interference from powerful officials or people with strong link to government. The journalist also requires special training about safety and be aware of the consequences that may arise from his action. The society also has a role to play in this regard in terms of the way it treats those in authority especially if they are found guilty, so that the effort of investigative journalists doesn't end at breaking news only. This point is important because as discussed in Chap. 1, among the features of scandal as identified by Lull and Hinerman (1997) is that apart from reporting the scandal widely in the mass media, the people involved should take responsibility for their actions, and the stories must attract public attention and response.

Consequences of Investigative Journalism

The respondents were also mindful of the consequences that might come with investigative journalism. Such consequences could mean losing one's job, the risk of losing life, as was the case with late "Dele Giwa, founding editor of *Newswatch*, the country's foremost newsmagazine, [who] was blasted to death in October 1986 by a letter bomb suspected to have been sent on orders of a top official of the military regime in power" (Ette 2000: 68), and the bombing of Bagauda Kalto, the correspondent of *The News* Magazine in Kaduna, allegedly for writing stories the military regime of the time was not comfortable with (Ibrahim 2003). And in some cases, those who manage to survive with their life might end up with a deformity for life as discussed earlier in Chap. 7.

Many journalists have the passion to uncover stories, but the economic situation of the country, the absence of a legal protection due to lack of an independent judiciary and the fear of the unknown might prevent journalists from investigating corruption scandals, even if they fully understand what it means, and so routine handout journalism might prevail. It is clear from the views expressed by the respondents that they have reservations on whether investigative journalism is actually practised by Nigerian journalists. As discussed by Waisbord (2000), investigative journalism has to stem from the effort of the journalist, by looking at information and facts such that the result of the investigation is worthy of changing the mood of the public.

In the words of one of the respondents from *Guardian* newspaper, "*Investigation is not something that even some of these young people have had about because we don't do it at all here. Investigation is not something that you start yesterday and that will end today*". The reference to "these young people", meaning young journalists who have not been in the profession for a long time confirms the reservation of many journalists on whether investigative journalism is practised at all in Nigeria.

As discussed by Lull and Hinerman (1997),[20] among the features of scandals is that those involved have to take responsibility for their action and feel the impact of their wrongdoing. What is perhaps clear is that within the context of Nigeria, and to a large extent many developing countries, there is need for a redefinition of investigative journalism from the ideal type of investigative journalism.

The inability of the media in developing countries to conduct investigative journalism in its "ideal" form may also be related to the economic situations in those countries because of the control of resources by the governments, which make it nearly impossible for media organisations to survive. Waisbord (2000) aptly described the situation where he points out that "the intertwined political and economic relations between news companies and the state made impossible the affirmation of the model of an "independent," "fourth estate" press, a model that views the reporting of official wrongdoing as one of its priorities and obligations. In countries where the state remained in control of vital resources for press economies, rarely were news organisations willing to criticise governments out of fear that such reporting would have damaging political and economic consequences. Additionally, the persistence of a heavily partisan culture ran against the consolidation of an "independent" press." (p. xxi).

The press in Nigeria has a history of taking adversarial stands against government positions from colonial to post-colonial days which may be one of the factors that keep the newspaper industry moving. However, the media is not completely immune from the factors described by Waisbord. A scan through Nigerian newspapers will reveal that the pages are full of adverts congratulating the government or the president on his birthday,

[20] See Chap. 1 for more details on the definitions and features of scandal.

independence celebrations, New Year celebration, democracy day or best wishes from cronies who want to maintain their relevance or use that to seek more favours. Such adverts are sought by commercial departments of the media organisations because it provides them with the revenue required to sustain themselves. As explained by one of the editors of the newspapers, sometimes when newspapers refused to cooperate, they were punished by being denied such advertisements.

This, as stated earlier, requires a negotiated definition that will either look at investigative journalism as conceived by journalists within their specific domain or come up with another definition or term that accommodates the realities of other countries. Perhaps this is where Waisbord's (2000) idea of watchdog journalism, which does not claim the "ideal" type of investigative journalism but lives up to the responsibility of disclosing official wrongdoing, becomes relevant. It is clear that Nigerian newspapers do try, within the limits of their resources and conception of investigative journalism, to expose the cases of corruption scandals; they do not completely agree that it is being practised. This is where the idea of watchdog journalism may provide a suitable alternative.

No matter how professional the media may be, and no matter the fashion from journalists to expose corruption scandals, they may only succeed if they are supported by other institutions in the society. If the judiciary is not strong enough to punish those who violate rules and procedure, and the legislator becomes a lame duck and unable to investigate and put pressure on erring officials, and the civil society becomes dull and ineffective, while the average person in the society is whirling in ignorance and poverty, coupled with the corruption within the media itself, the likely thing that will happen is the triumph of handout journalism. These challenges faced by the press whether in Nigeria or elsewhere do confirm the reservations of those who have concerns about the watchdog role of the media as the fourth estate of realm. This brings us to the obstacle faced by journalists when trying to investigate stories.

Obstacles

Nigerian journalists face numerous challenges. As discussed earlier and acknowledged by the respondents, those who try to uphold the principles of investigative journalism may risk their lives, especially if they want to attempt to follow the Anglo-American model of investigative journalism. The cases of Dele Giwa and Bagauda Kalto are typical examples of how risky it could be to be in the bad books of senior political figures. In Nigeria, especially during military rule, it was common to close down media houses, arrest and detain journalists or confiscate their working materials. Even under a civilian administration, the media was not free from government effort to scuttle their activities when the government perceived them to be over stepping their boundaries.[21]

The challenge of government interference undermines the ability of the journalists not only in unearthing corruption scandals, but also in their routine activities. This is more prevalent with the government owned news media. A respondent who was an editor formerly in two governments owned newspapers had a bitter experience with the chairmen of the board of directors who were the government representatives in both newspapers. According to the journalist's account, an editorial decision will be taken, but the following morning the journalist will see on the pages of the same paper a news headline and editorial different from the one agreed and written the previous day. This was happening at a time in the mid-1980s when the government was considering introducing the Structural Adjustment Programme which created a harsh economic situation in the country. The journalists had to resign in protest. In some newspapers and radio or television stations, some state governments gave instruction to the media houses to make sure they carry the stories featuring the state governor first before other stories. When journalists find themselves in this situation, it will be difficult for them to even contemplate anything near investigative journalism or writing reports that will implicate senior officials. The media houses in this case are simply part of the state bureaucracy.

But the media itself has its own internal problems. One of the respondents, a former president of the Nigeria union of journalists mentioned that in almost every story written there is a kickback. After covering an event, journalists normally wait for a post coverage fee, what is commonly known as "kwa", a neologism derived from communiqué into communi-kwa and then short-formed to "Kwa". The money is used for transportation and the purchasing of top-up cards for mobile phones; the amount is normally between 1000 naira and 5000 naira, this according a senior journalist from

[21] For a detailed account on the risk and intimidation including loss of life that happened in recent years under a civilian administration in Nigeria see World Press Freedom Review on Nigeria by the International Press Institute available at: http://www.freemedia.at/cms/ipi/freedom_detail.html?country=/KW0001/KW0006/KW0171/

the *Nation* newspaper does not indicate an intention to influence the story (though it does in away because the journalists may ignore the story if they did not receive the bribe), but when the journalist is given 100,000 naira, then it is a real bribe aimed at influencing the story. Many journalists establish a rapport with politicians through coverage of events, which in many occasions translate into appointment as press secretaries, special assistants and special advisers and so on.

The challenge of advertising revenue and lack of adequate training and modern equipment is a serious impediment in journalistic practise. Many journalists do not know how to use a computer and where they do, access to the Internet is not smooth such that they can easily get stories, although there is a significant improvement as many journalists either from personal effort or from loans given by their proprietors try to own laptop computers in order to ease their work. But on the job training remains a major challenge.

However, it is fair to say that journalists in Nigeria fall into the trap of politicians and news sources and sometimes being compromised, not necessarily because they intentionally decide to be corrupt. It is because they can't be different from the society they work in. where a journalists is underpaid, he doesn't have working materials, he cannot produce stories through magic, he has to find a means of survival. Many journalists carefully confirm that some newspapers, in particularly they mentioned *Thisday*, has a reputation of giving its staff identity cards and leaving them to survive on the favours of their news sources. Going by Gans' (1979) theory, it takes two tango; it is clear who will take a better advantage between the journalist and the source. The journalists are certainly not happy with the situation, and in the words of one of the respondents and a senior figure of the Economic and Financial Crimes Commission, he described journalists among the best Nigerians and among the most patriotic.

Corruption Within the Media

The fact that the journalists themselves point at the media as suffering from corruption internally poses the question as to whether corruption within the media is similar to corruption in politics. The answer may not be a definite yes or no. However, from the responses of the journalists interviewed, there could be some reasons that may provide indications as to the differences between corruption within the media, and corruption in politics which the media shows interest in reporting. There are at least five points that will be of interest here.

First is the anger of the journalists about corruption in politics. Of all the journalists interviewed, their body language, and the way they passionately respond to the questions suggests that they are not happy with the corruption in government, even if they contribute to the corruption within the media. In fact, two of the respondents, one from the *Guardian* and the other from the *Punch* said they are also not saints.

The second reason which could differentiate between corruption within the media and corruption in politics is the desire shown by the media in reporting these cases of corruption. Even if it is for commercial reasons, it was an indication that the press is concerned about political corruption and is willing to report it as much as possible. According to a respondent who is a senior executive in the Economic and Financial Crimes Commission, journalists are among the best Nigerians, and some of the cases investigated by the commission were a follow up of stories carried by the press, as such, if the journalists become corrupt, it is because it is hard for them to be different from the society they live in.

The third reason, which will also be highlighted later, is the lack of strong capital base, which will allow the media to have the strength to investigate stories, expose them and still survive the anger of authorities should they decide to punish the media by denying it government patronage like advertising and so on. A former president of the Nigeria Union of Journalists who was among the respondents suggests that the best way for the media to be independent in Nigeria is to have a reform that will bring consolidation so that different media organisations could merge and have a strong capital base as was done in the banking sector and which made the banks stronger.[22] (See Yusha'u 2018 on the capitalisation of the Nigerian media.) This argument by the journalist may have a merit, but there could be concerns that such an effort will hand over the media to few powerful individual organisations as the case is, for instance, in the West with Murdock's press or the Time Warner Company and other few conglomerates that monopolise the media industry.

[22]Another concern is that after Sanusi Lamido Sanusi took over as the Central Bank Governor of Nigeria from Professor Charles Soludo who introduced the consolidation of the banking sector, a lot of corruption was uncovered to the extent that the Central Bank had to sack some of the chief executives of the banks, and inject money up to 400 billion naira into the banks so that they did not collapse. See "Central Bank of Nigeria (CBN) Sacks 5 bank CEOs, injects 400 billion into banks" available at: http://www.chairmanking.com/central-bank-nigeria-cbn-sacks-5-bank-ceos-injects-400-naira-billion-banks-20090814/ downloaded 17/01/2010.

The fourth reason that may differentiate between corruption within the media and corruption in politics is poor remuneration. Journalists are underpaid; this is one of the points raised by many of the respondents. Among the few newspapers that have a large capital base, the earning of their staff does not correspond with the profit they make. This situation has the tendency to encourage journalists to use their profession to make money since their proprietors are exploiting them to make money.

The fifth reason is the pressure from the society. People pay attention to the type of work you do. It is easy, for instance, for people to assume that a reporter attached to the presidency, governor's office or the national assembly is making money, because the beat he is reporting from may be considered as lucrative. Even fellow journalists may have the same assumption and perhaps start looking for the time they will be given similar assignment. A luxurious lifestyle is attached to certain kind of jobs; in fact, friends and relatives may even suggest that this is the opportunity to take your share from the national cake, a term used by Nigerians to mean favour, gift, access to resources, though in reality it is another form of corruption. Such pressure may force journalists not only to accept bribes but also use their position to seek for government favours.

The five points above do not provide an excuse for media practitioners to become corrupt, especially the final point which may facilitate a stronger clientelist relationship between journalists and government officials. But what this suggests is that journalists are human beings with needs like people in other professions; the society in which they live also affects their thinking and ideological orientation.

Poor Capitalisation

The journalists interviewed have shown strong concern about the need for a strong capital base that will ensure a smooth running of the newspaper industry. This indeed is a valid argument. Perhaps the journalists are concerned about the encroachment of external influences that may take advantage of the weak financial base of the newspapers to satisfy their interests. Another issue that can be deduced from here is that perhaps journalists in Nigeria are looking up to other media conglomerates in the world, like CNN, BBC and so on, because they have a strong financial base which enables them to run their operations smoothly sometimes by rejecting expensive adverts.[23] And there could be a number of reasons for that. First is the influence of the Anglo-American media in Nigeria as both BBC and CNN are known in the country. The second is that many of the journalists as indicated in the interviews received their training in some of these big media organisations, or had even worked in them. The third reason could be that the university departments that train journalists in the country do train journalists based on the Anglo-American model as some of the teachers received their training either in England or the United States (Murphy and Scotton 1987). This view, though apt, may be simplistic in the sense that even the media in the West faces a lot of challenges in terms of the way it operates; a classical example can be found in the work of Franklin (2004) in his work on *packaging politics* where he cited examples of how the BBC received flaks during Margret Thatcher's government on license fee, or the informal censorship and the influence of spin during Tony Blair's government. Herman and Chomsky's work (1988) and (2002) on the *propaganda model* was an additional example of how capitalism may work against the interest of media organisations.[24]

What, however, may be needed in the case of Nigerian media is a high degree of social responsibility. This responsibility may occur in two ways. The first is by diversifying and encouraging the establishment of local newspapers that may satisfy local interests. This is possible by coming up with government policies that allow the starting of newspaper businesses to be flexible and have low taxation on the import of newsprints and machines needed for newspaper production. Nigeria can also follow the example of South Africa by establishing institutions similar to Media Diversity and Development Agency (see Chap. 4 for details). It is not easy to maintain a national daily in a country with a population of over 190 million people. To do so there is need for massive capital that ensures the employment of staff and offices in almost every part of the country. Transporting the newspapers as early as possible to states that are far away from Lagos and Abuja

[23] For example CNN rejected Barack Obama's 30 minutes infomercial aired in various television stations in the US. See 30-minute *Obama ad shows campaign muscle* available at http://edition.cnn.com/2008/POLITICS/10/29/campaign.muscle/ downloaded 29/11/2008.

[24] An example of the inadequacy of Western media can be found in the build-up of the war on Iraq where Judith Miller, the *New York Times* reporter was used as a "conduit" for writing stories that will be used by government officials as evidence that there are weapons mass destruction in Iraq. See Boyd-Barrett (2004) who used the propaganda model to critique what he calls "the buying out" of journalists by intelligence services or public relations agencies.

where the newspapers are printed. At the moment even the highly established newspapers are finding it difficult to cope; this results in some states in Nigeria receiving copies of newspapers of the previous day. This means that the news they read is twenty-four hours behind. The competition in the market also makes it difficult as the main source of advertising remains government parastatals and companies mostly based in Lagos. If local newspapers can be established and the cost of running is affordable, these local newspapers can survive on the sale of news copies and adverts generated from issues affecting the people like naming ceremonies, announcements, auctions and so forth. The second thing is to have a salary structure for journalists which employers must abide by and sanctions imposed on any newspaper that refused to adhere to the needs of its employees.

Having a strong capital base is a necessity for the running of media organisations. What, however, the respondents failed to see is that the strength of the media goes hand in hand with the strength of the economy. Therefore, it may not be as easy to generate the kind of capital the journalists think, when the majority of the newspapers are competing an already saturated market. Further illustrating how good policies and the running of local newspapers can help the newspaper industry are the habits of some readers, who may not be able to purchase the newspapers at their market price, but they are willing to pay 5 naira to the vendor and read the headlines and some parts of the story only, and the vendor keeps the newspaper. If the good policies are in place, which ensure the establishment of these local newspapers sold at a price that can be affordable to the person who is willing to pay five Naira to read the headlines, it means there is a market left which is not being explored due to the absence of these good policies and the insistence of newspaper proprietors to concentrate on establishing newspapers that are sold nationally.

Bad Working Conditions

Some of the factors responsible for the bad working conditions that the respondents complained about stemmed from the issues raised in poor capitalisation. But let us deduce more from the issues raised by the respondents. At least three things are clear from the respondents' views, which may suggest some of the factors responsible for the bad working conditions. These three factors are greediness, poor remuneration and lack of self-esteem. In terms of greediness, some of the proprietors have shown their desire to accumulate wealth using the newspapers, without regard for the profession and its credibility and the welfare of the staff working under them. The most common example given by the respondents is that of a proprietor who thinks the identity card given to his staff is enough for them without a monthly salary. This has the tendency of not only compromising the staff working under him, but such greediness easily causes the newspapers to become vulnerable in the hands of politicians. Such greediness has made some newspapers to introduce an annual ceremony in which awards are given to ministers, governors and other people holding senior positions in government. Leading this in Nigeria is *Thisday* newspaper which continues with such ceremonies despite criticism and displeasure expressed by the public. According to (Ikita) 2008:

> In *Thisday's* parade of the "Ministerial Front-liners" on its Tuesday (February 12, 2008) daily edition, the newspaper attempted to dress up activities of "intent" or "hoping/dreaming" projects embarked upon by ministers as reasons for "nominating" the ministers for "best" minister award. According to *Thisday*, "We painstakingly monitored the performance of the ministers throughout 2007". But what *Thisday* describes as a "painstaking" monitoring process is actually no more than shallow presumptuous statements that hold no substance among the veritable variables that can be factored into the calculus of good governance. What is there to assess about a minister that just got appointed a little over half a year ago? What is there to assess when policies or ministerial initiatives have caused pain than pleasure to more citizens?[25]

A good salary that is enough to take care of the needs of a person is an essential motivation. As explained by the respondents, journalists are not paid for months. Yet they are expected to continue with the daily routine of reporting, writing articles and analysis. In some newspapers, there are number of words which a reporter must write on a daily basis. These factors beclouding the journalist may force them into fabrication, sycophancy and so, and journalism will simply become a way of extortion and deception which leads to lack of self-esteem. Journalists are seen as beggars, as people who have no self-respect. The integrity of a profession goes hand in hand with the way a person handles such a profession. This situation may create an ethical dilemma between upholding the ethics of the profession and the search for daily bread. Oloruntola (2007) summarised the problems that contribute to the bad image that journalists have in Nigeria in the following words: "Despite the introduction of the code of ethics for

[25] See *Thisday Awards: Celebrating Mediocrity in Government* available at http://www.nigeriavillagesquare.com/articles/philip-ikita/thisday-awards-celebrating-mediocrity-in-gover.html downloaded 29/11/2008.

Nigerian journalists and the setting of Nigerian press council, there are other ethical issues which are part of the overall problems in the society. These include sycophancy, character assassination, pressure, bribery, moonlighting, sensationalism, self-censorship, plagiarism, advertorial, deception and faking stories among others" (p. 63).

Inadequate Professional Training

The views expressed by the respondents have suggested some of the key shortcomings faced by media practitioners. These shortcomings can be summarised into three issues: education, equipment and training. Concerning education one of the respondents even posed a challenge to the journalists as to the number of books they read. It will be difficult for a journalist to inform others when he is not himself informed. However, the educational shortcomings of the journalists may be linked to the kind of training they receive from the university (see Chap. 5 for similar situation in Kenya). At the moment there are a lot of universities offering courses in mass communications in different universities in Nigeria. An example of universities offering at least a first degree in mass communications include among others Bayero University, Kano, University of Maiduguri, University of Lagos, University of Nigeria Nsukka, Ahmadu Bello University, Zaria and Nnamdi Azikwe University. This is in addition to other state universities and polytechnics offering diploma courses in the same area. Underfunding and lack of equipment is a major problem affecting not only these courses but the university system in general. Some of the facilities required for training in these departments are outdated and therefore have little relevance to what exists in the field. Postgraduate programmes that will help with research and production of ideas are still struggling to take root; this might be one of the reasons that makes it difficult to digest "the tensions and solutions to the problem of craft versus scholarship" (Steel et al. 2007: 2) in journalism.

Journalism is a dynamic profession that is moving with technological advancement in the world. The medium of instruction remains the English language, and so with the falling standard in education, employers face the challenge of having not only to retrain university graduates, but also be concerned about the quality of their (English) language,[26] which the major-

[26] *Leadership* newspaper carried an editorial on November 29, 2008 about the falling standard of education in Kwara state-Nigeria. According to the editorial "Early last week, the Kwara State commissioner for education, science and technology, Malam Bolaji Abdullahi,

ity of the newspapers use as their means of communication. Many graduates do become acquainted with the practical aspect of journalism after they have been employed, and with the challenges faced by the industry, it will be difficult to raise the standard of these graduates to the level they can favourably compete with journalists whether within the country or in other parts of the world who already have been used to modern equipment right from their university days. This is for those who have a degree. So the method of journalism training in many universities not only in Nigeria, but in many African countries, needs to be boosted to meet contemporary challenges. For more on journalism education in Africa, see Banda et al. (2007), Berger (2007), Skjerdal and Ngugi (2007), Rooney (2007), McCurdy and Power (2007), Ogundimu et al. (2007) and Botha and de Beer (2007).

As stated earlier, working equipment is essential in the practice of journalism and these may include, for instance, recording devices and laptops. The Internet is playing an important role as well in the search for stories, receiving regular updates, and the use of emails makes sending reports easier, and since they are already typed it will simply be copied and pasted for layout. Where the Internet is slow, or the journalist does not know how to use a computer, there may be a delay in writing and sending news reports. Despite these challenges concerning equipment, there are significant signs of improvement here as many of the journalists, either through personal effort or from their organisations, do own laptops. And the increase in commercial Internet cafés also helps journalists in their work, especially reporters from regions that are far away from the headquarters. Having modern equipment is also crucial in terms of training.

Training is very important because it will help many of the journalists to confront the challenges of their time. Though some foreign media organisations like the BBC do help with the training of journalists as discussed earlier. But such training may not necessarily be conversant with the internal challenges faced by journalists, since it may provide more of an international angle. Also the training provided by the foreign media can only cater for few journalists, which makes it even harder for the majority of journalists to benefit from such efforts.

made a shocking revelation. Out of 19,125 teachers, including 2628 university graduates, who took a test designed for primary four pupils, only seven passed. Two hundred and fifty-nine teachers, including 10 university graduates, scored zero in the test which was in English and Mathematics. This is the barest manifestation of the utter decay in our education system." See A National Disgrace available at http://leadership.nigeriannewsservice.com/news/130/ARTICLE/3057/2008-11-28.html downloaded 30/11/2008.

Conclusion

This chapter has provided an analysis and insight from the perspectives and experiences expressed by the respondents in the previous chapter. It has brought additional meaning to the issues raised in relation to corruption scandals, fourth estate, journalism culture, clientelism, poor capitalisation, bad working conditions and inadequate professional practice. Additional classifications of the issues raised in the previous chapter were provided. Quotations from different newspapers in Nigeria were used to further substantiate some of the issues raised in the chapter and some of the theoretical insights provided by scholars.

What this discussion highlights is that journalism is a product of the culture in which it is practised, and that this impacts on the practices and processes as well as expectations and conventions. Moreover, the discussion has shown how interviews can serve as valuable means of identifying themes and issues in relation to journalism practice which they may not write or give prominence to in their day-to-day activities. This highlights the importance of this research as a contribution to the wider literature on journalism in Africa, and the internal dynamics in terms of culture, religion, politics and economy that makes Nigeria distinct from other societies. The chapter has also further highlighted the difficulty in adopting models developed in other parts of the world and then applying them directly, without modification, in other settings.

Therefore, as discussed by Bourdieu, that journalistic field is part of cultural production (Schultz 2007c), the analysis that stemmed from the data suggests that beyond information dissemination, journalism practice is an exhibition of the cultural ethos of the society. The complexity of the way newspapers operate in Nigeria as discussed by the respondents adds impetus to the postulation that sees journalism as an avenue of cultural production.

As such it is important to understand that the issues raised in earlier chapters on the historical landscape of the press in Nigeria and the literature review which provided additional insight into the character of African media remained fairly consistent. The complex nature of the Nigerian press should not be viewed in isolation; it is part of the historical process of the evolution of Nigeria. Therefore, the reporting of corruption scandals should be viewed from this perspective rather than be seen as something that can be reported in a manner different from the political, economic and cultural factors that shape the thinking of the journalists and the media environment itself. The implication of this is that it will take a long time before journalism practice in Nigeria improves to a standard that will avoid the influence of certain forces in the society that the journalist as an individual cannot avoid.

References

Banda, F., et al. (2007). Contextualising Journalism Education and Training in Southern Africa. *Ecquid Novi. African Journalism Studies, 28*(1&2), 156–175.

Bayely, D. H. (1966). The Effects of Corruption in a Developing Nation. *The Western Political Quarterly, 19*(4), 719–732.

Behrendt, S. D., Lathan, A. J. H., & Northrup, D. (2010). *The Diary of Antera Duke: An Eighteenth-Century African Slave Trader*. Oxford: Oxford University Press.

Berger, G. (2007). In Search of Journalism Education Excellence in Africa: Summary of the 2006 Unesco Project. *Ecquid Novi. African Journalism Studies, 28*(1&2), 149–155.

Botha, N., & de Beer, A. S. (2007). South African Journalism Education: Working Towards the Future by Looking Back. *Ecquid Novi. African Journalism Studies, 28*(1&2), 198–205.

Boyd-Barrett, O. (2004). Judith Miller, New York Times and the Propaganda Model. *Journalism Studies, 5*(4), 435–449.

Brennen, B. S. (2000). What the Hacks Say: The Ideological Prism of US Journalism Texts. *Journalism, 1*(1), 106–113.

Diamond, L. (1989). (Book Review). Democracy and Prebendal Politics in Nigeria: The Rise and Fall of the Second Republic. *African Affairs, 88*(351), 284–286.

Ette, M. (2000). Agent of Change or Stability? The Nigerian Press Undermines Democracy. *The Harvard International Journal of Press/Politics, 5*(3), 67–86.

Franklin, B. (2004). *Packaging Politics: Political Communication in Britain's Media*. London: Bloomsbury Academic.

Gans, H. J. (1979). *Deciding What's News: A Study of CBS Evening news, NBC Nightly News, Newsweek, and Time*. New York: Pantheon.

Goddard, P. (2006). 'Improper Liberties': Regulating Undercover Journalism on ITV, 1967–1980. *Journalism, 7*(1), 45–63.

Hallin, D. C., & Mancini, P. (2004). *Comparing Media Systems: Three Models of Media and Politics*. New York: Cambridge University Press.

Hallin, D., & Papathanassopoulos, S. (2002). Political Clientelism and Media: Southern Europe and Latin America in Comparative Perspective. *Media, Culture and Society, 24*, 175–195.

Hanks, W. F. (2005). Pierre Bourdieu and the Practices of Language. *Annual Review of Anthropology, 34*, 67–83.

Hunter, L., & Oumarou, C. E. (1998). Towards a Hausa Verbal Aesthetic: Aspects of Language About Using Language. *Journal of African Cultural Studies, 11*(2), 157–170.

Ibrahim, J. (2003). Democratic Transition in Anglophone West Africa. CODESRIA Monograph Series. Council for the Development of Social Science Research in Africa. Dakar, Senegal. Retrieved April 10, 2008, from www.codesria.org/Links/Publications/monographs/Ibrahim.pdf

Joseph, R. A. (1988). *Democracy and Prebendal Politics in Nigeria: The Rise and Fall of the Second Republic.* Cambridge: Cambridge University Press.

Latham, A. J. H. (1973). *Old Calabar-16001891: The Impact of the International Economy upon a Traditional Society.* Oxford: Clarendon Press.

Lull, J., & Hinerman, S. (1997). The Search for Scandal. In J. Lull & S. Hinerman (Eds.), *Media Scandals: Morality and Desire in the Popular Culture Marketplace* (pp. 1–33). Cambridge: Polity Press.

Mancini, P. (2007, July 17). *Journalism Culture: A Two Level Proposal.* Sent by the Author via Email to This Writer.

McCurdy, P. M., & Power, G. (2007). Journalism Education as a Vehicle for media Development in Africa. *The AMDI Project. Ecquid Novi. African Journalism Studies, 28*(1&2), 127–147.

Murphy, S. M., & Scotton, J. F. (1987). Dependency and Journalism Education in Africa: Are There Alternative Models. *Africa Media Review, 1*(3), 11–35.

Ogundimu, F. F., Oyewo, O. Y., & Adegoke, L. (2007). West African Journalism Education and the quest for professional standards. *Ecquid Novi. African Journalism Studies, 28*(1&2), 191–196.

Oloruntola, S. (2007). Mass Media Ethics in Nigeria: The Problems Facing the Nigerian Journalists. *Lagos Papers in English Studies,* 1, 58–68. Available at http://www.artslasu.org/journal_eng/contents/vol_1/oloruntola.pdf downloaded 29th/11/2008

Oyovbaire, S. (2001). *The Media and Democratic Process in Nigeria* (1). Available at http://www.waado.org/nigerdelta/Essays/Oyovbaire.html. Downloaded 15 Aug 2006.

Quarts Africa. (2016). *Lagos Is Africa's 7th Largest Economy and Is About to Get Bigger with Its First Oil Finds.* Retrieved 17 May 2018. Available at https://qz.com/676819/lagos-is-africas-7th-largest-economy-and-is-about-to-get-bigger-with-its-first-oil-finds/.

Rooney, R. (2007). Revisiting the Journalism and Mass Communication Curruculum: Some Experiences from Swaziland. *Ecquid Novi. African Journalism Studies, 28*(1&2), 207–221.

Sandcholtz, W., & Koetzle, W. (2000). Accounting for Corruption: Economic Structure, Democracy, and Trade. *International Studies Quarterly, 44*, 31–50.

Sanusi II, HRH Muhammad Sanusi. (2017). *Nigeria Between the Past and the Future: Culture, Governance and Development*. SOAS Africa Conference 2017. 100 Years Anniversary. School of Oriental and African Studies, University of London. Retrieved 11 May 2018. Available at https://www.youtube.com/watch?v=ciV5Vi-3Adw.

Schultz, I. (2007a, May 28). Craft and Conversation: Features of Danish Journalism Culture. Using Filed Theory as Framework for a Sociology of Journalism Culture. Paper Presented at the Political Communication Section, International Communication Association Conference, San Francisco.

Schultz, I. (2007b, May 24–28). Context in Newsroom Ethnography: Reflexive Sociology and the Concept of Journalistic Field, News Habitus and Newsroom Capital. Paper Presented at the International Communication Association Conference, San Francisco.

Schultz, I. (2007c). The Journalistic Gut Feeling: Journalistic Doxa, News Habitus and Orthodox News Values. *Journalism Practice, 1*(2), 190–207.

Skjerdal, T. S., & Ngugi, C. M. (2007). Institutional and Governmental Challenges for Journalism Education in East Africa. *Ecquid Novi. African Journalism Studies, 28*(1&2), 176–189.

Steel, J., Carmichael, B., Holmes, D., Kinse, M., & Sanders, K. (2007). Experimental Learning and Journalism Education Lessons Learned in the Practice of Teaching Journalism. *Education + Training, 49*(4), 325–334.

Tumber, H., & Waisbord, S. (2004). Political Scandals and Media Across Democracies, Volume I. *The American Behavioral Scientist, 47*(8), 1032.

Ujorha, T. (2014). *Calabar: Is This Africa's Oldest Press?* Retrieved 11 May 2018. Available at https://www.dailytrust.com.ng/daily/feature/14745-calabar-is-this-africa-s-oldest-press.

Waisbord, S. (2000). *Watchdog Journalism in South America: News, Accountability, and Democracy*. New York: Columbia University Press.

Yusha'u, M. J. (2018). Poor Capitalization and Corruption Within the Nigerian Press. In H. Mabweazara (Ed.), *Newsmaking Cultures in Africa* (pp. 185–205). London: Palgrave Macmillan.

CHAPTER 9

Conclusion: Comparing Nigeria, Kenya and South Africa

Media systems study attracted the attention of media scholars through the work of Siebert, Peterson, and Schramm (1956), the famous *Four Theories of the Press*. Blumler and Gurevitch (1995) carried on from the *Four Theories of the Press* and further strengthened the debate on comparative media research.

The work of Hallin and Mancini (2004) was groundbreaking. They expanded the study to cover eighteen countries in Europe and North America. The media systems theory that came out of the study rested the arguments raised in the *Four Theories of the Press* and reviewed and refined the comparative research framework suggested by Blumler and Gurevitch (1995). The comparative research framework suggested by Hallin and Mancini were the development of media markets and development of strong or weak mass circulation press, political parallelism, development of journalistic professionalism and the degree of state intervention in the media systems of a country.

A point of departure between this book and that of Hallin and Mancini is trying to explore the media systems theory within an intranational context. Although the frameworks suggested by Hallin and Manicni are quite useful, and are needed to evaluate media systems, a critical look at them suggests their root and focus was more relevant to European and North American contexts.

Take for instance the first framework: the development of media markets and the emergence of strong or weak mass circulation press. In any

M. J. Yusha'u, *Regional Parallelism and Corruption Scandals in Nigeria*, https://doi.org/10.1007/978-3-319-96220-7_9

country that has a media system, most have developed media markets gradually. But the development of media market and mass circulation press did not develop in a vacuum in Europe and North America where Hallin and Mancini conducted their studies.

The development of media markets and mass circulation press in Europe was a long historical process. It was linked to the development of printing press, the role of the Roman empire and was used as a tool for propaganda in Germany and the Ottoman empire. By the seventeenth century newspaper markets were developing in Europe across different cities: "rudimentary newspapers soon appeared in other European countries: Switzerland (1610), the Habsburg domains in central Europe (1620), England (1621), France (1631), Denmark (1634), Italy (1636), Sweden (1645), and Poland (1661). English and French translations of Dutch *corantos* were also available. But signs of official intolerance emerged fairly soon, and censorship stifled newspaper development in the late seventeenth century and into the eighteenth century in continental Europe" (Encyclopaedia Britannica 2018: 2).

This process in Europe continued up to the 1800s during the era of the industrial revolution when news consumption had become part and parcel of the culture of people. By 1814, you have major newspapers like the *Times* in London producing 5000 copies an hour. The development of the Fourdrinier machine made it easier for mass production of newspapers. (Encyclopedia Britannica 2018). In the United States, mass circulation presses were transforming the media landscape in the 1890s by developing a new form of journalism that focused on celebrity culture and popular journalism (Williamson 2012).

This is the climate under which the mass circulation press developed until the current era of online publications which is changing the nature of media consumption globally, and in some instances, as discussed by Sambrook (2017), even threatening to stop printing completely. Newspapers like the *Independent* in London have already ceased printing and focus on online publication, while online newspapers like *Huffington Post* have moved from an alternative online media into the mainstream.

The experience of African countries is different. As discussed in Chaps. 2 and 3, the development of media markets in African countries, at least from the examples of Nigeria and Kenya, and even South Africa, was related to missionary activities, colonial administration and later the involvement of post-independent governments and private proprietors. Taking the framework on the development of media markets and mass circulation press and applying it on the African context assumes the universalisation of the framework without any modification, which is precisely the criticism of Hallin and Mancini (2004) in the *Four Theories of the Press*.

Political parallelism is a major feature of media systems in many countries. But it also has a core European history, as discussed by Hallin and Mancini (2004) and Artero (2015). Political parallelism coincides with the interest of political parties and social organisations, movements and ideologies with the interest of newspapers. In other words, these newspapers and media organisations promote the interest of these political parties and social organisations. According to Hallin and Mancini you find these features in countries where the Polarised Pluralist Model and the Democratic Corporatist Model prevail, although it is decreasing, especially in the Democratic Corporatist countries.

The support of the *Daily Mirror* in Britain for the Labour Party and the *Telegraph* for the Conservative Party is an example of political parallelism. However, it is diminishing. The *Daily Mirror* opposed the war on Iraq in 2003 supported by Tony Blair's *New Labour*, and the *Telegraph* led in exposing the expenses scandal of British parliamentarians including conservative politicians. Perhaps one of the reasons for the diminishing of political parallelism in Britain is the increasing commercialism of the news media. It is apt, therefore, for Hallin and Mancini to place Britain within the Liberal Model. As a result of the expenses scandal, the circulation figures of the *Telegraph* increased by 600,000 copies (the Guardian 2009).

The history of African countries differ from those of Europe and North America. This book has shown that the news media in Nigeria is more regionally inclined. Political reporting is influenced by the regional interest of the newspapers as we have seen in the reporting of corruption scandals. This is a historical phenomenon. After political independence, newspapers like the *Nigerian Tribune* which still publishes, and the *New Nigerian* were representing the regional interest of the Western and Northern Regions even though they were sold nationally. Even after the takeover of the Nigerian military of the *Daily Times* and the *New Nigerian* newspapers, the *Daily Times* remained southern in orientation and the *New Nigerian* very northern in orientation, though they were supposed to be national in orientation because of the change of ownership under various military governments.

A case in point which illustrated the regional division of the two newspapers was the Daboh-Tarka scandal in the early in 1970s. Godwin Daboh was a Nigerian businessman who accused a federal commissioner in the government of General Yakubu Gowon, J S Tarka, of using government resources to enrich himself. The two leading newspapers in Nigeria at the time, the *Daily Times* and the *New Nigerian*, dedicated enough space to the story. While the core issue of the story was allegation of corruption and embezzlement of public office, the reporting of the scandal took a regional tone. *The Daily Times* was vehement on exposing the alleged excesses of Chief J S Tarka, while the *New Nigerian* focused on how southern interests were behind Godwin Dabo to demonize Tarka and request for his resignation through the pages of the *Daily Times* (Jibo and Okoosie-Simbine 2003).

After the return of Nigeria to a civilian administration in 1999, several scandals have taken place, among them was the certificate and age forgery by the former speaker of the federal house of representatives who increased his age and claimed to have a degree from Toronto University. An investigation by the *The News* magazine from Southern Nigeria found that Salisu Buhari lied and this led to his resignation as speaker. Another newspaper from the north, *Today*, also published another story about certificate forgery by the then Governor of Lagos State, Bola Tinubu. Yet the news media was silent about this story, unlike the case of Salisu Buhari that generated national furore. According to Jibo and Okoosie-Simbine (2003: 184):

> The most effective way in which the media helps a country to fight graft is to beam the searchlight on those in authority to expose their criminal acts and double standards. This opportunity was lost in the "Speakergate" scandal probably because *The News* did not want to damage the Obasanjo presidency. On the other hand, the *Today* newspaper, owned by a northerner, also pursued what appeared to be revenge by publishing similar allegations against a Southern Governor, Alhaji Ahmed Bola Tinubu of Lagos State. The interesting development was that these allegations against Tinubu were ignored by *The News* and were half-heartedly reported in the other Southern-owned media. It is thus significant that, whereas Buhari was forced to resign, Tinubu has remained in office and enjoys a good press, as a perfunctory glance at it, since the allegations were made, will reveal. This leads one to wonder if there are no double standards in the Nigerian media's fight against graft in the fourth republic.

In the case of Kenya, we have seen how tribal and ethnic interests are reflected in the newspapers especially during election violence that characterized elections in 2007 and more recently in 2017. The demographic composition of journalists working in media organisations themselves was reflective of the regional divide in the country as the study by Ireri (2017a) confirms that Kikuyu, Luo, Lunha, Kalenjin and Kamba have the majority of journalists working in various newsrooms, with journalists coming from the Rift Valley region constituting 21.4% of working journalists; the next region, which is the Western province had 19.5% of journalists (see Chap. 5 for details on the Kenyan media system).

This book does not cover the demographic composition of Nigerian journalists, but it was clear during the interviews with journalists for this book, that the composition of journalists in Nigeria was representative of the regional dynamics of the country. It was also clear during a visit to the offices of *Thisday*, *Guardian*, *Daily Trust* and the *Nation* newspapers that majority of employees in each of these newspapers reflects the region where the newspaper comes from. Therefore, it would be too simplistic to adopt political parallelism and apply it within an African context.

South Africa has more unique feature compared to Nigeria and Kenya. The influence of apartheid has created what was described earlier in Chap. 4 as racial parallelism. This was because a section of South African newspapers under the apartheid regime were reflecting the views of the apartheid regime, while the liberal and black press was reflecting or promoting anti-apartheid views in their newspapers. But that was changed after the defeat of apartheid and the establishment of black majority rule in 1994. Some of the Afrikaans newspapers that were supportive of the apartheid regimes even established newspapers like the *Daily Sun*, which cater for the needs of black working-class readers. A case of reversed racial parallelism influenced by commercialism.

Therefore, situating the Nigerian media from the framework suggested in Chap. 1, about the development of media during colonialism, the development of nationalist press to fight for independence, and the regional parallelism as opposed to political parallelism was useful in this book. This has helped in understanding the regional character of the Nigerian and other African media. It was clear from the information that even within Nigeria, the media developed in Southern Nigeria during colonial times was ahead of the Northern Region. Early newspapers such as *Iwe irohin*, the *Anglo-African*, the *Lagos Times*, the *Lagos observer*, the *West African Pilot* were all developed before a single newspaper was established in Northern Nigeria. *Gaskiya Ta fi Kwabo*, published in the Hausa language, was almost exclusively the newspaper from Northern Nigeria that fought and survived during colonial times.

In post-independent Nigeria, there had been more newspapers from Southern Nigeria than there are newspapers from Northern Nigeria as discussed in Chap. 3, and the analysis in Chap. 8 gives credence to this.

Of course, the issues discussed are not mutually exclusive. There are several exceptions and further research is required to prove that.

The dynamics of Nigerian politics is changing. In 2015 during the elections between the People's Democratic Party and the All Progressives Congress new alliances in Nigerian politics were forged. For the first time in Nigerian political history, South West Nigeria and Northern Nigeria came into a successful political alliance that produced a government in a presidential system. The alliance was led by Muhammadu Buhari from Northern Nigeria and Bola Tinubu from Southern Nigeria. During the elections in 2015, the media from the southern part of Nigeria, with few exception of newspapers like *Guardian*, *Thisday* and *Vanguard*, which had soft spot for Goodluck Jonathan, provided a more positive coverage to a candidate from Northern Nigeria. Was this further evidence of the influence of regionalism among Nigerian newspapers? Would these newspapers provide a semblance of a more positive tone in 2015 elections if there was no political alliance between the two regions? These are areas of interest for further research.

Despite all the challenges mentioned, Nigerian media remains one of the most vibrant in Africa. The commercial media in particular, which shows more resilience compared to the political-clientelist newspapers as discussed in Chap. 3, provide more hope for the future of journalism. Issues of professionalism, weak capital base and corruption within the media remain challenges that need to be tackled. Hallin and Mancini's media system theory has contributed greatly in widening the debate about media systems globally. From what we have seen so far in this book, more research needs to be done to determine the exact nature of media systems in Africa. A key question that needs to be answered is whether the entire African continent should be treated as a one-stop shop with the same entrance and exit door, or if it should be treated as a large complex with multiple entries and exits. As we have seen in the diversity between Nigeria, Kenya and South Africa, the nature of media systems are more diverse and complex than many people envisaged, and applying a single method will not provide tangible answers. My take is that communication scholars in Africa should conduct more soul searching about the media systems in the continent. This soul searching should be done without the constraint of pre-determined theoretical biases. Rather, an in-depth and comprehensive research that looks at the media system of each country in the continent should be conducted. The outcome of the research should guide the evolution of the theories that will explain the media systems in Africa. Hallin and Mancini's media system theory has not outlived its usefulness yet; but a good starting point is to write an epitaph to existing Western-centric theories and explore a new paradigm that develops from within the continent, until a clear and unambiguous theoretical explanation of African media system is achieved.

References

Artero, J. P. (2015). Political Parallelism and Media Coalition in Western Europe. Reuters Institute for the Study of Journalism. Retrieved May 18, 2018, Available at https://reutersinstitute.politics.ox.ac.uk/sites/default/files/2018-01/Political%20Parallelism%20and%20Media%20Coalitions.pdf

Blumler, J. G., & Gurevitch, M. (1995). *The Crisis of Public Communication*. London/New York: Routledge.

Encyclopedia Britannica. (2018). Newspaper Publishing. Retrieved May 18, 2018, Available at https://www.britannica.com/topic/publishing/Newspaper-publishing

Hallin, D. C., & Mancini, P. (2004). *Comparing Media Systems: Three Models of Media and Politics*. Cambridge/New York: Cambridge University Press.

Ireri, K. (2017a). A National Survey of Demographics Composition of Kenyan Journalists. *Journalism, 18*(2), 241–261.

Jibo, M., & Okoosie-Simbine, A. T. (2003). The Nigerian Media: An Assessment of Its Role in Achieving Transparent and Accountable Government in the Fourth Republic. *Nordic Journal of African Studies, 12*(2), 180–195.

Sambrook, R. (2017). Stop Press: Last Words on the Future of Newspapers. Retrieved May 15, 2018, Available at https://theconversation.com/stop-press-last-words-on-the-future-of-newspapers-72027

Siebert, F. S., Peterson, T., & Schramm, W. (1956). *Four Theories of the Press. The Authoritarian, Libertarian, Social Responsibility and Soviet Communist Concepts of What the Press Should Be and Should Do*. Urbana/Chicago: University of Illinois Press.

The Guardian. (2009). MP's Expenses Scandal Gains Telegraph More than 600,000 Sales. Retrieved May 18, 2018, Available at https://www.theguardian.com/media/2009/may/20/telegraph-mps-expenses-circulation

Williamson, M. (2012). When 'Popular' Was 'Radical': The Mass Circulation US Press in the 1890s, Emerging Celebrity Journalism and Popular Tastes. *Media History, 18*(2), 115–127.

Index[1]

[1]Note: Page numbers followed by 'n' refer to notes.

M. J. Yusha'u, *Regional Parallelism and Corruption Scandals in Nigeria*, https://doi.org/10.1007/978-3-319-96220-7

The manufacturer's authorised representative in the EU is Springer
Nature Customer Service Centre GmbH, Europaplatz 3, 69115 Heidelberg,
Germany. If you have any concerns regarding our products, please
contact ProductSafety@springernature.com

Printed and bound by CPI Group (UK) Ltd, Croydon, CR0 4YY
05/10/2026
02228140-0008